SL- IS FOR SLEAZE BUT SN- IS

The Meaning Behind English Consonant Clusters

Les paroles seules comptent. Le reste est bavardage.

(Only words count. The rest is idle chatter)

Eugène Ionesco

This self-astonishment is achieved when, by some process I can't fathom, common words are moved, or move themselves, into clusters of meaning so intense that they seem to stand up from the page, three-dimensional almost.

Geoffrey Hill

To all the people who have humoured me when I've swaggeringly declared that sw- describes oscillating motion and ostentation.

PV13

ISBN-13: 978-1985830899
ISBN-10: 1985830892

Contents

Foreword

Do the consonant sounds we use actually mean anything? We are all familiar with a threatening *grrr* or a hissing *ssss*. But when we put consonants together and go beyond the mimicry of onomatopoeia with its snap, crackle and pop, we find meaning hiding just below the surface – a *phonosemantic* meaning intrinsic to the letters themselves. So while *grrr* and *growl* are onomatopoeic, *grate, gripe, grimace, gristle* and *grouch* are not, but they all start with the *gr-* cluster and all carry a sense of *grumpiness*. It feels right that the *Grinch* steals Christmas, a *Sminch*, *Plinch* or *Twinch* wouldn't work.

In this book, we will go on a sightseeing tour to look at the consonant clusters of English. At each stop, we will see that each and every cluster has its own integral senses. I had various lightbulb moments and smiles of recognition along the way: *cl-* clings, *pr-* prods and *sm-* smirks, just as you would expect. The focus is on clusters rather than single consonant sounds because the phonosemantic themes of the clusters are easier to see and conform much more regularly to discernible patterns. Millions of words begin with an *s*, but most of them won't hiss at you. If you take *sp-*, on the other hand, you are much more likely to find words that will *spurt, spew* and *spit*: they share a common theme.

Languages continually evolve; they are always in a state of flux. As I've looked deeper into consonant clusters, I've become amazed by the staying power of their fundamental meanings in the face of this constant change. For me, language is an endlessly fascinating topic, with numerous enticing meanders to explore. I hope you enjoy reading *Sl- is for Sleaze, but Sn is for Sneeze!* as much as I've enjoyed researching and writing it!

Introduction

I find it difficult to believe that words have no meaning in themselves, hard as I try.

Stuart Chase, *Tyranny of Words*

Are there any clues to deciphering the meaning of an unfamiliar word? In this book, we will discover that you can often gauge the general meaning of a word just by looking at how it is spelt or listening to how it is pronounced. Obviously, this is not always the case, or else we would have no need of dictionaries or thesauruses once we had reached a certain level of proficiency in a language. Even so, we will find that there are a lot of words with a *phonosemantic meaning* – we can get an idea of what they mean by looking at how they are spelt or listening to how they are spoken, even if we have never encountered them before.

I've always been interested in languages: my BA was in French and Arabic and I've been lucky enough to study linguistics and live in several countries, learning the different languages as I've travelled around, working as an English teacher. One day in 2013, I was browsing the web for lesson resources when I came across a five-page extract from a paper by John Lawler entitled *Women, Men, and Bristly Things: The Phonosemantics of the BR– Assonance in English* (Lawler, 1990). In spite of (or perhaps, because of) this rather formidable title, I clicked on the link, (www-personal.umich.edu/~jlawler/assonances.pdf) and was captivated immediately. It highlighted the phonosemantic themes of the br-cluster (outlined here in chapter 5), and provided a statistical analysis of the frequency that br- words corresponded to them. The link included a single page named *Phonosemantic Coherence in English Assonances*, which grouped certain letter combinations according to a list of what Lawler calls "semantic embodied images". This piqued my curiosity and I decided to see if I could find any evidence for these semantic images or indeed more plausible alternative images. I also wanted to find phonosemantic themes for the many consonant clusters which were not listed, as well as examine any etymological history to see why such groupings might have occurred. This research led me to produce blog posts for my students on the school website, which outlined a consonant cluster, its phonosemantic theme(s), word etymologies and a number of exercises to help students assimilate the new vocabulary. It also whetted my appetite to look deeper into the subject, which is how this book came about.

This book's main focus will be on the sound symbolism of English *onset clusters* – the consonant clusters at the beginnings of words – with the idea that specific combinations of initial letters carry specific inherent meanings or *phonesthemes*: **gl-** words will *glow*, *glimmer* and *glitter*, while **sw-** words will *swing* their hips, *swivel* and *swagger*. In concentrating on onset clusters, we can also avoid the thorny issue of whether a specific *medial cluster* – a cluster in the middle of a word – is intra-syllabic, that is, within the same syllable, e.g. *lumpen, windy* (lump-en, wind-y), or inter-syllabic and across two syllables, e.g *blacksmith, implode* (black-smith, im-plode). This is not always as simple as it looks and English spelling certainly doesn't help: a numeral is a *number*, with its /mb/ inter-syllabic cluster (num-ber). However, if your feeling of numbness increases, you get *number* (numb-er), with *m* + *b* in the same syllable and a silent *b* to boot! Frankly, medial clusters bring me out in a cold sweat, or as the Germans would say *Angstschweiss* – a word with a particularly beautiful inter-syllabic medial cluster of its own! Like medial clusters, many word final consonant clusters do not seem to carry phonosemantic meaning so clearly, and they are also outside the scope of this book.

Most English onset clusters can come before both words and syllables, but the few that are present only at the beginning of syllables – the /gw/ of *language*, the /vw/ of *reservoir* – will receive limited attention, as it is doubtful whether they carry any phonosemantic meaning. In addition, combinations of consonant plus /j/, e.g. the /mj/ of *mute*, or the /pj/ of *pure*, will not receive special attention either: this is usually a feature of pronunciation of consonants before the vowel /u:/ rather than an indication of separate consonant clusters in themselves.

In dispensing with /j/, we are in fact in line with a long-term trend in English, so-called *yod dropping*, from the Hebrew letter *yod* ' /j/. With yod dropping, the /j/ sound has gradually been dropped after the initial consonant. Nowadays, few dialects of English differentiate between *chews* and *choose* and *yew* and *you*, for example, though certain Welsh English accents do still have a /ɪʊ̯/ diphthong as opposed to a /u:/ for *chews* [tʃɪʊ̯z] and *yew* [jɪʊ̯], so here differences remain. The /j/ has also largely disappeared after *l*, as can be seen by the now yod-less *blue* and *lunatic*, although it lingers in many pronunciations of *lurid* and *lewd* and is still commonly pronounced after *l* when there is a syllable break before the /j/, as with *value* and *volume*. That yod dropping is an ongoing process can be seen by differing pronunciations of *suit*, *salute*, *assume*, *enthusiastic*, *superstition* etc. Most American accents now drop the /j/ of *tune*, *student*, *during*, *nuclear* and *tutor* too, but the most consistent yod-droppers are in East Anglia, where *new*, *produce*, *music* and *cube* often have /j/ elision. In the 1980s, Norfolk farmer Bernard Matthews even brought yod dropping to the national consciousness with a series of TV ads about his *bootiful* turkey products!

The standardisation of spelling with the advent of printing marks the boundary between Late Middle English and Early Modern English. It is also important because the first printers preserved the spelling of words as they were pronounced at that time. This means that we can tell that the wh-, wr-, kn- and gn- clusters had yet to be reduced to single consonant sounds, unlike other attested clusters, which had clearly disappeared by that point. This includes the h-clusters (see chapter 2) and the wl- cluster of *wlanc* "proud, stately", *wlatsom* "disgusting" and *wlite* "beauty, splendour", all of which had died out. Very few descendants of wl- endure, although *lisp* from ME *wlispen* is a notable exception. As we will see, the remaining clusters wh-, wr-, kn- and gn- still have strong phonosemantic themes, despite the fact that their pronunciations have been simplified.

Early printers, such as William Caxton (c.1422-1491) and Richard Pynson (1448-1529), did enjoy a certain degree of flexibility, however. Despite being influenced by the so-called Chancery Standard used by bureaucrats and officials of 15th century London, printers in the Late Middle English period were not averse to tinkering with spelling. Although spellings were usually altered to fit in with apparent rules and by analogy with existing patterns, changes could lead to confusion when they were not firmly based on pronunciation or etymology. This sometimes happened because many printers of this era were not English at all, but spoke Dutch or Flemish as a first language. Caxton himself lived in Bruges for over twenty years and was influenced by Flemish spelling conventions. He has been credited with the *h* of *ghost* and by extension *aghast* and *ghastly*. Although this was consistent with contemporary Flemish spelling norms, as in *gheest* "ghost", the *h* is superfluous in English when we consider that earlier Middle English spellings were *gost*, *agast* and *gastlich*.

The phonosemantic themes attributed to English consonant clusters have been in place for centuries, if not millennia, and are deeply embedded in the language. They are found throughout our rich dialects, as well as in Standard English, as in the Scots and north-eastern English *clarts* we shall come across in chapter 8 – sticky, malodorous mud which is perfectly aligned to the *clay*, *clag* and *clods* of the cl- cluster. The words at the core of the phonesthemes are usually Germanic, and can be traced back to an earlier Proto-Germanic era. Phonosemantic parallels can often be drawn to similar clusters in other Germanic languages. For example, the sn- cluster's focus on the nose is the same in the Scandinavian languages, Dutch and Frisian and has its German counterpart in schn-. Sometimes, phonosemantic connections can even be made between words in different language groups. If we take the st-cluster, then many words describing standing, stability and steadiness carry a st- onset cluster, as the following words for "steady" illustrate: German *stetig*, Slovak *stály*, Greek *σταθερά* (*statherá*), Italian *stabile* and Hindi स्थिर (*sthir*). Of course, many such words share a common etymology, so it is hardly surprising that they resemble each other. The "steady" words cited above are all thought to descend from the Proto-Indo-European root **sta-* "stand, make firm", as we shall see in more detail in chapter 1.

Although etymology plays an important role in determining phonesthemes, we will see that there are many instances where neat etymological links cannot always be traced. This is the case with the aforementioned consonant cluster br- (see chapter 5), which has "brawny masculinity" as one of its phonosemantic themes. Languages as diverse as Irish with *briomhar* "strong, vigorous", Norwegian *braut* "burly, boastful", and Latin *brutalis* "savage, stupid" demonstrate this theme, to which we can also throw in a Swiftian *Brobdingnagian*. Of course, it is easy to cherry-pick, but this is not an isolated example, and the sheer quantity of apparently unrelated words with similar clusters and shared sound symbolism should lead us to discount coincidence as a reason for so many close parallels.

Because the key words at the heart of each consonant cluster have been in the English language for such a long time, it is perhaps unsurprising that words with similar meanings have developed by analogy with them, converging to reflect the underlying phonosemantic concept. This may involve changes in sound and spelling, or the abandonment of parallel forms. One example of this occurred with the consonant cluster fn-, which Old English inherited from Proto-Germanic *fneusana* "breathe, pant". Words with this cluster, such as *fneosan* "sneeze", *fnoren* "snore" and *fnorten* "*snort*", merged with the sniffing, snivelling, snottily nasal sn- cluster (see chapter 6) to leave *sneeze*, *snore* and *snort* respectively when fn- disappeared. This change may also have been hastened by the visual resemblance of the letter *f* to so-called *long s* – written ∫ in the Middle English period.

Some clusters have more than one phonestheme; here one theme may have evolved from another or themes may have developed independently. Relations between phonesthemes can often be constructed, but without attested semantic links, these remain speculative. It is also true that some consonant clusters have more easily identifiable (and indeed quantifiable) phonosemantic meanings than others, with fr- (see chapter 30) being particularly tricky to pin down. As might be expected, the more frequent the cluster is in English, the greater the likelihood that there will be more than one phonestheme and a greater number of words that do not conform to the phonosemantic model. On the other hand, the rarer clusters are more closely in sync with a single phonestheme: wr-, spr-, spl- and thr- being good examples.

Numerous factors can lead to the convergence of words carrying a specific phonosemantic theme around a particular cluster. Some words may look and sound similar because new coinages may be mispronunciations of older words, or they may be imitative forms. In such cases, it is to be expected that similar initial clusters denote similar meanings. Hence, we have small variations between near synonyms like *slap* and *slam* and *clank* and *clunk*. New words can also be created by blending words together to create a *portmanteau* (see chapter 10). In such cases, English usually prefers to put the cluster first, so we have *smog*, rather than *foke* for a mixture of *smoke* and *fog*; *spork*, rather than *foon* for a piece of cutlery that combines a *spoon* with a *fork*; and *skitching* – *hitching* a ride by holding on to the bumper of a moving car while *skateboarding* or wearing roller *skates* – rather than *hating*, for obvious reasons! New terms can also be coined by analogy with existing words with similar sounds or similar patterns. For instance, *floriculture*, *horticulture* and *apiculture* were created by analogy with *agriculture*. Words which sound similar to each other may even merge, especially if their meanings are quite close. The weak Old English verb *dyfan* "dip, immerse, submerge" merged with the strong verb *dufan* "dive, sink" to produce *dive* with its two past forms; the weak regular *dived* and the strong irregular *dove*, the latter occurring by analogy with *drive*, *drove*.

Sometimes, phonic similarity is used for humorous effect, as with puns – plays on words beloved by Christmas cracker manufacturers – "Why did the scientist put a knocker on his door?""He wanted to win the No-bell prize"; malapropisms – the mistaken use of similar sounding words – "illiterate him quite from your memory" (*illiterate* instead of *obliterate*); and spoonerisms – where the initial sounds of two or more words are transposed – "we'll have the hags flung out" for "we'll have the flags hung out". Slips of the tongue may also bring words closer together, as when

American politician Sarah Palin inadvertently coined the word *refudiate*, conflating *refute* and *repudiate* to produce the *New Oxford American Dictionary*'s "Word of the Year" in 2010.

Words also converge towards existing themes by simpler methods. New verbs are created from existing nouns and vice-versa, much to the disgust of traditional grammarians. Expecting them to accept these forms is a big *ask*. New classes of word are also created by *back-formation*, a process of conversion whereby new lexemes (units of meaning) are created by the removal of affixes. For example, the noun *pathogen* is a back-formation from the adjective *pathogenic*, the verb *cremate* is a back-formation from the noun *cremation*, and the adjective *difficult* is a back-formation from the noun *difficulty*. Of course, the opposite process, that of affixation, creates even more words related to a common root: *economy, economic, economical, economist, economise*, etc.

Another way in which words produce offshoots with the same phonosemantic themes is through frequentative forms (see chapter 7) indicating repeated action. The English frequentative suffixes are *–er* and *–le*. Hence, we have *clutter* as the frequentative of *clot*, with the same *clogged-up, clustered* theme, and *draggle* "make wet by dragging along the ground", with its derived form *bedraggled* from *drag.* Similarly, we have reduplicative words with the same theme. These can be identical forms found in "baby talk", as in *choo-choo* and *wee-wee*, or more commonly by combining two different vowel grades from the same word in a process known as *ablaut*. Nearly always in these combinations, there is a high vowel, usually /ɪ/ followed by a lower vowel e.g. *chit-chat, shilly-shally, flip-flop, pitter-patter, riff-raff, criss-cross, flim-flam* and *zigzag*. Ablaut is also responsible for the vowel gradations in Germanic strong verbs, preserved in the irregular verbs loved by English students worldwide, like *sink-sank-sunk*, and *swim-swam-swum*, as well as the vowel differences in a number of irregular plurals like *tooth*, *teeth* and *louse*, *lice*.

Finally, a warning. Once you start noticing phonosemantic meaning, you'll find it everywhere. Politicians and spin doctors like simple messages which stick in the mind. In July 2017, Labour Party leader, Jeremy Corbyn accused the Prime Minister, Theresa May of "*flip-flopping* and *floundering*" on the public sector pay cap, two uncomplicated metaphors that nevertheless exemplify the *flimsily* inconstant phonosemantic nature of the fl- cluster. This contrasts sharply with the Conservative Party's mantra of the 2017 General Election campaign that they were the party of "strong and stable" government, with the st- cluster invoking *steadiness* and *sturdiness*. Clearly, alliteration plays a part too – phrases like "coalition of chaos" and "magic money tree" were also extensively bandied around, but the power of the phonesthemes should not be dismissed. Phonosemantic meaning is everywhere – in the media, marketing, advertising and the arts – *Sl- is for Sleaze but Sn- is for Sneeze!* will show how deeply ingrained phonosemantic meaning is in the language that we use every day.

In this book, I've attempted to avoid overly-technical linguistic terminology while not overly-simplifying or "dumbing down" – occasionally a difficult balancing act. The appendices include some diagrammatic explanations, as well as a brief look at some of the phonological features of English consonants and phonotactics for reference purposes.

A quick note on the text: words prefaced with an asterisk are ancient, reconstructed roots, put together by linguists on the best available evidence. Words in the Latin alphabet appear, diacritics and all, without a phonetic transcription. Words in other alphabets are written as they appear in the usual script of the native language, with their transliteration afterwards in brackets. An exception to this is Gothic, as unfortunately my computer doesn't do runes. Any mistakes in transcription are, of course, my fault alone.

Sound Symbolism

Yossarian − *the very sight of the name made him shudder. There were so many esses in it. It just had to be subversive. It was like the word* subversive *itself. It was like* seditious *and* insidious *too, and like* socialist, suspicious, fascist *and* Communist.

Joseph Heller, *Catch 22*

The idea that there is phonosemantic meaning integral to certain combinations of letters is controversial as it flies in the face of the theories of Ferdinand de Saussure (1857–1913), a pioneer of semiology – the study of signs and symbols – and justly regarded as one of the founders of modern scientific linguistics. In de Saussure's notion of signs, there is the *signifier* (the letters that make up a word or phrase) and the *signified* (what the word or phrase actually means). For him, "le signe est arbitraire" – the relation between the signifier and the signified is arbitrary; the word itself carries no inherent meaning. Hence, there is no reason why the word *crab* should mean "a crustacean, found chiefly on seashores, with a broad carapace, stalked eyes, and five pairs of legs, the first pair of which are modified as pincers" (OED) – the combination of letters is meaningless in itself. De Saussure did recognise that onomatopoeic words were exceptions to his notion of signs, but he has often been challenged for his unwillingness to accept any other form of sound symbolism. The celebrated Danish linguist Otto Jespersen (1860–1943) was an early critic of de Saussure and a proponent of phonosemanticism. He wrote that: "There is no denying that there are words which we feel instinctively to be adequate to express the ideas they stand for" (Jespersen, 1922), and believed that there were often rational associations between the signifier and the signified. Similarly, American linguist Dwight Bolinger (1907-1992) in *Aspects of Language* (1968) writes: "Given a particular word for a particular thing, if other words for similar things come to resemble that word in sound, then, no matter how arbitrary the relationship between sound and sense was to begin with, the sense is now obviously tied to the sound."

It is also worth remembering that the sign in early alphabets (not to mention Chinese characters) is anything but arbitrary. The Phoenician alphabet is the ancestor of the Greek alphabet, from which the Latin and Cyrillic alphabets were derived. However, Phoenician letters were derived from Egyptian hieroglyphs, themselves descended from pictograms – pictorial symbols that represent words or phrases. Furthermore, Phoenician letters, although representing individual phonemes, resembled simple drawings themselves. For example, *tēt* ⊗ (which later became the Greek *theta* – Θ) meant "wheel", and was the Phoenician hard "t". Even in the Latin alphabet, it feels somehow right that *s* is snake-like, *z* zigzags and *o* resembles lips that are rounded in surprise.

Whether individual consonants actually "mean" something is a more contentious matter of debate. We can tentatively say that the way consonants are articulated influences word meaning. The vehement "popping stops" of *b* and *p* (or more accurately, the *bilabial plosives* – see appendix), are more likely to be *pompous*, *pugnacious* and *bombastic*, *bright*, *blaring* and *prickly* – essentially, in your face. *Sausages* will *sizzle* because sibilant consonants *buzz*, *hiss*, *chatter* and *shush*, but it is also true that this will not happen every time that we meet an *s*, *z*, *tʃ* or *ʃ*.

In his highly acclaimed *Cambridge Encyclopedia of the English Language*, David Crystal argues that "if a sound is credited with a certain intrinsic meaning, the meaning should exist whenever the sound appears" and he concludes that "there are no totally convincing cases of this" (Crystal, 1995). Much as I admire Professor Crystal's brilliant work, I would take issue with this. Language evolves, word senses develop and diverge, foreign words are borrowed and assimilated into the language, and pronunciation changes. No other lexical "rule" conforms to such constrained (str- *stringent*, *straitened*, *strong*, *strict*) parameters, requiring a 100% burden of proof for it to be generally true or to be at the very least a discernible tendency. English is full of "exceptions that prove the rule", and it would be frankly amazing if there *weren't* multiple examples of words which do not seem to conform to an underlying phonosemantic theme. When Professor Crystal lists forty words with the sl- cluster (see chapter 17) conveying "downward movement, direction and position" and "generally negative association" and then lists ten words that "seem to lack these associations", he quantifies the phonosemantics: most words with the sl- onset cluster fit the pattern. He is at pains to reiterate that "before reaching a conclusion, it is essential to consider the existence of words with the same phonetic shape which do *not* convey the range of meaning suggested" (his italics). While this point is irrefutable, sometimes it boils down to a question of arithmetic: if a high enough proportion of words with the same consonant cluster have a particular sense, it is likely that there is some phonosemantic relation between them.

In fact, the occurrence of certain consonant clusters for particular phonesthemes is statistically significant. Numerous studies have shown that these clusters occur at far more frequent rates than random variation or the laws of probability would dictate. For example, Benjamin Koppel Bergen found that 60% of the most common gl- words were related to light and/or vision (Bergen, 2001). It is also likely that conceptual metaphor adds to the word stock of a particular phonestheme. Common ideas, such as "happiness is light" or "crookedness is abnormal" may have

18

added *glee* and *glad* to the gl- cluster, and *crank* and *crackpot* to the crooked cr- cluster respectively.

Some languages have phonosemantic meaning built-in to their consonant combinations. Arabic and other Semitic languages have so-called "radical root systems" whereby a sequence of three (or occasionally four) consonants or "radicals" carry an explicit phonosemantic meaning. Hence, in Arabic, the consonants د, ر and س /d/, /r/ and /s/ combine to have a phonosemantic meaning of "study". There are then standard models of word formation which expand the root in a systematic fashion. So on top of دَرَسَ (*darasa*) "study, learn", we find دَرَّسَ (*darrasa*) "teach", مَدْرَسَة (*madrasa*) "school", دَرْس (*dars*) "lesson", مُدَرِّس (*mudarris*) "teacher" etc.

There are also overt ways of borrowing words to make them fit in with the dynamics of the host language. One method is through a phenomenon known as phonosemantic matching (PSM), where the sounds of the borrowed word are matched with a word in the host language that is similar in sound and meaning. This can camouflage the fact that the parallel term has been borrowed, as it sounds "natural" in the target language. Such terms are very rare in English, though *chaise lounge*, an American corruption of French *chaise longue*, literally "long chair" has been identified as a PSM. Similarly, Dutch has transformed the Spanish word *hamaca* "hammock" into *hangmat*, which seems to describe a hammock pretty well, and *anchova* "anchovy" has been turned into *ansjovis*, with the final syllable *vis* being "fish" in Dutch.

Other languages make more deliberate use of phonosemantic matching. Sapir and Zuckermann (2008) point out that Iceland has formalised language planning with the Icelandic Language Council, a body which applies a puristic language policy and actively coins new terms based on existing Icelandic models. This is done in consultation with specialists, the media and the public so that new words are given a wider exposure and so stand a greater chance of being accepted. Icelandic PSMs include *ratsjá* "radar" from English *radar*, but combines Old Icelandic *rata* "find" with *-sjá* "-scope"; *eyðni* "AIDS", from the English acronym *AIDS*, but aligned with the existing Icelandic verb *eyða* "destroy" and the nominal suffix *-ni*; and *tækni* "technology, technique" from Danish *teknik*, but matched with Icelandic *tæki* "tool" and the *-ni* ending.

There are pitfalls and opportunities when it comes to marketing and PSMs. The Toyota MR2 was hastily renamed MR in French speaking countries when MR2 was associated with its homophone *emmerdeur* "pain in the arse", and its *merde* "shit" root. Another cautionary tale involves Coca-Cola in China. Before marketing executives could agree on an acceptable Mandarin transliteration of *Coca-Cola*, local shopkeepers were choosing characters that matched the pronunciation of the product. Unfortunately, this meant that *Coca-Cola* was translated as "bite the wax tadpole" and "wax-flattened mare". The marketeers quickly settled on a PSM character combination that translated as "allow the mouth to rejoice". Those involved in marketing spend colossal sums naming new products so that the brand name carries certain desirable associations, as well as for reasons of euphony. This is why we have the cleaning products *Fairy* and *Ariel* rather than *Troll* and *Lucifer*.

Chinese characters and Arabic radical roots are obviously semantically meaningful, and *neologisms* (newly coined words) and compound forms are frequently created in line with these semantic and phonosemantic connotations. Yet, we will discover that a great number of English words have phonosemantic links too. Of course, the red herrings that are folk etymologies muddy the waters (though they also illustrate popular eagerness to explain word origins, and interest in the topic), and many English words have common etymologies, so common phonosemantic themes are to be expected. Even so, I believe that there are very often phonosemantic meanings embedded within English consonant clusters that go above and beyond these shared Proto-Indo-European roots. *Sl- is for Sleaze but Sn- is for Sneeze!* will take a closer look at this.

Folk etymology is the term applied to changes in a word's form or pronunciation due to popular belief about its derivation. This often occurs when parts of a word or phrase fall out of use, or sound dissimilar to contemporary forms, so changes are made to their spelling to match with their perceived origins. Folk etymology was prevalent in the past due to a lack of knowledge about linguistic sound changes. It differs from phonosemantic matching in that PSMs are *consciously* matched to existing words which are deemed to be similar in sound and meaning to the adopted loanword. Folk etymology is the mistaken belief that a given word derives from the same source as a word which is similar sounding, but is, in fact, unrelated.

Folk etymologising is not a new concept. The flowering plant *groundsel* is believed to have undergone folk etymology, morphing in Old English (OE) from "pus swallower" to "ground swallower". It changed from an older OE form *gundæswelgiæ*, from *gund* "pus" and *swelgan* "swallow", in line with its use as a poultice, to the later *grundeswyliġe*, by association with OE *grund* "ground", indicative of its invasive growth. Another Old English word to undergo folk etymologising is *hleapewince* from *hleapan* "leap" and **winc-* "totter", which quite accurately described the flight of the more familiar *lapwing*, a bird whose wings may flap, but they certainly don't lap! The ancestor of *blindfold*, the OE verb *blindfellian* "strike blind" had become *blindfell* by the Middle English (ME) period, and was used to describe covering someone's eyes with a bandage. Its past participle *blindfelled* was mistaken as a present form and by analogy with *fold* became *blindfold*, relating to the folding of the bandage to go around the head. A similar transformation occurred with OE *scamfæst* "firm in modesty, restrained by shame", which became ME *shamefast* – with the "fixed" *fast* we see in *steadfast* and *fasten*. This was then altered due to folk etymology to *shamefaced*, and the meaning "embarrassed by shame" took over from the earlier meaning of "bashful".

Words borrowed from other languages are also subject to folk etymology, as demonstrated by a number of borrowings from Old French. Old French *crevice* "freshwater lobster" (Modern French *écrevisse*) was borrowed by English as *crevis*, but soon became *crayfish*, despite not being a fish; Old French *femelle* derives from the Latin diminutive of *femina* "woman", but became *female* through the influence of *male*; Old French *berfrei* "wooden siege tower" became *belfry* due to its association with *bell*; and Old French *apentis* "attached building" (from the same root as *appendage*) became Anglo-Norman *pentiz*, and then *penthouse*, by association with *house*.

Meanings can alter quite radically once folk etymology comes to the fore: Spanish *cucaracha* became *cockroach* in spite of having nothing to do with *cocks* or *roaches* (as in the fish) or even *caca* "excrement", as some folk etymologists would have it; a *mongoose* is not related to a *goose*, but is borrowed via Portuguese *mangus* from an Indian language such as Marathi मुंगूस (mungūs); a *forlorn hope* now generally means "hopeless undertaking", but comes from Dutch *verloren hoop* "lost troop, storming party"; and a *Jerusalem artichoke* isn't from Jerusalem, but comes from Italian *girasole articiocco* "sunflower artichoke" (Although the Italians were wrong too, as it isn't an artichoke either!)

Some of the most pervasive folk etymologies are now widely accepted as factual, even though there are attested histories of their evolution that gainsay this "common knowledge". *Caesarean* does not stem from Gaius Julius Caesar being born by caesarean section but from *caesus*, the past participle of the Latin verb *caedere* "cut". In Roman times, caesarean deliveries were only carried out if the mother was dead or dying. However, Gaius's mother Aurelia Cotta gave birth to the boy who would become Julius Caesar when she was twenty, yet lived till her mid-sixties. The origin of the word *Caesar* itself is lost in the mists of time, but one (possibly equally unlikely) suggestion is that it is derived from *caesaries* "hair", due to baby Gaius apparently having a full head of hair when he was born. Similarly, although a man called Thomas Crapper was a renowned plumber in Victorian times, he neither gave his name to the slang *crapper* "toilet" or to the *crap* that goes down it. Instead, the word *crap* is related to *crop* and meant "chaff, thing cast off" and *crapper* is a variant of *cropper* (see chapter 12). Staying on this idyllic pastoral theme, the bird known as a *wheatear* does not get its name from flitting around ears of wheat. Rather more prosaically, *wheatear* is a more socially acceptable version of Middle English *whit ers* "white arse", due to the bird's prominent white rump, and hence exactly how the French refer to the same songbird – cul-blanc.

1.   st- standing and stiffness

Stand firm, don't flutter!

Benjamin Franklin

St- *stands* firm, an *upstanding* model of *stability*. It is rigid and unbending, the consonant cluster of the *stiff* upper lip. The st- form is found across the Indo-European language group with hundreds of thousands of st- words connected to this underlying concept. In English, this is seen in some of our most basic and common words, with verbs: *stand, stay, step*; nouns: *stick, staff, sting*; and adjectives: *still, steady, stiff. Stems* and *stalks stand* tall, *staunch stalwarts* adopt a *stable stance* and *statesmen* should be concentrating on the global *status* of their *states* and increasing *standards*. They are the *steadfast stewards* of our democracy after all; their focus should be here, rather than aimed at *establishing* country *estates* without *obstacles*. These st- words have entered English from a variety of different sources, but almost all can be traced back to reconstructed Proto-Indo-European roots.

Of these roots, the PIE root **sta-* "stand, make firm, set down" is the most prolific, being the source of a plethora of descendant roots across the Indo-European languages, (including one of the most ancient Indo-European languages with a substantial written documentary record, Sanskrit, where the root स्था (*sthā*) means "stand, stay"). The consensus amongst scholars is that the Indo-European homeland is the Pontic-Caspian steppe – a large area of grassland north of the Caucasus Mountains in what is now eastern Ukraine, southern Russia and western Kazakhstan. They believe the Proto-Indo-European language goes back to the 4th or 5th millennium BCE. This is also thought to be where and when the horse was first domesticated. Travelling on horseback gave the early Indo-Europeans a massive advantage, enabling them to migrate from their homeland to Europe and South Asia, passing on features of their language and culture wherever they went. Horses certainly seem to have had a special place in Indo-European life, and many st- words in English reflect this importance: *stud*, *stall*, *stallion*, *stable*, *stirrup*, *steed*, for example.

Seven countries in Central Asia and a large number of regions have names ending in *–stan*, the Proto-Indo-Iranian for "place, state", literally "where one stands". Persian influence on this part of the world, especially in the time of Darius the Great c. 500 BCE, when the Persian Empire was at its peak, has left the area littered with *-stans*: *Afghanistan*, *Pakistan*, *Kazakhstan* etc. *Stan* remains current in a number of Slavic languages, meaning "state" in Polish, "tent" in Czech and Slovak, "apartment" in Croatian, Serbian, Macedonian and Bosnian and "camp" in Bulgarian.

The English name *Stan*, as a short form of *Stanley*, isn't directly related to the Slavic and Persian *stans*, but it does match the upstanding firmness of the st- cluster. *Stanley* is a compound of Old English *stan*, the forerunner of *stone*, and *leah* "meadow". Several settlements near "the standing stone in the meadow" were named *Stanley*, and the name was passed on to the people who lived there. This makes the accident that befalls Stanley Lambchop, the hero of Jeff Brown's children's classic *Flat Stanley* (1964) even more shocking. It is Stanley of the standing stone that is flattened by a bulletin board; *Flat Nigel* wouldn't have the same ring. Flat Stanley does console himself by posting himself to his friends in California in an envelope, entering locked rooms by sliding under the doors, and being used by his younger brother as a kite, but eventually the novelty wears off.

The Ancient Greek for "cause to stand", ἵστημῐ (*ístēmi*) is another direct descendant of the PIE *sta-* root. As well as providing Greek with a host of derived terms, many other words from this root have found their way into English. These include *stasis* from στᾰσῐς (*stásis*) "stasis, standing", *ecstasy* from ἔκστασις (*ékstasis*), literally "standing apart" – as the ecstatic are wont to do in comparison with the rest of us – *static* from στατικός (*statikós*) "static, coming to a standstill" and *stadium* from στάδιον (*stádion*). The latter was a fixed measure of length – the running track at Olympia was one stadion long – and the sense of the word evolved to mean *race track* and from there to its modern meaning.

From -στατης (*statis*) "standing, stationary", English has taken the suffix -*stat*, used for scientific instruments involved in regulating and stabilising. The first of these was the *heliostat*, a device which continuously reflects sunlight to a fixed point. Other -*stats* include *thermostat*, *hydrostat*, *aerostat* and *photostat*. Further st-borrowings from Greek include *stereo* from Greek στερεός (*stereos*) "solid", and *stoic*, which is yet another child of the PIE *sta-* root (see boxed text below).

Stoic comes from Ancient Greek Στωϊκός (*Stōïkós*) from Ποικίλη Στοά (*Poikílē Stoá*) or "painted porch" of the Agora in Athens, which was decorated with frescoes depicting the Battle of Marathon. It was here where the philosopher Zeno of Citium lectured from about 300 BCE. As founder of the Stoic school of philosophy, Zeno built on the ideas of the Cynics, teaching that peace of mind and happiness were achieved through observing a virtuous life in accordance with Nature and that destructive emotions were the result of errors in judgement through insufficient self-control and a lack of fortitude.

Stoicism was a popular doctrine of Roman Greece and the Roman Empire for the next eight hundred years, advocates including Cato the Younger, Seneca and the Emperor Marcus Aurelius. According to Diogenes Laërtius, Zeno bowed out in a memorable way too. Apparently after leaving his school, he tripped and fell, breaking his toe. He immediately proceeded to quote a line from Aeschylus's *Niobe*: *I come, I come, why dost thou call for me?* Then, he held his breath until he died – an impressively stoic thing to do. He lives on not only as the Father of the Stoics, but also in astronomy, as one of the Moon's largest craters has been named "Zeno" after him.

The word *steel* can be traced back to Proto-Germanic **stahlijan* "made of steel" and further back to PIE **stak-* "be firm, rigid", and then inevitably to the ubiquitous **sta-*. The Russian for *steel* is its close relative сталь (*stal'*), and the possessive form equating to the *'s* of English is -ин (*-in*). Ethnic Georgian Ioseb Besarionis dze Jughashvili adopted the alias *Stalin* in his writings from when he was around 32 years old and setting out on his monumental and megalomaniacal rise to power. Whether calling himself "man of steel" and carrying out murderous purges were to compensate for his pock-marked face, small *stature* (he was 5 feet 6 inches tall) and withered left hand can only be guessed at.

From the Proto-Germanic descendants of PIE **sta-,* Old English took *standen* "stand", *steall* "stall for animals", *stow* "place" – as in the British towns of *Stow-on-the-Wold*, *Chepstow* and *Walthamstow*, and *sted* "place" – found in many compounds, such as *homestead*, *instead*, *bedstead* and *Hampstead.* In addition, Old English had a huge number of *stif* "stiff" and *stæþþig* "steady" things, including: *stæf*, the forerunner of "staff" and "stave"; *sticca* "stick"; *staca* "stake"; *starian* "stare, look fixedly at"; *stapol* "tree trunk", the origin of *staple*; *stearc* "stiff, severe", which evolved into both *stark* and *starch*; and *steorfan* "die, become stiff", which narrowed in meaning to become Modern English *starve*.

Steering, OE *stieran*, is also connected to the idea of "stiffness" as the guiding of vehicles was often done with a stiff rudder, *stýri* in Icelandic. The *stern* or rear of the boat is obviously where the rudder was and hence where the steering was undertaken.

Starboard also comes from *steer* – OE *steor* plus *bord* "side of a ship". Ships had their steering oar on the right-hand side, and so needed to dock on their left hand "port" side to stop the steering oar getting in the way. The *steerage* part of the ship was originally in front of the chief cabin towards the stern of the ship, where the steering apparatus was. When the deck wheel was invented in the 18th century and the steering moved forwards, the steerage part of the ship also moved to the front and so is where the *steerage accommodation* on a ship, i.e. the cheapest cabins, has come to be found.

One of the world's most iconic birds, the *stork*, is famous for its stiff, upright posture, on its *stilt-like* legs or on its nest atop a tall *pedestal*, perhaps a telegraph pole or chimney *stack*. *Stork* is thought to be derived from the stiff PIE **ster-* root and its Proto-Germanic descendant **sturkaz*, as numerous Germanic cognates – words with a common ancestor – demonstrate: Icelandic *storkur*, German *Storch*, and, most familiarly of all, *stork* in Swedish, Norwegian, Danish and Dutch. Other European languages have borrowed from this Germanic root e.g. Latvian *stārķis*, Bulgarian *щъркел* (*shtŭrkel*) and Slovene *štorklja*.

The feet are clearly important in the st- world for steadiness and support – it would be difficult for us to *stand* being without them. Household appliances and other objects that need to be held in an upright position need *stands* to add *stability*. To stand still, we need to *step* into a *stable* position. Otherwise, we may *stagger*, *stumble* off balance and lose our foothold. *Stairs* and *steps* will help us to climb steadily, but care should be taken, especially if they are *steep*. Ideally, we need to take steps to tread firmly, but *stamping* or even *stomping* will be considered as undue pressure and not something we should *stand for* in polite society – in fact, we should *stamp out* these practices!

The word *style* can be traced back to Latin *stilus* "pointed instrument, stake" – from the PIE root *steigh-* "step, stride, rise", from which we have *stile* and German has *steigan* "climb". *Styluses* made of pointed reeds were used by the ancient Mesopotamians to write in cuneiform script on clay tablets. Various words for "pen" come from this ancestor, such as English *stylograph*, French *stylo* and Italian *stilografica*. Latin *stilus* was influenced by Greek στῦλος (*stûlos*) "pillar, column" (yet another *sta-* descendant) and with their shared rigidity and vertical orientation, their meanings merged. From here we have the sense of *style*, as in not just "manner of writing", but also "architectural style" and by extension, "manner, fashion" in general.

There are also a varied group of st- words from PIE *steu-* "push, knock, stick, project". Some relate to high and pointy things, such as *standard* and *steeple*, while others concern things that have been blunted, cut down or *stunted* like *stoop*, *stubble*, *stump*, *stock* and *stub*. The stumpiness of *stub* is highlighted by the fact that you can stub a toe, but not a foot, and you can stub out a cigarette, but not a fire. The verb *stint* "to be sparing" originally had the meaning of "cut short" and so also belongs to the "stunted" group. *Stab*, on the other hand, comes from the "pushing, thrusting" sense, as does *stutter*, emphasising the difficulty in which words are enunciated. The verb *study* came to English via Old French *estudiar* and Latin *studeo* "I strive after, I study". It has been traced further back to the PIE *steu-* root, with its idea of "thrusting forward eagerly" and hence "striving after, dedicating oneself to", bringing forth an image of the class swot.

Several ancient Germanic st- words have undergone a semantic shift. *Stale*, for example, was originally a positive word and was used in relation to beer and wine, meaning "free of dregs or lees" because it had "stood long enough to clear", though I'm not sure how tempting stale beer sounds! *Stark* has also kept only its more negative connotations in English, as "severe, bare, sheer", whereas in Modern German, *stark* is also used in a more positive sense for "strong, powerful".

Latin and its daughter languages, particularly French, have enriched English with a vast number of st- words. The Latin verb *stare* "stand, stay" together with its related verbs *sistere* "cause to stand" and *statuere* "set up, erect" and their derived forms have given English thousands of terms. These include (deep breath): *stage, state, status, statue, stature, station, substance, instance, circumstance, distance, existence, persist, insist, desist, assist, subsist, exist, cost, constant, arrest, contrast, constable, rest, resist, superstition, constitute, destitute, prostitute* and *substitute* – and that is just scratching the surface!

St- is an ancient cluster, *steeped* in history, like *stalactites* and *stalagmites*. For this cluster, all the (Indo-European) world's a *stage* – st- stands stiffly upright everywhere. A free-standing chair or *stool* is *Stuhl* in German, *stolica* in Slovak, and *стул* (*stul*) in Russian; a *stem* is *stelo* in Italian, *стебель* (*stebel*) in Russian and στέλεχος (*stélekhos*) in Greek, and a *station* is *stacja* in Polish, *estação* in Portuguese and *stasjon* in Norwegian. Of course, some of the closest similarities exist between st- words in English and other Germanic languages: *stiff* is *stev* in Danish, *steif* in German and *stijf* in Dutch, for example. Even so, a quick comparison of the words for "stand" indicates the enduring nature of st- right across the Indo-European board and in particular the remarkable *staying power* of **sta-*, from which all of the following are descended: *estar* (Spanish), ایستادن (*istâdan*) (Persian), *stehen* (German), *стоя* (*stoja*) (Bulgarian), *stát* (Czech), στέκομαι (*stékomai*) (Greek) and, nearer to home, *stå* (Swedish and Danish).

2.   wh- whirls and whips

"A whizzpopper!" cried the BFG, beaming at her. "Us giants is making whizzpoppers all the time! Whizzpopping is a sign of happiness. It is music in our ears!

Roald Dahl: *The BFG*

Although the windy Big Friendly Giant admonished Sophie not to "gobblefunk around with words", he might well acknowledge that the **wh-** of *whizzpopping* farts is beautifully descriptive. The wh- cluster is often onomatopoeic, in that the rush of air produced when wh- is pronounced imitates the sounds of the *whacks*, *whoops* and *whumps* characteristic of this cluster. This means that wh- is a favourite cluster for cartoonists, with *whew! whine!* and *whoosh!* featuring prominently in cartoon strips alongside perennial favourites like *bang! crash!* and *boing!* Wh- words *whistle* and *whoosh* and are often connected with the fast movement of air or water.

The traditional pronunciation of the wh- cluster was /hw/, (also written in the International Phonetic Alphabet as /ʍ/), and this is still the typical pronunciation in many parts of Scotland and Ireland, in some southern states of the USA and among older speakers in New Zealand. This traditional pronunciation can be seen in Old English spellings such as *hwæt* "what", *hweol* "wheel" and *hwæte* "wheat". In the rest of the English-speaking world, the pronunciation of this cluster has been reduced to /w/ in what is known as the *wine/whine merger*, whereby the /hw/ sound was reduced to a simple /w/.

A different type of reduction occurred in the Middle English period when the wh- came before a rounded vowel – a vowel that is pronounced when the lips form a circular opening – such as /u:/ or /o/. Here, /hw/ was reduced to /h/, giving us *who* [hu:], *whose* [hu:z], and *whom* [hu:m]. The morphing of the spelling of question words did not immediately settle at *wh-* in the parts of Britain where the distinction between the pronunciations of *wine* and *whine* remained. Scots and some northern English dialects preferred the spelling *quh-* to *wh-* up to the late 17th century. Hence, they had *quhen, quho, quhere* for "when", "who" and "where" and similar *quh-* forms for other question words. This echoes the spelling of the corresponding terms in Latin, which declined in many different ways, but commonly used qu-, as with *qui, quae* and *quod*. All of these Indo-European question forms have a common origin with the PIE form **kwo-* being the origin of *who, which, what, why, where, when* and *how*. Vestiges of the *quh-* spelling for the wh- cluster can still be found e.g. in *quiff*, which is etymologically a variant of *whiff*. The sound change from Latin /kw/ to Germanic /hw/ was explained by the great linguist Jacob Grimm as part of what came to be known as *Grimm's Law* (see next chapter).

In the most part, the wh- words relating to the fast movement of air and water are descended from earlier hw- equivalents and have since had their pronunciations reduced to an initial airy /w/. *Whisk* is an exception here, being a descendant of Old Norse *visk*, from Proto-Germanic **wiskaz*, "hay, wisp of straw". Although superficially like *whirl* and *whirr* in that it relates to rapid circular movement, *whisk* (and *whiskers*) took on the wh- spelling by analogy with these and similar terms. This is a key feature of phonosemantics: word spellings take on existing forms that carry the sound symbolism in the DNA of the cluster.

Having said this, the 16th century English seemed to take to the wh- cluster with boundless enthusiasm, as words that had no apparent semantic connection suddenly adopted a wh- spelling.

They clearly didn't know quhat they were doing. For example, *whole* is an unetymological alteration of Middle English *hool* "whole, sound, healthy", but the h- spelling is more appropriate as the word is related to *hail*, *healthy* and *hale* (not to mention *heil* in German). Similarly, Middle English *hore* became *whore,* being used repeatedly by Shakespeare – in *Hamlet*, *Othello*, *Macbeth* and many other plays – and in the King James Bible with its wh- form.

Many of our "spinning" wh- words can be traced back to Old English *hweorfan* and Old Norse *hverfa*, both meaning "turn", and to their common ancestors Proto-Germanic **hwarfaz* and PIE **kwerp* "turn, revolve". *Whirr*, *whorl* and *whirl* fit this category as do the compounds *whirlwind* and *whirlpool* and the short-lived but brilliant *whirlybird* "helicopter". Old English had *hwyrfepol* and *wirfelmere* for "whirlpool" while *whirlwind* is first recorded in the 14th century, probably modelled on the Old Norse *hvirfilvindr*. *Wharf* can be traced back to late OE *hwearf* "embankment, shore" and its verb *hweorfan* "turn, revolve" with its sense of "bustle" – wharves being hives of activity. *Wheel* goes back to a similar PIE root **kweklo-*, meaning "revolve, move around", as do the Greek κύκλος (*kúklos*) (from which English takes "cycle") and the Sanskrit चक्र (cakra/chakra) literally "circle, wheel", and in Indian religions, vortexes of spinning energy.

When referring to fast, more direct movement, wh- indicates a *whizzing* or *hissing* of air, often accompanied by a high-pitched sound. *Whistle* and *whisper* go back to Proto-Germanic **hwis-* and PIE **kwei* "hiss, whistle", also the ultimate source of *whine*. Imitative of *whining* are various wh- words for cajoling or complaining, such as *wheedle*, *whinge*, *whinny* and *whimper*. *Wheezing* is also related to hissing, again with an Old Norse connection *hvæsa* "hiss", while *whip* comes from Middle English *whippen* "flap violently", again with the idea of rushing air and with an audible high-pitched noise. *Whips* make *wheals*, raised swellings on the skin, although *wheals* have now been almost entirely superseded by *weals*. From *whip* we get *whippets*, fast dogs that can run at a *whipcracking* speed. Even *whittling* a stick and *whetting* a knife on a *whetstone* involve fast, rhythmic movement, and the sound of the rush of air.

Although the *h* is still present in most of the words that were formerly spelt *hw-*, albeit now after the *w*, the other h-clusters of Old English lost their *h* during the Middle English period. This coincided with a change in pronunciation as *hl-, hr-* and *hn-* were reduced to *l-, r-* and *n-* and three more consonant clusters were lost in word initial position. This meant that the alien-looking *hlæder, hrost* and *hnecca* were simplified to *laddere, rost* and *nekke* on their way to becoming *ladder, roost* and *neck*. Similarly, *hlud* turned into *loud*, *hræfn* turned into *raven* and *hnappian* became *nap*.

H loss shows little sign of abating. All the initial h-clusters may have disappeared, but initial letter *h* has also been under attack in some dialects, such as Cockney, for centuries, with the phenomenon known as *h dropping*. This results in *'ill, 'arm* and *'all* for *hill, harm* and *hall*. Furthermore, Modern English shows almost universal h dropping in short unstressed words in phrases such as "where does he [dəzi:] live?", particularly when the *h* follows a fricative consonant (see appendix). In fact, the pronoun *it* is a reduced form of the Old English neuter 3rd person singular pronoun *hit*, reflected in Old Frisian *hit* and Dutch *het*.

H-clusters were common in Proto-Germanic, which explains their presence in Old English and in most of its contemporary continental equivalents. Proto-Germanic **hlaupan* gave OE *hleapan*, the ancestor of the verb *leap*. This is *hlaupa* in Old Norse, *hlapa* in Old Frisian, and *us-hlaupan* in Gothic. Nevertheless, h dropping became widespread across the Germanic languages: Old Norse *hlátr* "laughter" (OE *hleahtor*) becomes Norwegian *latter*, Old High German *hriot* "reed" (OE *hreod*) becomes Modern German *Ried*, and Old Frisian/OE *hlid* is now *lid* in both modern languages. By the Middle Ages, h clusters were in retreat everywhere in the Germanic world, with the exception of Iceland, and to a lesser extent the Faroe Islands, whose languages are, to some degree, fossilised versions of Old Norse. Hence, Icelandic has *hringur, hrár, hneta* for Old English *hring, hreaw* and *hnutu*, the forerunners of *ring, raw* and *nut*. *Hw-* was the last h-cluster to change in English, which is why traces of the hw- pronunciation are still common in some dialects.

The phonotactics – permissible sound combinations – of Old English rather than Modern English are used by Richard Adams in his constructed Lapine language, spoken by the rabbits in the 1972 classic novel *Watership Down*. According to Adams, the Lapine language (from French *lapin* "rabbit") came from his subconscious, but he wanted the words to sound "wuffy, fluffy as in the word *Efrafa*", which was one of the rabbit warrens in his book. This means that Lapine has h-clusters, especially hr- and hl- which hark back to the Old English period. In Adams's Lapine society, rabbits can count only up to four, the number of their claws. Any number above four is *hrair*, which is also translated as "thousand" in the name of the rabbits' mythical hero *El-ahrairah*, glossed as "Prince with a Thousand Enemies". Other hr- words include *hraka* "droppings, excrement" and the onomatopoeic *hrududu* "motor vehicle". Words with hl- include *hlessi* "wandering rabbit with no permanent hole" and *hlao* "depression in the ground holding moisture".

The flip side of *h dropping* is *h insertion*, a form of hypercorrection, whereby *h* is placed in front of words beginning with vowels, producing *hever* for *ever* and *hafternoon* for *afternoon*, not to mention *haitch*, for the letter itself! Some words borrowed from French used to have a silent *h* but have since had the /h/ reinserted: few people would now drop the *h* in *hotel, horrible* and *harmony*, but the British and the Americans differ in their pronunciation of *herb*, while the British can't agree about how to say *historic* amongst themselves!

As many of our wh- words are onomatopoeic, they lend themselves easily to memorable turns of phrase and idioms. *Whop* "slap down" belongs to the onomatopoeic group, but is also the source for the derived form *whopper* "something huge" or "outrageous lie". Often a *whopper* combines both definitions as in "the fish I caught last week was three metres long". A *whiff-sniffer* was a prohibitionist in 1920s America – a guardian of public morals

35

who would try to detect the smell of alcohol on a drinker's breath. Management gurus, personal trainers and other sadists will happily *whip you into shape*, so that you can be a *whizz-kid* in your chosen field (as long as you *get a fair crack of the whip*, that is). *Gee whiz!* And finally, those of an unenlightened *wham-bam-thank-you-ma'am* disposition may decide to signal their interest in members of the opposite sex by *wolf-whistling* at them. This practice apparently originated with American sailors, who no doubt had their hands full. However, that's enough of that, if you want any more examples, I'm afraid you can *whistle for* them. On to the next chapter!

3.   fl- flowing, flapping and flags

Float like a butterfly, sting like a bee. The hands can't hit what the eyes can't see.

Mohammad Ali

Fl- *flits* in without a by-your-leave. It is a cluster of quick, *fluid* movements, *flighty* and inconstant, a creature of ebb and *flow*. Fl-words travel on currents of water and air. The currents may be gentle – *flags flutter* from their poles, light objects *float* on the water or the air, *fledglings flap* their tiny wings and fly; or more turbulent – rivers *flood*, missiles are *flung* and people are *flogged*. Fl- tends to have a horizontal orientation: flags flutter *sideways*, buoyant objects float *on the surface* of the water, and birds fly *across* the sky.

This leads us to a second, related strand of the fl- cluster, which concerns two-dimensional space and objects that are *flattened out* or lateral. Upstanding Stanley becomes *flat*; Mohammed Ali knocks sturdy opponents to the *floor*. Other flat or lateral examples include *flannel, flank, flan* and *flange*. Many fl- words also have clear parallels with words in the pl- cluster (see chapter 19), which shares many of the features of fl-.

The link between Germanic *f* and Latin *p* was first noted by the philologist, poet and philosopher Friedrich von Schlegel at the beginning of the nineteenth century, sparking a new interest in comparative linguistics – you can't get much (Germanic) *flatter* than a (Romance) *platter*. Schlegel's ideas were extended to other Indo-European languages by the Danish linguist Rasmus Rask, and then by Jacob Grimm, who outlined the regular correspondences between German, Latin and Greek stops and fricatives (see appendix for more details about how the letters of the alphabet are classified). This system of sound changes is known as the First Germanic Consonant Shift, or Grimm's Law.

Jacob Grimm (1785-1863) was an impressively knowledgeable polymath. As a linguist, his first real labour of love was the *Deutsche Grammatik "German Grammar"* (1817-1839). In this weighty tome, he explains many of the changes to Germanic consonants that occurred during the first millennium BCE and which distinguish Germanic languages from other branches of the Indo-European group. Some examples are /p/ becoming /f/ – PIE *ped* becomes English *foot* and German *Fuß* compared to Sanskrit पद् (*pád*) and Latin *pedis*, as in *pedal*; /k/ changing to /h/, PIE *kerd-* becomes English *heart* and German *Herz*, in contrast with Latin *cor* and Greek καρδιά (*kardia*), as in *cardiac*; and /d/ morphing to /t/ – PIE *dent-* becomes English *tooth* and Dutch, Danish and Swedish *tand*, as opposed to Sanskrit दन्त (*danta*) and the Latin *dens* of *dental*.

Jacob also spent many years compiling the frankly massive *Deutsches Wörterbuch "German Dictionary"*, in collaboration with his younger brother Wilhelm (1786-1859). The early volumes of this monumental undertaking were published in 1854 after sixteen years of work. Jacob had single-handedly finished the entries for A, B, C and E (Wilhelm having done D) and had got up to the entry for *Frucht* "fruit" at the time of his death in 1863. Work on the *Deutsches Wörterbuch* was then taken up by a succession of scholars, academics and institutions, until it was finally completed in 1961, 123 years after it had started. The finished dictionary had 320,000 keywords and weighed 84 kg.

Jacob was also a linguist, mythologist and lawyer, but is undoubtedly best known as the one of the two editors of Grimm's Fairy Tales, again alongside Wilhelm. The tales were published in 1812, after years spent recording and researching village oral storytelling. Although hugely popular, the tales were heavily criticised when first published for not being suitable for children, perhaps in keeping with the brothers' surname, which means "wrath" in German (see chapter 26). Early editions were later modified to remove such elements as Rapunzel becoming pregnant after late night trysts with her princely night-time visitor!

Jacob's devotion to academic studies is truly outstanding. As well as the decades spent on the dictionary and the folktales, he also spent many years working as a librarian and in a number of prestigious universities. He even had an early stint working as a royal librarian for Napoleon's brother, Jérôme, King of Westphalia. Somehow, he also found the time to study German language history and work towards finding principles that explain the evolution of Indo-European linguistics and the sound shifts specific to Germanic languages.

One of the key starting points when examining the fl- cluster is the Proto-Indo-European root *pleu-, meaning "flow" It's a cracker of a root, responsible for a multiplicity of descendants, exemplifying the interconnected nature of Indo-European languages. Sanskrit has प्लवते (plavate) "swim, float"; Old Church Slavonic has плово (plovo) "swim, navigate" – passed down into contemporary Slavic languages such as Bulgarian, which has плавам (plavam) "float" and плувам (pluvam) "swim"; Latin took pluvia "rain", (from which English took pluvial and interestingly, plover – a bird that literally "belongs to the rain"), and Greek has πλέω (pléō) "float, sail" and πλοίο (ploío) "ship". Following the changes consistent with Grimm's Law, PIE pl- became Proto-Germanic fl- for these flighty, flowing words, (spelt vl- in Dutch). Hence, English has flow, Dutch vloeien and German fließen. The same root is the ancestor of the verb fly, Dutch vliegen and German fliegen, as well as various Germanic words for "bird", such as the Dutch and German vogel, Danish and Norwegian fugl and English fowl.

The range of meanings derived from PIE *pleu- and represented by the fl- cluster is well-illustrated by the different meanings of fleet. This first appeared as a verb, descended from Old English fleotan "float, drift". Although this sense is now obsolete, the next sense "fade, vanish" is still with us in its present participle form fleeting. Another meaning of the verb is "move quickly, fly" as those who are fleet of foot. The noun fleet comes from Old English *flota*, which meant both "ship" and "sailor" before becoming "group of ships under one command". Languages as diverse as Spanish, Polish and Serbian (amongst others) still use *flota* for "naval fleet", and from Spanish we have also borrowed *flotilla*, or "little fleet". A further meaning of *fleet* was "estuary, tidal inlet" as in various Kent –fleets, the village of Fleet in Dorset and Fleet Street, the former home of the British press. This was located by the River Fleet, which is now a subterranean tributary of the Thames.

Other roots contribute to the *flowing* nature of fl-. The Latin root *fluo* "flow" gave English *fluid, flux, flush, flume, fluctuate* and *fluent*, (along with *effluent, confluence, affluent* etc.), not to mention *fluvial* "pertaining to a river". The idea that speech flows like a river in the mouths of fluent speakers is echoed in many languages. "Rivers flow and rivers run", as Karine Polwart sings, somewhat tautologically. In French, fluent speakers speak *runningly* (*couramment*), while *courant* "running" also means "current", borrowed by English as a synonym of "flow". *Fluo* ultimately goes back to the prolific PIE root **bhel* "swell, blow" (the star of the show in chapter 22, where we look at bl-) a root which is also responsible for *flower, flour* and *flourish* via Latin *flos* "flower", itself the origin of *Florence* and that city's gold coins, *florins*. In both cases there is an outpouring; the flood of the river and the blossoming of the flower.

*Bhel- is also the ancestor of *flame, flamethrower* (a calque, or literal translation, of German *Flammenwerfer* – see chapter 11) and *flagrant* along with a number of other *flashy* words with the fl-cluster. One of these is *flamingo*, which English borrowed in the sixteenth century from Portuguese. This in turn can be traced back via Spanish to Provençal *flamenc* "flame-coloured" and that language's source word *flama* "flame". The Camargue region in the Rhône delta of Provence is home to the largest colony of greater flamingos in the Western Mediterranean. *Flamingo* may also be

related to the famous Andalusian *flamenco*, due to the fiery, passionate nature of the dance. Having said this, there are multiple suggested origins for this word, including *Fleming*, as the Spanish court of the time had a number of Flemish nobles, due to Spain's ownership of Flanders. What they were doing dancing a Morisco peasant dance is a matter of conjecture. Other sparky *flashers* lay bare different fl-origins to show us what they are made of. These include *flicker* and *flare* and the rock used for millennia to create a spark, *flint* (discussed further in chapter 10).

Another subset of the *flock* of fl- words is connected with the concept of *fluffiness*. As with other members of the fl- fraternity, this group float lightly on the breeze in *flurries*. Some of these words can be traced back to the PIE root **pleus-* "pluck, feather" which had become **flusaz* in Proto-Germanic. This became Old English *fleos* (and Dutch *vlies*) from which it had little distance to travel to reach its modern spelling of *fleece*. *Fleecing* as in "cheating, swindling" comes from the idea of stripping a sheep of its fleece – stripping people of their money, or indeed taking the shirt off their backs. **Pleus-* is also the source of *plume*, probably *floss*, and by association, Beatrix Potter's *flopsy* bunnies.

Further down our list, we arrive at the inadequate *flotsam* – the *floating* wreckage of the fl- cluster. Here we find the *flim-flam* and the *flustered flunkies*, where the cluster reveals its lack of constancy. Fl- *flaunts* its lack of respect for convention, displaying everything from mildly risqué behaviour to a downright tarty side. Fl- is the home of the fashionably *flirtatious flappers* of the 1920s, determined to *flout* the rules of a priggishly stuffy society and under the admiring gaze of *flamboyantly* attired *flâneurs*. A few steps down the social ladder, we reach the *flighty* young *flibbertigibbets*, *flouncing flippantly* through life and not averse to a moonlight *flit* if needs must. Lastly, we arrive at the brazen *floozy*, *flashing* her wares at unsuspecting passers-by.

As touched on earlier, a final major group of words beginning with the fl- cluster concerns the notion of *flatness*. In the Middle English period, there was *flet* "dwelling, ground floor" alongside *flat*, the familiar adjective. These words converged when the former, under the influence of Scots, came to mean "apartment". On the same theme, the Old Norse word *flatr* "slab of stone, flake" gave English *flake*, *flagstone*, *floe* and *flaw*, which originally meant "flake, thin cake of ice", before coming to mean "crack" and then "defect". *Flat* words ultimately derive from the PIE root **plat-* "spread", which we will look at in more detail with the pl- cluster in chapter 19. Most of the "flat" words beginning with fl- are Germanic, having been altered to fl- by Grimm's Law. Even so, the flow between languages has been fittingly *fluid* – Germanic languages have moved from pl- to fl-, but kept borrowing both pl- and fl- words. Pl- words embracing the *flatness* theme, such as *plan*, *plane* and *plinth* tend to have been borrowed into English from Romance languages at a later date. A good example of this dichotomy can be seen with *flounder* (Germanic) and *plaice* (Old French *plaise*) both of which originally just meant "flatfish", aka *fluke*, from Old English *floc* "flatfish".

4.   thr- thrusting through

Fame can take interesting men and thrust mediocrity upon them.

David Bowie

Thr- *threads* its way along a groove in the tongue before being *thrust through* the *throat* and *thrown* into the air. This cluster indicates a struggle to get through the bottleneck, and it is therefore fitting that it is a battle to get thr- out of the mouth. In the English language classroom, it is sure only to produce frustrated students and plentiful amounts of spittle. Words like *throughout* and *thriftless* are English's answer to those words in foreign language classes that seem impossible to pronounce. When I was teaching, thr- was my payback for the delighted laughter at my pitiful attempts at French *écureuil* "squirrel" and Czech *čtyři* "four", not to mention my tortuous struggles trying to distinguish between French *dessus* "above" and *dessous* "below", and Portuguese *avô* "grandfather" and *avó* "grandmother", though that's another story!

The **thr-** cluster exists in English, some Scandinavian languages, Greek and a handful of others. It also occurs in Old Persian, while Bengali, for some unfathomable reason, appears to have decided to borrow thr- from English, but it is very scarce everywhere else. English actually added to its store of thr- words in the Middle English period, when a small number of words with the pattern *th + vowel + r* underwent a process known as metathesis. This meant that the *r* swapped places with the vowel so *thir-* became *thri-* (as with *thrill* from Old English *þyrel* – the thorn *þ* representing the /θ/ sound of *thick*) and *thur-* became *thru-* (as with *through* from OE *þurh*).

Metathesis is the process whereby sounds or syllables are rearranged in a word, eventually resulting in the creation of new forms. It is a phenomenon found in many languages, and continues to be seen in English today. It can lead to parallel forms with the same meaning, like *pretty* and *purty*, and parallel forms whose meanings diverge, like *patron* and *pattern* (both from Latin *patronus* "model to be imitated"), and the closer pair *skirmish* and *scrimmage*. Pronunciation is also affected, as with [æstərɪks] for *asterisk*, which is the opposite of the way Chaucer and Caxton's *ax* was transformed to Modern English *ask.*

Metathesis is common with the liquid consonants *r* and *l*. Sequences where an *r* is followed by a short vowel are especially prone to metathesis, although similar sequences with a long vowel usually remain unchanged. This explains why *three* from OE *þreo, þri, þrie* (all long vowels) is unmetathesised, but *third* and *thirty* from OE *þridda* and *þritig* (both short vowels) metathesised. Similarly, *thirteen* only metathesised once the long vowel from Old English *þreotiene* had shortened to Middle English *thrittene.* Other examples of this ilk include *dirt* from ME *drit* "excrement, mud" and *curd* from *crud* "coagulated substance". The latter is interesting as *curd* remetathesised back to *crud* in 1920s US slang for "venereal disease", and then moved back into mainstream speech as "nonsense", "disgusting substance". This spawned the adjective *cruddy*, with its phonosemantic similarity to the *crudeness* and *crustiness* of the cr- cluster undoubtedly playing its part (see chapter 12).

Metathesis happened in the other direction with the *r* moving ahead of the vowel before Old English –ht /xt/. Hence, *beorht, fyrhtu, wyrhta* and *worhte* became *bright, fright, wright* and *wrought*, although unmetathesised and metathesised parallel forms existed for hundreds of years. In fact, this happened in numerous cases, with *bird* overcoming *bridd, wren* supplanting *wærna, burst* outlasting *brest* and *grass* prevailing over *gærs* only after centuries of nip and tuck. This kind of metathesis was common in other languages too, one interesting example being French *fromage* "cheese", which is from Old French *formage* "forming".

One way of *thrusting through* the thicket of *thorns* is by making a hole through which you can escape. The Old English word for "hole" was the aforementioned *þyrel*, hence *nostril*, literally "nosehole" from *nosu* + *þyrel*, which overcame other challengers like *nosethirl* and regrettably, *nosethrill* on the way. *Thirl* still exists in some dialects as a verb "pierce, bore", as a noun as "hole, aperture", and in toponyms – place names – such as *Thirlmere* in the Lake District. *Thrill* comes from OE *þyrlian* "make a hole" and only later developed its meaning of "excite" as the thrilled were metaphorically pierced with emotion. *Thrill* now lives happily side by side with the related *drill*, although their meanings have become distinctly separated. *Through* wasn't clearly separated from *thorough* until the early Modern English period. Thus, we have *drive-through* and *throughway*, but also *thoroughfare*. *Thorough* was initially used adjectivally, meaning "from end to end" from which "exhaustive, careful" is only a small step as thorough things are carried through to completion. However, the concept of *through* is not universal across Indo-European. Many Romance and Slavic languages do not distinguish between *through* and *across*, (French *à travers*, Italian *attraverso*, Polish *przez*). It is Germanic languages where *through* and its cognates imply a constricted, bounded journey and *across* is an easier movement from one side to the other.

Throat and *throttle* come from Old English *þrote*, "throat", which is related to OE *þrutian* "swell". Cognates in other languages include Icelandic *þroti* "swelling", Dutch *strot* "throat" and Italian *strozza* "throat", itself borrowed from Germanic. A sore and swollen throat will *throb* painfully, and thr- often does seem to smart a bit, whether you are on the wrong end of a painful *thrashing* or flailing about in your death *throes*. *Throes* can be traced back to the Old English noun *þrea* "affliction, threat, torment" and its cheery related verb *þrowian* "suffer, endure", cognate with German *drohen* "threaten".

The Old English ancestor of *threat* is *þreat*, "crowd, pressure, trouble, force", which resembles contemporary Icelandic *þraut* "annoyance, complaint, struggle". The OE forerunner of *throng*, *þrang*, "crowd, press" also has the idea of uncomfortable pressure leading to discomfort, so fits in with the idea of constriction intrinsic to thr-. The PIE root of English *threat* is *treud-* "push, press, squeeze". This root has also spawned a lot of words in Indo-European languages, such as *mpyд/trud*, the word for "effort, labour" in most Slavic languages, and the Latin *trudo* "push, shove", from which English later took *extrude*, *intrude*, *protrude* etc.

Another group of thr- words involve "beating" or "rubbing". *Threshing* is the process of loosening the edible grain from the chaff before the winnowing (separating) stage. Prior to industrialisation, it was a labour-intensive, time-consuming process in which some unfortunate peasant would repeatedly trample on the cereal or beat it with a flail on the threshing floor. It has been suggested that a *threshold* was originally a threshing area adjacent to the living area of a house rather than the entry point. A dialect form of *thresh* was *thrash*, although the latter is now primarily used for "whip" or "give a severe beating" – the world is an altogether better place when Newcastle United give Sunderland a good thrashing – and for *thrash metal*, an aggressive subgenre of heavy metal music in which the artists wear black, thrash their instruments and rant incoherently. Proto-Germanic *threshkana* is the source for cognates in all the contemporary Germanic languages for words for *thresh* as with German *dreschen* "thresh" and Icelandic *þreskja*.

The *threshkana* root is thought to be a descendant of the PIE megaroot *ter- "rub, turn". *Ter-* is the source for thousands of words across the Indo-European language group, a sizeable number of which have evolved new senses and been borrowed by English at various stages. These include *diatribe, termite, trite, detrimental, attorney, contour, tournament* and *tourniquet. Throw* can also be traced back to **ter-*, but in its Old English guise *þrawan* was much closer to **ter-* meaning "turn, twist" rather than "throw". The modern sense of *throw* may have developed via the notion of whirling a missile around before throwing it, as in hurling a stone from a sling. Slings are known to have been used as weapons since the Neolithic era, and a similar throwing action can still be seen in the Olympic field event of the hammer. This original sense is still preserved in ceramics, where the clay is still *thrown* around the potter's wheel – i.e. it is turned and rubbed. *Thread*, as "twisted yarn" is another descendant of **ter-*, as is the dialectal term *tharm* "bowel, gut", which leads us back to the (hopefully not critically) constricted path through which thr- must travel. *Thairm*, the Scots equivalent of *tharm*, denotes the intestine used for making instrument strings and haggis. On which picturesque note, we'll skip on to the next chapter!

5.   br- brides, brothers and brushes

'That's enough to begin with,' Humpty Dumpty interrupted: 'there are plenty of hard words there. "Brillig" means four o'clock in the afternoon — the time when you begin broiling things for dinner.'

Lewis Carroll, *Through the Looking-Glass*

Br- is a potent *brew* of *breasts*, *bristles* and *braggadocio* – a somewhat eclectic mix, I think you'll agree. As Lawler (1990) explains, the cluster appears to have three distinct phonesthemes. Firstly, there are two clear themes that seem to have been assigned either "masculine" or "feminine" meanings, according to traditional gender roles. The male br- words show man as the territorial, aggressive fighter, a world where *brawn* comes before *brains* and where bands of *brothers brag* of their *bravery*. The female br- words show woman as the homemaker, primarily in charge of feeding and *breeding*. The new *bride* makes the *bread*, looks after the *brood* and weans the babies at her *breast*. A third use of br- is for *bristly* things, and there are a whole host of these too. Br- is neatly encapsulated by Brer Rabbit's taunt at the end of the American folktale *Brer Rabbit and the Tar Baby* (1880): "I was born and *bred* in the *briar* patch, *Brer* Fox!" Here, all three phonosemantic br- meanings are rattled out in quick succession.

First, let's take a look at the *brutes* that have got too big for their *britches*. The word *brute* comes from the extinct Oscan language of southern Italy, a sister language to Latin. From Latin *brutus* "heavy, dull, stupid" it acquired the meaning of "belonging to the lower animals" and *brute* and *brutal* spread throughout Europe from Portuguese *bruto* to Bulgarian брутален (*brutalen*). *Brutus* was also the surname of one of the most celebrated families

48

in Rome, the *gens Junia*, a clan descended from the last king of Rome, the brilliantly monikered Lucius Tarquinius Superbus, or more mundanely, Tarquin the Proud. The most famous descendant is undoubtedly Marcus Junius Brutus, one of the conspirators involved in the assassination of Julius Caesar. In Shakespeare's *Julius Caesar*, the emperor's dying words are a despairing *"et tu Brute?"* when he sees Brutus join in the stabbing. Mark Antony does later call him "the noblest Roman of them all", but Brutus has already rather blotted his copybook by this point, not to mention killed himself by running onto his servant's sword.

Brutal men *break* things, and the reconstructed ancestor of *break*, the Proto-Indo-European root **bhreg* "break" is a source word for many of the masculine br- words, including *brick*, *bruise*, *braggart*, *brittle* and *breeches*. In a manner which will raise a smile from aficionados of national stereotypes, it seems that the medieval French prided themselves on their manhood: Middle French *braguette* referred to codpiece armour, while its verb *braguer* meant "flaunt, brag". The former gave English *bracket* – apparently the architectural supports resembled these armour-plated codpieces, whereas the latter is the source of *braggart*, a boastful fellow, especially one who would *brandish* his breeches (and presumably, their contents).

The Old Italian verb *brigare* "brawl, fight" and its noun *briga* "trouble, bother" are the source of further testosterone-fuelled br-words. Derived nouns from this root include *brigata* "company, troop", and *brigante* "irregular soldier". However, while the former kept its discipline and was borrowed by French and then English as *brigade*, the latter gave French and English *brigand* – a result of the chaos disbanded and irregular soldiers have caused on numerous occasions throughout history. Other derivatives from *brigare* include *brigandine* "body armour" and *brig*, originally fast, skirmishing ships, later used as prisons.

Brave comes from Italian *bravo* via French *brave*. This etymology is interesting because *bravo* as a noun in Italian meant "desperado", and as an adjective originally meant "savage" before acquiring the meaning of "bold". *Bravo* probably comes from a fusion of Latin *pravus* "crooked, depraved" and *barbarus* "wild, uncouth". Medieval Latin *bravus* meant "villain, cutthroat", and this has its echoes in the derogatory attitudes held by European settlers towards the North American Indian *braves*, who were considered to be primitive warriors.

One way in which our more knuckle-headed *brethren* can display the fact that they are *all brawn and no brains* is through *brawling*. *Brawn* now chiefly refers to muscular strength and power, but this derives from its older meaning of "slab of meat" from the same Germanic source that gave the Germans their *Bratwürste*. **Brawl** has its parallels in the Low German and Dutch verb *brallen* "brag, boast" – fighters flaunting their muscles prior to the brawl and if victorious, strutting in triumph afterwards. Contemporary boxers and wrestlers still go through the same ritualised swaggering today. The Yorkshire dialect word *bray* also means "crush, beat up", and the winner of a brawl may *bray* about his victory like the ass he is. The latter *bray* was taken from Middle French *braire* which also describes the cry of a donkey, but this in turn comes from the Proto-Celtic **bragu* "break wind", bringing to mind the unreconstructed, farting meathead who epitomises the *brash* masculine br- cluster, and is "built like a *brick* shithouse". In an entirely coincidental accident of juxtaposition, this seems like an apt moment to point out how effortlessly the terms *Brexiter* and *Brexiteer* have been absorbed into the national vocabulary – another example of how newly-coined words are quickly accepted when they fit an existing phonestheme.

Although it was the men who typically brought the meat home, it was usually the women who cooked it (although this may be hard to believe when you see how territorial and protective modern man gets around his barbecue). The verb *braise* comes from Old French *brese* "embers, live coals", and tending the hearth tended to fall under the woman's remit. Women as homemakers *braised* and *broiled* the meat and *brewed* the *broth* and the beer, possibly in a *bronze* pot. *Brandy* also fits into this category, coming into English from Dutch *brandewijn* "burnt wine", i.e. wine that has been distilled over a fire.

In Indo-European tradition, the newly married *bride* went to live with her husband's family, hence the link between Old English *bryd* "bride" and its Gothic cognate *bruþs* "daughter-in-law", both of which can be traced back to Proto-Germanic *brudiz* "bride, daughter-in-law". It may well have been the new daughter-in-law's job to cook, brew and make broth for her *brydguma* "bridegroom" and his family. Somewhat surprisingly, *bridal*, although now exclusively used in reference to weddings, is not the simple adjective that it seems. In fact, it comes from the Old English noun *brydealo* "wedding ale, wedding feast" from *bryd* "bride" and *ealu* "ale, feast". The *brydealo* was an occasion marked by copious ale-drinking and riotous festivity, which may ring a few bells with attendees at modern wedding receptions!

Braise, *brew*, *brandy* and *brimstone* go back to the PIE root *bhre- "burn, heat, incubate". As well as the fiery *burn*, the noun *burn* meaning "stream" is also thought to come from this root, along with is doublet *bourne*, as in *Bournemouth*. The semantic connection is apparently through the image of spray from flowing water resembling smoke. Thus, Norwegian *brenning* and Swedish *bränning* mean both "burning" and "surf". *Brood* and *breed* also come from the *bhre- root. The original meaning of *brooding* was "sitting on eggs to make them hatch". This idea of "nursing" led to the later figurative idea of nursing a grievance or a grudge, as resentment was "incubated in the mind". *Broody* women were "ready to breed", but *breed*, from Old English *bredan* originally meant "warm to hatch, cherish", as the woman as homemaker fulfilled her main roles of feeding and nurturing to *bring up* the *brood*. However, too many children could put a strain on the maternal instinct as outlined in the nursery rhyme "There was an Old Woman Who Lived in a Shoe":

> There was an old woman who lived in a shoe.
> She had so many children she didn't know what to do;
> So she gave them some *broth* without any *bread*;
> And she whipped them all soundly and sent them to bed.

No doubt the little *brats* deserved it.

Loaves and *bread* cause problems for English language learners. What English speakers casually call "a loaf" is what speakers of other languages would simply call "a bread", as in French *un pain*, Polish *jeden chleb*, Danish *et brød* etc. Yet, while these languages can count out *breads*, English must count out *loaves*, much to the bemusement of students of English – many a time I have heard the plaintive lament "what is this loaf?" However, the root of the word for "bread" in many Slavic languages is the same as the root for *loaf*, Proto-Germanic *(k)hlaibaz*. This root gave Old English *hlaf*, Old Norse *hleifr* and Gothic *hlaifs* "bread, loaf baked in an oven". Proto-Slavic *xlěbъ* (*xlěbŭ*) is a borrowing from a Germanic source, and the antecedent of Russian хлеб (*xljeb*), Czech *chleb* and Bulgarian хляб (*hljab*).

After the Old English period, the consonant cluster *hl-* was reduced to *l-*, so OE *hlaf* became ME *laf* and Modern English *loaf*. The Anglo-Saxons also celebrated *hlaf-mas*, "loaf-mass", the festival of the new wheat harvest, every August 1st. On this day, a loaf was made from the new crop to be taken to church and blessed. This festival survives in some areas of English and Scotland as *Lammas*, although it is also celebrated by Wiccans and other neo-pagans as the harvest festival of *Lughnasadh* and is believed to be of pagan origin.

By the 13th century, *bread* had replaced *hlaf* as the generic term for "bread". There are two theories regarding the origin of the word *bread*. One theory is that it is from Proto-Germanic **brautham*, which would mean it comes from the Proto-Indo-European root of *brew*, **bhreu*, thus connected to Old English *beorma* "yeast" and so referred to the leavening process. An alternative theory posits that bread comes from Proto-Germanic **braudaz*, "broken piece, fragment", from PIE **bhera*-"split, break off,"and so means "piece of food". If this interpretation is correct, then *bread* is connected to Old English *breotan* "break off" and related to *break* and *brittle*. Recognisable cognates of *bread* abound, especially in Germanic languages e.g. *Brot* (German) and *bröd* (Swedish), but there is also French *brioche* (from Old French *brier* "break, knead"), Albanian *brydh* "crumb" and Latin *frustum* "crumb, morsel" amongst many others.

Bread equates to power; the *breadwinner* commands respect. For many cultures, the person who controls the bread supply is the master of the household. The Old English *hlafweard* was the "loafward" – guardian of the loaves. *Hlafweard* was then reduced to *hlaford* "master of the household, superior". With the loss of the hl- cluster, this became *laford/lowerd* and by the close of the Middle English period, the word had morphed to the familiar *lord*. *Lady* took a similar route to reach its current form. The second element of Old English *hlæfdige* is equivalent to "kneader, maker of dough", which later acquired the meaning of "maid, female servant". As with *hlafweard*, the initial h- of *hlæfdige* was lost, and in the 14th century, the *f* disappeared too. In the meantime, *dæge* moved via *deie* to *dey* resulting in *hlæfdige* becoming *lady*. So next time you feel intimidated or envious of "lords and ladies" remember that they are basically "breadkeepers and doughkneaders"! At least bread guardians and bread kneaders had some respected function, though. The Old English term for "household servant" was *hlafæta*, "loaf-eater", reflecting the disdain felt by the aristocracy for each of their domestic minions as "another mouth to feed".

The PIE root *bhreus- "swell, sprout" is the ultimate source of both *breast* and *brush*. In Proto-Germanic, this had become *brust- "bud, shoot". This is one of the bridges between the feminine br- and the bristly br- as it is only a short hop from *brust- to both *breast* and *brush*, with the connecting theme of budding new growth. Br- often focuses on the spiky thorniness of young plant growth – the sprouting *underbrush* providing *brushwood* and *broom*. The verb *browse* also can be traced to this new growth as it originally meant "feed on buds". At the same time, many of these prickly plants were fashioned into tools to be used by the woman as homemaker, *brushes* and *brooms* featuring heavily in her domestic armoury. Outside of the home, with less domestically-minded women, the br- connection remains, as *broomsticks* are witches' preferred means of transport!

There are many of these sharp, bristly br- words in English – pointy things that are ready to trip, scratch and entangle the unwary like *briars* and *bracken*. The modern English *bristle*, comes from Old English *byrstel*, which has cognates in Swedish *borst* and German *Borste*. *Bur* "prickly seed vessel" and *barley* are also etymologically related to *bristle*. Sometimes, there is also some crossover between this phonosemantic meaning and the spiky, aggressive display of the *brash, brusque* male, fiercely defending his territory. Primitive man will *bristle* with anger if you *brush* past him, before demanding if you spilt his pint.

The PIE root *bhrem "spike, point, edge," has been pinpointed as another common source of many of the bristly br- words in English, while other items undoubtedly developed by analogy with the large body of similar br- terms. *Bhrem* is the source of *broom* and *bramble*, both of which have similar cognates in Germanic languages. For instance, German *Brombeere*, Icelandic *brómber* and Dutch *braam* all mean "bramble, blackberry". This PIE root is also the source of *brim*, *brink* and the German city of *Bremen*, which is located at the brimming water's edge, on the banks of the river Weser. Other spiky br- words abound throughout contemporary Indo-European languages, with Slovenian *brst* "bud", Spanish *brezo* "heather" and German *Bruiere* "briar" just the tip of a very large, and yet somehow bristly, mixed metaphorical iceberg!

6. sn- snivelling snouts

Laugh and the world laughs with you, snore and you sleep alone.

Anthony Burgess

Sn- *snorts* and *snuffles* its way out of our *schnozzles* – it is the nose phonestheme. Almost everything that we do with our *snoots*, *snouts* or *snitches* is prefaced by the sn- cluster. When the nose is irritated, we will *sneeze*, when it is blocked we will *snore*, *snuffle* or *snivel*, and when we want to inhale something we will *sniff* it or *snort* it up our noses. Likewise, if something or someone really gets up your nose, you may well dismiss the offender with an arrogant *sniff* or a disgusted *snort*.

If we look to the past and among English speaking dialects, there are even more sn- examples. Old English had the noun *snofl* "mucus", the ancestor of *snivel*, and the verb *snytan* "wipe or blow the nose", cognate with Old Norse *snyta*. This verb survives in Scottish English and some other dialects as *snite* "wiping or blowing the nose without bothering with a handkerchief" – think Premier League footballer evacuating a nostril. (In an ideal phonosemantic world, you would now be thinking of Robert *Snodgrass* or Ian *Snodin*, but my money is on Wayne Rooney.)

Many of these nasal sn- words have been traced back to Proto-Germanic *snut-* "snout", the source of numerous contemporary cognates: German *Schnauze*, Dutch *snuit*, Saterland Frisian *Snuute*, Norwegian *snute* and Danish *snude* all mean "snout". The Baltic languages of Lithuanian and Latvian also have sn- snouts, possibly due to Prussian influence, with *snùkis* and *snuķis* respectively. *Snot* and *snoot* join *snout* as obvious English descendants of *snut-*, but there are also a number of imitative sn- words, which have been

56

likened to the sounds of the breathing through the nose, such as *snore*, *snort* and *snooze*.

Centuries before yuppies were *snorting* lines of cocaine, the aristocracy were funnelling tobacco up their delicate noses in the form of *snuff*. Snuff was brought back to Europe from the Americas by the Franciscan monk Ramón Pané, who accompanied Columbus on his second voyage to the New World in 1493. Pané had observed the Taino and Carib people of the Lesser Antilles taking snuff, and he resolved to try it out for himself. Thoroughly enamoured by the experience, Pané brought snuff back to Spain, whence it spread swiftly to the Royal Courts and palaces of Europe. An early convert was the French Queen, Catherine de' Medici, who was introduced to ground tobacco snuff in 1561. She found that it relieved her persistent headaches and was so impressed with its healing power that she gave it her royal seal of approval. She proclaimed that it would henceforth be known as *Herba Regina*, which led to the French nobility eagerly shovelling it up their hooters from dainty little *snuff-boxes*.

The burnt part of the candle wick is also known as the *snuff*, while the instrument used to extinguish the candle is the *snuffer*. It is from this meaning that the colloquial *snuff it* "die" is thought to originate, and this is also a cognate of Dutch *sneuvelen* "perish, die in battle". Furthermore, we have the slang verb *snuff out* "kill, murder" which is one of a number of English sn- words that have a shady, underworld character. These include *snooper*, *snitch* "informer, stool pigeon", *snatch* "steal", *snaffle* "purloin, acquire illicitly", *snag* "seize, obtain" and *sneak*, which can be either "con artist" or "informer".

In a roundabout way, *snuff* may also be the origin of terms beginning with sn- which relate to drinking strong alcohol. The warm nasal reaction to a pinch of snuff was associated with the similar feelings triggered by a *snifter* or *snort* of whisky, a quick *snootful* or a shot of *Schnapps*. A snifter is likely to clear the nose and prevent *snuffling* or *sniffling*, but a strong dram may provoke a *sneeze*. *Sneeze* is interesting in that it is the descendant of the now obsolete *fnese*, from Old English *fneosan* "sneeze, snort". The English fn- cluster was used with words to do with breathing, but was always rare and merged with the sn- cluster without difficulty in the Middle Ages (see introduction). Fn- does exist in other Germanic languages, as for example, Dutch *fniesen* "sneeze" and Old Norse *fnysa* "snort", but even here it isn't commonplace.

Many sn- words *snap* or *snip*. In line with the nasal theme, these words derive from Middle Dutch and Middle Low German *snavel* "bill, beak" and pertain to the beak itself and its cutting, biting and feeding functions. Thus, *snap* means "quick sudden bite or cut", but also in Northern English "food to be eaten in a work break", when you could *snatch* some time to eat. Other related words include *snack*, *snaffle*, *snook* and *snoop*. The *snipe's* most prominent feature is its long and slender beak, so it is unsurprising that it fits in with the nasal sn- theme, or that it has similar cognates in Germanic languages, such as Dutch *snip*, German *Schnepfe*, and Swedish *snäppa*, which means "sandpiper", a bird of the snipe family. Snipe shooting was practised by British soldiers in India, who would stay out of view of the birds in special hides. It is from here that we get the word *sniper*.

Pejorative sn- words are also common, possibly from the idea that you wrinkle your nose in disgust when confronted with the unpleasant or that you *look down your nose* on those people who you despise. *Snivelling snotnoses* are routinely *sneered* at and are the butt of *snide* remarks and *snotty* comments. Those who enjoy this kind of *snarky sniping* will ridicule their unfortunate victims and *snigger* or *snicker* at those whom they disdain. The lower classes may be derided by the *snootier* members of the elite, who may regard them as mere *guttersnipes* whose efforts to improve their social status must be *snubbed* and *sneezed at*.

The word *snob* has travelled a long way in a relatively short time. In the late eighteenth century, it meant "shoemaker" or "cobbler", but by the 1790s it was being used by students at Cambridge University in a contemptuous sense to refer to the local merchants and townsmen. By the Victorian era, *snob* was being used for "person who apes his social superiors", but the meaning then again broadened to "person who insists on his superior social status" and by the early 20th century, had acquired its current meaning of "one who despises those considered lower in rank, status or taste" – a 180° turn from its 1790s meaning. Snobs must abound throughout the world, because the English word has been exported to a plethora of languages: French, Serbian, Bulgarian, Italian and Dutch to name but a few.

The sn- cluster's association with the nose remains strong in Germanic languages, as attested by the vast numbers of similar sounding words we can find there. For instance, *snuffle* comes from Middle Dutch *snuffelen* "sniff about, sneak", which is related to *snuffen* "sniffle". These terms equate to *schnüffeln* and *schnuppern* in German. *Sniff* is *sniffa* in Swedish, *snuiven* in Dutch and *snuse* in Danish. Similarly, *snore* is *snarka* in Swedish, *snorke* in Norwegian and Danish, *snurken* in Dutch and *schnarchen* in German. *Snot* gets up people's nose as *snor* in Sweden and as *snot* in the Netherlands, where an irritating Dutch whippersnapper may be dismissed with the equally familiar *snotneus*. What's more, sn- is still productive in the nose department. The word *snorkel* is a 20th century coinage from German navy slang for the airshaft of a submarine, *Schnorchel* "nose, snout". The nasal sn- seems to be a very Germanic phenomenon, however. Other language families largely avoid it for words relating to the *snoot*, unless the beak is the source behind the naming of Irish *snag* "treecreeper" and the derived terms *snag breac* "magpie" and *snag darach* "woodpecker", *breac* meaning "piebald" and *darach* "oak".

A less common phonestheme with the sn- cluster is derived from PIE *sneg-* "crawl, creep". Its descendants include *snake, snail, sneak* and *sneaker*, the shoe so-named because of its noiselessness. Another possible relation is Lewis Carroll's invented beast the *snark*, which may well be a portmanteau – word blend – of *snake* and *shark* (see chapter 10). Again, Scandinavian languages share this root, so we find cognates for "snail" in Icelandic *snigill*, Danish *snegl* and Swedish *snigel*; and cognates for "(grass) snake" in Icelandic *snákur*, Danish *snog* and Swedish *snok* (see also chapter 20 where sm- overlaps here). Interestingly, Swedish *snok* is also slang for "nose", so the two themes *cock a snook* at etymologists and interlink here.

The sn- cluster's particularly evocative sound symbolism has also been responsible for the naming of a number of famous fictional characters. Along with the sneakily elusive *snark,* the cartoon beagle *Snoopy* has a very impressive schnozzle, *Snidely Whiplash* is the stereotypical villain in The Rocky and Bullwinkle Show, and Professor *Severus Snape* in the Harry Potter series is a sneering, sarcastic bully. The dialectal verb *snape* and its variant *sneap* mean "rebuke, chide, bite, offend", or in other words, "put someone's nose out of joint", altogether a perfect summary of the phonosemantic significance of Severus Snape's character and the snide aspects of the sn- cluster as a whole.

Authors often give their characters evocative names to indicate their personalities. Most simply, many children's books embrace this concept, notably Roger Hargreaves's *Mr Men* series and its spin-offs. The same applies to children's comics such as *The Beano*, with characters such as *Lord Snooty, Dennis the Menace, Minnie the Minx, Billy Whizz* and *Plug* (from *plug-ugly*) leaving us in no doubt of their defining personality traits. Other authors use phonosemantics in the naming of their characters: it is no coincidence in *A Christmas Carol* that Dickens portrays *Ebenezer Scrooge* as *scrimping* and *scraping*, *scrabbling* around for every penny, while his underpaid and abused clerk *Bob Cratchit*, is made to *cringe* and *crawl* for his tyrannical master.

Various sportsmen and entertainers also choose or are awarded nicknames relating to success in their chosen profession e.g. Phil "The Power" Taylor (darts), James "Bonecrusher" Smith (boxing), and Ernie "The Big Easy" Els (golf). Then there is the light-hearted theory of *nominative determinism*, which has been propounded by *New Scientist* magazine since 1994. This theory states that people will gravitate towards areas of work and patterns of behaviour that match their names. Some fabulous examples have been found: an article on urology by researchers named Splatt and Weedon, a meteorologist named Storm Field, and naked jogger Donald Popadick, charged in an Ottawan court with indecent exposure.

Although it is clearly far-fetched to say that our lives are predetermined by our names, some phonosemantic matches are very tempting: Usain Bolt is the fastest man on the planet. The President of France, Emmanuel Macron married Brigitte Trogneux in 2007. The Trogneux family are chocolatiers, whose flagship product is macaroons, specifically *macarons d'Amiens*, pointing Brigitte Macron towards her destiny. As for FIFA ex-President Sepp Blatter, his period of *bloated* office was marked by rampant corruption, lavish overspending, bribery and excess, in accordance with the *bling* and *bluster* of the bl- cluster. While the English word *blatter* is a variation on *blather*, i.e. "chatter volubly and excessively", in German, the surname Blatter actually means "someone who lived on a plateau", specifically from the Swiss town of Blatten. However, one of the meanings of the German noun *Blatter* is "pock, pustule", which seems curiously appropriate.

While it is fun to speculate about clusters and nominative determinism in this way, it does stretch the bounds of credibility. It is certainly true that Australian footballer Danny Invincible was a regular scorer at the start of the century for Swindon Town and Kilmarnock, but it is also true that his compatriot Lorraine Crapp was an Olympic swimming champion in 1956, and was not, therefore, crap at swimming!

7.   gl- glowing glances

Personality is the glitter that sends your little gleam across the footlights and the orchestra pit into that big black space where the audience is.

Mae West

   Wise old heads and slaves to cliché tell us "all that *glitters* is not gold". And in fact, we have been saying this for a very long time: Shakespeare tells us that "all that *glisters* is not gold" in *The Merchant of Venice*, and earlier still, Chaucer declared that "hit is not al gold, that *glareth*" in his poem *The House of Fame*. Yet, despite the stale proverb, it is true to say that very many words that begin with **gl-** will indeed *glitter*, *glimmer* or *glisten*, and that *glitter* and *gold* ultimately derive from the same root. The gl- cluster is the light fantastic, covering the perception, production and reflection of light. Over time, the number of gl- words has multiplied to the extent that there is now a separate word for almost every conceivable type of light. The light may be fleeting, as when you catch a *glimpse* of it, or it may last for a longer time as it *glows*. Gl- is also a smooth combination, it *glides* hither and thither and *gleams* like *glass*.
   Many of the words carrying this cluster can be traced back to PIE **ghel-* "shine, yellow, glimmer". The Old English word for "yellow" is *geolu*. Here the "soft g" has become /j/, which also happened with *yolk* from OE *geolca*, a sound change probably due to Viking influence. The words *gold* and *gild* come from the same root, as do the words *gall* and *bile*, both of which refer to the yellow-green fluid produced by the liver to aid digestion. From this root, Greek took χολή (*kholē*), from which we get *cholera* and

melancholy, two of the four temperaments derived from the "humours", or vital fluids, according to Hippocratic medical theory. Up until the 19th century, it was commonly believed that the humours had to be in balance to keep the body healthy. Melancholy came from black bile, produced in the spleen, while a choleric or angry disposition came from an excess of yellow bile, from the gall bladder.

If we look at other Germanic languages, the yellow and gold gl-connection becomes even clearer. *Yellow* in German is *gelb*, while *gold* is the same word as in English. The Dutch equivalents are *geel* and *goud*, while Swedish has *gul* and *guld*. In a process known as *satemisation*, Proto-Indo-European *g^h and *g became Proto-Balto-Slavic sibilants *$\acute{z}^h$ and *$\acute{z}$. Hence, *yellow* and *gold* become *žluté* and *zlato* in Czech, *žuto* and *zlato* in Croatian and желто (*želtó*) and золото (*zóloto*) in Russian. The currency of Poland, the *zloty*, comes from *złoto* "gold", while the Polish word for yellow is *żółty*.

Linguists divide Indo-European languages into *centum* and *satem* languages, according to the pronunciation of the initial consonant in the word for "hundred". Centum languages maintain a hard initial /k/ as in the original pronunciation of Latin *centum*. (The hard k is not the only important change in Latin pronunciation. Julius Caesar's *veni*, *vidi*, *vici* boast sounds a bit pathetic in its classical Latin guise of *waynie, weedy, weaky*!) Satem languages are named after the word "hundred" in Avestan, the language of Zoroastrian scripture, where *satem* is pronounced with an initial /s/. Broadly speaking, the "eastern" branches of Indo-European, particularly Indo-Iranian and Balto-Slavic, were satem languages while the "western" branches of Hellenic, Italic, Celtic and Germanic were centum languages. Later developments cloud the picture, as in Romance languages, where Latin /k/ has been palatalised – moved forward towards the hard palate – in a satem-like manner, producing the intermediate /tʃ/ of Italian *cento* and a step further forward, the /s/ of French *cent* and Portuguese *cem*. English is a centum language, which goes some way towards explaining why *g* is so common in comparison with *z*, and why our gl- cluster is so productive, whereas zl- and zhl- are non-existent.

Old English gl- was a rampant cluster, and many Modern English words have undergone only minor change since the Old English era over a thousand years ago. Old English *glæm* becomes *gleam*, *glowan* becomes *glow* and *glæs* becomes *glass*. Similarly, *glom* produces *gloom* and *gloaming*, while *glisnian* produces *glisten*. All of these Old English words have their ultimate source in the ubiquitous PIE root **ghel-*. By the Middle English period, many of the glimmering gl- words had gained the extended meaning of "stare, gaze upon", in part influenced by other Germanic languages. The Old English word *glær* originally meant "amber" before becoming today's *glare*, influenced by Middle Dutch and Middle Low German *glaren*, "to gleam". Old Norse *glóa* "glow" had become *glo* in Danish, meaning "stare, glare, gape", which is thought to have influenced English *glower*, originally a *frequentative* of *glow* (see boxed text), In the 18th century, the word *glim*, a back-formation of *glimmer* or *glimpse* had its brief day in the sun. It was a slang word meaning both "candle" and "eye", and illustrates the close link between looking and the light.

Frequentative forms indicate repeated or frequent action. Although less productive than in the past, historically this was a very common method of coining new words from an original stem. Clearly, this also adds to the number of words with close meanings and the same initial consonant clusters, reinforcing the phonosemantic theme. English frequentative verbs were usually created merely by adding either the suffix *−er* or *−le* to the existing word. For example, *flutter* "move with quick flapping movements" derives from the verb *float*, *waddle* comes from *wade*, and *scuffle* comes from *scuff*. Sometimes, there is very little difference between the stem word and the frequentative, as in the pairs *wag/waggle, chat/chatter* and *prate/prattle*. Many other frequentatives have stayed close to their source words, like *crumble* "break into crumbs", *gobble* "stuff food into your gob and swallow it quickly".

However, some pairs have moved quite far apart as senses evolve, as with *top/topple* where *topple* was originally "tip forward headfirst" and *mud/muddle* where *muddle* was originally "bathe or wallow in mud". In other cases, the frequentative is still in use, but the original root has become obsolete, as with the frequentative *tumble*, "fall down; perform acrobatics", which derives from the Old English verb *tumbian*, "dance; leap", and *mutter* from OE *motian* "utter, converse, speak" which now only survives as a dialectal relic in the verb *moot*. Still other frequentatives have developed figurative meanings, like *dabble*, which originally meant "dip into water" from *dab*, but now has acquired the sense of *dip into* as "do casually or superficially". *Dribble* in the sporting sense of "use many skilful touches to take the ball past opponents" has had a similar figurative jump from its source *drib*, a variant of *drip*, though many skilful dribblers are dripping with talent! Sporting dribble has spread across the world, as Italian *dribblare*, Bulgarian *дриблирам* (*dribliram*) and Japanese ドリブル (*doriburu*) testify.

Frequentatives are also formed by reduplication of a monosyllable as in *coo-coo, hush-hush* and *bye-bye*, and in "baby talk" – *tum-tum, neigh-neigh* etc. (Many studies have shown that reduplication in "baby talk" helps children to acquire new vocabulary more rapidly, both because of the words themselves and the high tone of voice we use when saying them, which no doubt helps explain the popularity of characters in the BBC children's TV series *In the Night Garden*, where *Makka Pakka, Iggle Piggle* and the *Ninky Nonk* reign supreme.) One interesting case of reduplication which occurs across Indo-European languages is with *murmur*, which has been traced back to the Proto-Indo-European reduplicative root **mormor* "mutter". This produced Latin *murmurare* "murmur, hum, roar", Bulgarian *мърморя* (murmorja) "grumble, carp", Lithuanian *murmėti* "murmur, grumble" and Sanskrit मर्मर (marmara) "rustle, murmur, crackle", among many others.

The same link between the gl- cluster and the eye is also present in Slavic languages. The Russian for "eye" is глаз (glaz), and глазеть (glazet') means "stare, look", while the resemblance of eggs sunny side up to eyes is found in глазунья (glazun'ja) "fried eggs". An egg when beaten will form a smooth glaze on food, or in Russian, глазурь (glazur'). In Bulgarian, the verb for "watch, look at" is гледам (gledam), while in Croatian and Bosnian it is gledati, and in Macedonian гледа (gleda). These verbs have been traced back to a Proto-Slavic form *ględati and ultimately back to our old friend *ghel-.

Fine differences in the meanings we attribute to the glints we perceive have grown up as more and more words are added to the gl- repertoire, and the connection between reflected light and the eye has become firmly established. Not many people like to be on the receiving end of a glower; we get annoyed by a gloat; but a gleeful light will gladden our hearts. You can show that you find someone attractive by giving them the glad eye, for which you may be rewarded with a come-hither glance or a baleful glare. The word glad originally comes from Old English glæd, meaning "bright, shining and filled with joy". Glad is also the source of glade, a bright open clearing in a forest, or if you are from the Florida Everglades, an endless tract of low marshy grassland teeming with alligators. Even when the glint fades and the twinkle recedes, gl- is still there to chronicle our eyes glazing over and the vacant, glassy-eyed gaze: the eyes are open but the lights are out – a glum end to an evening, a life or indeed, a paragraph.

Glide is also related to this smooth, gleaming group of gl- words and has many close cognates in Germanic languages, for example Swedish glida, Dutch glijden and German gleiten. The latter is very close to the Yiddish גליטש (glitsh) "glide, slip" which is the source of glitch. Hence, glitch has slid down the slippery slope until its very smoothness has caused a slip-up.

Away from the *doom and gloom*, the bright lights and *glitter* of Hollywood and the rich and famous have taken on a lot of gl- words. We talk *in glowing terms* about the *glamour* of the film industry and high fashion, with the idea that there is a magical, sparkling ambience and a magnetic attraction. Top actors and models are *glorified* by the media as they strut around in their *glad rags*, although it is certainly true that we look at their world through *rose-tinted glasses*. In the 1970s, a new, and fortunately short-lived, style of music, *glam rock*, appeared, made famous by singers like David Bowie and the disgraced Gary Glitter. Performers delighted in adopting extravagant clothes, hairstyles and make-up, along with implausible, but outré second identities.

On the other hand, gl- also represents the shallowness of the tinseltown world. The *glitterati* are obsessed by the *glare* of publicity and the fawning reviews they get in *glossy* magazines. Things are said to be *glitzy* when they are showy but superficial and the *glib* speeches of actors at the Academy Award ceremony are fluent but lacking in depth. The glorification of this gilded world also lends itself to arrogance as the rich and famous respond to requests for autographs with a *glacial stare* or breeze past their fans *without a backward glance*.

8.   cl- clinging and clumping

You're as soft as clarts... and your ma's soft as clarts, and your da's soft as clarts!

Catherine Cookson, *Kate Hannigan: A Novel*

Cl- has a handshake so *clammy* that you want to wipe your offended hand surreptitiously down the back of your trousers. This cluster is all about adherence: it *clings* on tight and sticks fast, *clasping* and *clamping*, so that things *clot*, *clump* or *club* together. English has hundreds of words starting with cl-, and a significant proportion of them deal with sticking, fastening, holding or indeed, *clustering*.

The Proto-Indo-European root **glei* "stick, paste together" has been pinpointed as the source of *clay* and many of the other English cl- words. Following Grimm's Law, PIE /g/ became Germanic /k/, leading to the Proto-Germanic form **klajjaz* "clay". This later became Old English *clæg*, and then Middle English *clay*. Despite being superseded by *clay*, *clæg* held on in many northern and eastern parts of Britain, influenced by Danish *klæg* "glue, paste", and it is still going strong in some dialects, along with *claggy* "sticky, tacky". Although our *cloying* descendants of **glei* usually now begin with cl-, there are a few sticky words that have kept the gl- cluster, notably *glue* and later borrowings from French and Latin, such as *gluten* and *glucose*.

Languages are living entities that borrow from each other all the time. Foreign words may fill a gap in the native vocabulary or seem better-suited than existing terms, but they can also be adopted because another language is seen as dominant, prestigious, or merely cool or fashionable.

Linguistic *reborrowings* occur when words are borrowed from a language and then some time later borrowed back by the original donor language. When this happens there is often still a similar-looking doublet in the originating language, increasing the stock of words with similar forms and thus similar consonant clusters with related sound symbolism. More rarely, a word may fall out of use after it is loaned, and it is then reborrowed to fill its own gap. An alternative scenario is when the meaning of the loanword acquires an extended meaning in the borrowing language and the word is borrowed back with its new sense. This happened with *club*, borrowed by English from Old Norse *klubba* with the meaning "cudgel, heavy stick used as a weapon", which tallied nicely with related *cloddy* cl- words like the ancestors of *clump*, *cloud*, *cluster* and *clot*. When *club* acquired the sense of "association of people", i.e. "people who club together", it was reborrowed by Norwegian as *klubb*, hence all the *fotballklubber* in Norway.

Sometimes, the reborrowed word acquires a more specific meaning than the original loanword: *animation* was borrowed by Japanese from English as アニメーション (*animēshon*), which was then abbreviated to アニメ (*anime*) and borrowed back as *anime*, the artistic style associated with Japanese animation. This process can go on indefinitely, as reborrowings are themselves reborrowed. We can see a good example of this if we look into the etymological history of Old French *cotte* "outer garment with long sleeves". *Cotte* is a borrowing from a Germanic source, possibly Frankish **kotta* "coarse cloth, coat" or Old Saxon *kot* "woollen mantle". English later borrowed *cotte* from French as *coat*, one type of which, the *riding coat*, was reborrowed by French as *redingote* "frock coat", since borrowed once more by English as *redingote* "tightly-fitting double-breasted topcoat".

Far more common than reborrowing is repeated borrowings from the same source. Latin *discus* "quoit, discus" was borrowed by Old English as *disc* [dɪʃ] "plate, dish" – now spelt *dish*; and has since been plundered for its doublet, *disc*, as well as *dais*, *desk*, *disk* and *discus* itself. Sometimes the word in the host language evolves in spelling and/or pronunciation and is borrowed at different times in its development and so produces distinct doublets. This happened with many English words that were borrowed first from Norman French and later from standard French. Examples include the doublets *wallop/gallop*, *ward/guard*, *pocket/pouch*, *warranty/guarantee*, and *reward/regard*. In each of these pairs, the earlier Norman French borrowings include Germanic features like /w/, reflecting the influence of the Norsemen (who the Normans are named after), and the Franks. The /w/ becomes /g/ in later borrowings, reflecting the pronunciation of standard French.

The words *cleave* "stick, adhere", *clod*, *clammy* and *clot* can also be traced back to the **glei-* root, as can *clover*, which gets its name from its sticky nectar. *Clothes cling* to the body, so Germanic languages have a lot of cl- cluster cognates for *clothing*, including North Frisian *klaid*, German *Kleid*, Dutch *kleed* and Danish *klæde*, all of which mean "dress". The old proverb "ne'er cast a *clout* till May be out" advises the English not to take off their winter clothing until May has finished, *clout* here meaning "article of clothing" rather than "smack round the head". These are wise words when considering the notorious British climate where the rain is plentiful and sticky clods of earth, or in Geordie and Scottish dialects, *clarts*, pile up underfoot. The soft stickiness of *clarts* leads to the simile in the quotation at the start of this chapter, the put-down: *as soft as clarts*, as in "that Cristiano Ronaldo, he's as soft as clarts". In 1811, when Sir Walter Scott started building Abbotsford House in the Scottish borders, he was building on the site of the earlier farm of Cartleyhole. This had been renamed "clarty hole" by irreverent neighbours, possibly because the land had been reclaimed from a duckpond! The old well, still called "clarty hole", can be found beneath a transparent panel in the floor of Abbotsford House to this day.

Germanic cl- stickiness abounds: the word *sticky* is *klæbrig* or *klistret* in Danish, *klebrig* or *klissete* in Norwegian, *klebrig* in German and *klibbig* in Swedish. There are also close parallels with *cleave* in German *kleben* and Dutch *kleven*, which mean both "stick" and "cling". Similarly, clay is *klei* in Dutch, and *klaai* in West Frisian. Slavic languages are not affected by Grimm's Law, so the gl- cluster is maintained in their sticky mud. Hence, the word for "clay" is *глина/glina* in a great number of Slavic languages, including Bulgarian, Russian, Serbian, Polish and Slovenian.

Other related *clingy* Old English cl- roots are sources for numerous contemporary English words: OE *clamm* gives us *clam* and *clamp*; *clyppan* is the source of *clasp* and *clip*; while OE *clyccan* gives us *clutch*, *clinch* and *clitch*. The ancestor of *clench*, OE *beclencan*, is the causative of OE *clingan*, the ancestor of *cling*. Causative forms have an intrinsic "make someone/something do" meaning, and in the Old English period, this could be expressed by a vowel change in the verb stem, often from /ɪ/ to /e/. There were a lot of such pairs in Old English, but in many cases one of the verbs has fallen by the wayside. The surviving pairs include *settan/sittan* "set/sit", *drencan/drincan* "drench/drink", *stencan/stincan* "stench/stink" (here *stench* is obsolete in its verbal "make stink" form), and *lecgan/licgan* "lay/lie" – the causative verb being the first in each pair (see chapters 23 and 27 for more on this).

Another interesting derivation is that of the word *climb*, which was originally more concerned with holding on, rather than going upwards: *clutching* the *clods* with your *claws*, rather than *clambering* to the *cliff* summit. We know this because the forerunner of *climb*, Proto-Germanic **klimbana* "climb, go up by clinging", is a nasalised form of PG **klibana* "stick, cleave" and so yet another descendant of PIE **glei-*. This means that *climb* is also closely related to *clay* and *glue*. More surprisingly, the word *clever* can also be traced to *cleave*. In the Middle English period, the East Anglian dialect word *cliver*, meant "expert at seizing". The sense later broadened to "dexterous, skilful with the hands" and then "intelligent, bright", as the clever person *catches on*.

Cl- remains very prominent in Germanic languages for climbing, clinging and clasping. Swedish has *klättra* for "climb, clamber", *klatre* is the Danish and Norwegian equivalent, while in Dutch it is *klimmen*. When it comes to fastening things together, English *clip* and German *Klammer* "clamp, paperclip" have travelled far and wide: Czech has *klip*, Russian has *клип* (*klip*), Romanian has *clemă*, and Portuguese has *clipe*.

Another set of cl- words involves things that are in a solid block or that have been *clumped* together. In the Middle English period a *clogge* was a block of wood, and the verb *clog* meant "restrict movement by attaching a block of wood to an animal's leg". It was only later that the verb extended its sense to "block up with *clutter*" and the noun became "wooden shoe", now associated with the Dutch *klompen* footwear, and the brilliant but obscure expression *pop your clogs*, one of hundreds of euphemisms for "die". One ingenious yet speculative explanation for this idiom is that one of the senses of *pop* is "pawn" and that when a worker was about to die he would have no further need of his footwear so he could *pop his clogs*, presumably leaving the money to a grateful heir or putting money towards his funeral expenses.

Cleat and *clout* come from Proto-Germanic **klautaz* "firm lump", which also goes back to the influentially sticky PIE **glei-* and ultimately to its predecessor PIE **gel-* "ball up, clench". *Clot* shares the same etymology, and also brings to mind the extended senses of many of these "blockhead" cl- words, that of "*clumsy* idiot". A 17th century *clodhopper* was a derided peasant rather than a *clunky* shoe, and *clodpate* and *clodpoll* were common insults for *clownish* dolts until relatively recently. Similarly, English has taken *klutz* from Yiddish קלאָץ (*klots*) "wooden beam" a cognate of German *Klotz*, which means both "lump, block" and "clod, boor".

The descendants of Proto-Germanic **klautaz* are naturally widespread across Germanic languages: Icelandic *klumper* means "clump, lump"; Swedish *klimp* means both "dumpling" and "clot"; and German *Klumpen* means "clod". Another word which goes back to **klautaz* is Old English *clud* "mass of stone, boulder". This was extended by metaphor to describe masses of evaporated water in the sky – *clouds*. *Club* in the sense "thick stick used as a weapon" comes from the same root. As mentioned in the boxed text above, the idea of a social or sports club grew from this concept – people "assembling in a club-like mass". *Clubs* as a suit in cards is derived from the Italian and Spanish tradition of playing cards, whereby *cups*, *coins*, *swords* and *clubs* were the suits, the clubs here being cudgels – Italian *bastoni* and Spanish *bastos*. When English adopted the French suits, *cœurs* "hearts" took over from *cups*, *carreaux* "tiles", later to be renamed "diamonds" took over from *coins* and *piques* "pikes", later "spades", took over from swords. However, with *trèfles* "clovers", the suit took the French trefoil design, but kept the direct translation of the Italo-Spanish suit with "clubs".

Old English *cliewen* "sphere, skein" still exists in Northern English and Scottish dialects as *clew* "ball of thread or yarn". In Greek mythology, Ariadne gave Theseus a clew in order to find his way out of the Minotaur's labyrinth, as Chaucer describes in *The Legend of Ariadne*, the sixth part of his epic poem *The Legend of Good Women*:

Therto have I a remedie in my thoght,
That, by a clewe of twyne, as he hath goon,
The same wey he may returne anoon,
Folwing alwey the threed, as he hath come.

This *clew* transformed into *clue* "sign that which points the way", although most people are *clueless* about the word's origin!

Many of the balled-up clumpy words came to English directly from Latin or from other Romance languages. In such cases, Grimm's Law again does not apply, so the gl- cluster is consistent.

Hence, we have *globe*, *glob*, *agglutinate*, *conglomeration*, *glebe* and *globule* among many others. Perhaps it is not surprising that cl- and gl- are also well-represented in slang words for testicles. English has taken *goolies* from the Hindi word गोली (*golī*) meaning "bullets, balls". Geordie has the word *clem*, which refers to both "testicle" and "idiot" and Ulster English has *clinkers* for "balls". Elsewhere, Dutch has *kloten* for "bollocks" and Antwerp Flemish has *kloete*. I am sure there are other examples across the Indo-European world, but putting "foreign testicles" into an internet search engine comes up with some fairly unpalatable results, so balls to that. Excuse my English or pardon my French.

Cl- also has a large stock of words relating to impact, such as *clomp*, *clack*, *clobber* and *cleave* of the *cloven*, *cleft* variety meaning "sever, split". Many of these words are onomatopoeic and describe various types of noisy collision – *clapping*, *clashing* and *clanging*. This appears to be a common Germanic phenomenon. German has *klappen* "clap", *klappern* "clatter, rattle" and *Klatsch*, which means both "slap, smack" and "gossip"; Dutch has *kleppen* "chatter", *klinken* "ring" and *kletteren* "rattle, clang"; and Swedish has *klicka* "click", *klirra* "clink, jingle" and *klinga* "tinkle".

The ablaut series *clink clank clunk* (see introduction) also gives an indication of the relationship between vowel sounds and the noises they describe. Basically, the further forward the tongue is in the mouth when the vowel is pronounced, the higher-pitched and more resonant the sound denoted by the onomatopoeic word. Here *clink* with the front vowel /ɪ/ describes a high-pitched tinkle of glass on glass; *clank* with its vowel /æ/ articulated further back gives us the bang of metal on metal, as in a moving suit of armour; *clunk* with its back vowel /ʌ/ is a dull, hollow thud. In fact, *tinkle*, (tinny and light), *bang* (solid and substantial), and *thud* (heavy and nonresonant) also illustrate the same sound progression inherent in the vowels, as do *jingle* and *jangle*, but alas, not *jungle*. Other onomatopoeic cl- words include *clatter*, *cloppety-clop*, and *cluck*, as well as the imitative *claque* and *clique.* The latter two nouns come from French *claquer* "clap", a *claque* originally being a sycophantic group of people hired to attend performances and applaud or boo – a description which could also ring a few bells with observers of certain cliques today!

9. sp- spurts and spikes

Would thou wert clean enough to spit upon!

William Shakespeare, *Timon of Athens (Act 4 Scene 3)*

Sp- is a *spiky* malcontent: an irate, red-faced, old man of a cluster, *spouting* invective with *spittle* flying out of his mouth in an angry *spat*. This cluster *spits* out at us and *sputters* across the page. Its combination of the sibilant /s/ and the bilabial plosive /p/ explodes out of our mouths with a hiss and a pop. Sp- has clear links with the similarly volatile three-part clusters spl- and spr-, and sometimes it is difficult to distinguish between them. The waters are muddied by the slippery liquid consonants /l/ and /r/, which are frequently subject to metathesis (see chapter 4). For example, Proto-Indo-European **sper-* "strew" is the source of *spore* and *sperm*, but also has an extended form **spreud-* which is the source for *spurt*, *spray* and *sprout*. Nevertheless, sp-, spl- and spr- do have semantic differences, so we will examine them separately in this chapter and the two that follow it.

The stand-out group of sp- words are those that ultimately derive from the Proto-Indo-European root **spyeu-*, which is imitative of the sound of *spitting*. This form has given us *spew*, *spit* and *spatter*, as well as producing Latin *spuere* from which we get *sputum* and *cuspidor* "spittoon", the latter via Portuguese. In addition, **spyeu-* is the possible source of a number of other words related to the sudden outflow of liquid, such as *spate*, originally a Scottish and northern English term for a "sudden flood", *spume* and *spout*. As well as meaning "gushing forth", *spout* is also a dated slang term for the lift that took pawned items up for storage in a pawnbroker's shop. Hence, if you are forced to resort to pawning your goods, your plans are *up the spout.*

The expressive nature of sp- lends itself to abusing others by *spewing bile* at the target of our derision. Latin *spasticus* gave English *spastic* "affected by spasms, affected by spastic paralysis". By the mid-20th century, this was being used as an insulting put-down, as were related derivatives such as *spaz, spazmo, spack* and *spacker*. These terms remain taboo in British English, although they are comparatively inoffensive to Americans. Milder insults include *spanner, spoon* and (an insult coined in our house) *spangalang*. Other slightly derogatory 20th century slang words include *spawny* "undeservedly lucky", *specky-four-eyes* "wearer of glasses", *specky* "swotty, overly studious" and *spod* "swot".

The unattractive connotations of the sp- cluster may not have enhanced the sales of the canned precooked meat product *Spam*, challenging the mantra that "there is no such thing as bad publicity". US soldiers have derided it as "ham that didn't pass its physical" and "meatloaf without basic training", as well as awarding it some unfortunate backronyms (see boxed text below), such as "Something Posing As Meat". A 1970 *Monty Python* sketch built on this image by portraying Spam as an inescapable, foul-tasting horror in a restaurant skit in which Spam appears on the menu in every dish and Vikings periodically interrupt other clients by singing "Spam, Spam, Spam, Spam, Spammity Spam, Wonderful Spam." This apparent ubiquity of unwanted Spam led to its name being given to *spam email* and other unsolicited bulk electronic messages, passed on, of course, by *spammers.*

The word *backronym* is a blend of *back* and *acronym*, and is essentially an acronym that is created after a word is already well-established. This can happen in two ways. The first method is when a word that isn't an acronym is taken to be one and a full form is invented, as with *dweeb* "Dim-Witted Eastern-Educated Boor" and *rap*, which after its emergence was said to be an acronym for "rhythm and poetry". The second, less common method of forming a backronym is when an acronym already exists, but a new alternative form is made up to supersede or supplement it. This happened with the acronym relating to the safety standards for two-engined planes travelling over water for long periods, ETOPS – "Extended-range Twin-engine Operational Performance Standards", which soon became "Engines Turn Or Passengers Swim" in aviation slang.

Backronyms are often created for humorous effect: car maker Ford being the butt of the backronyms "Fix or Repair Daily" and "Found on Roadside Dead" and rival Fiat suffering "Fix It Again Tony". Operation Telic, the codename for the 2003 UK military operations in Iraq, was given the backronym "Tell Everyone Leave Is Cancelled", while the city of Cary, North Carolina has been given two backronyms: "Can't Afford Raleigh Yet" and "Containment Area for Relocated Yankees".

A backronym was also shoehorned into the USA Patriot Act passed by Congress in 2001. It became the ludicrous "Uniting and Strengthening America by Providing Appropriate Tools Required to Intercept and Obstruct Terrorism Act". Often backronyms are created a long time after a term has gained currency. For example, Steve Jobs named one of his Apple personal computers "Lisa" prior to its 1983 release. Only later was the backronym Local Integrated Software Architecture dreamt up. Similarly, American hip hop artist KRS-One was born Lawrence Parker, but was dubbed "Krisna" by the residents of the South Bronx homeless shelter where he lived in the early 1980s, due to his interest in Hare Krishna. His graffiti tag at that time was "KRS-ONE", possibly to distinguish himself from others with the tag "KRS". The phrase 'Knowledge Reigns Supreme Over Nearly Everyone' grew out of the tag, and became Parker's stage name.

Spitting PIE *spyeu-* remains remarkably prevalent in modern European languages. Naturally, Germanic languages are most similar to English, with Swedish *spotta*, Danish *spytte*, German *spucken*, and the brilliantly evocative Old Frisian *spedelspring* "outpouring of spittle". Romance languages also have close cognates with Italian *sputare*, Portuguese *cuspir* and Catalan *escopir*. The Slavs take [plju:] from **spyeu* to have Croatian *pljuvati*, Bulgarian, плюя (*pljujá*) and Russian плевать (*plevát'*). The Poles have the choice to spit with or without sp-, choosing from either *pluć* or *splunąć* to expectorate.

Roasting meat may also spit out juices or fat when rotating on a *spit*, the latter being a pointed rod which skewers the meat to be cooked over a fire. This second *spit* is one of a large number of sharp, pointed objects which also carry the sp- cluster, and comprise the second major phonestheme of sp-. Included in this group is our third and final *spit*, a narrow *spur* of sandy land that stretches out into the sea, such as *Spurn Head*, a narrow sand spit that extends over three miles into the North Sea at the mouth of the Humber estuary.

Finally extricating ourselves from *spit*, let's wash our hands and move on to the other *spears*, *spikes* and *spars* that exist in Modern English. Many of these come from the PIE root **spei-* "sharp point, sharp stick", including *spike*, *spoke* and *spire*. The phrase *spick and span* "neat and tidy, spotlessly clean" comes from *spick-and-span new*, literally meaning "as new as a recently made spike and chip of wood". It is an imitation of the Dutch *spiksplinter nieuw*, the common idea being that *span new*, from a Scandinavian source, is "as new as a ship just split". The German for "spike" is *Spitze*, from which we get the Pomeranian dog breed the *spitz*, whose name comes from its tapering spiky muzzle. Other close European cognates for *spike* include Swedish *spik*, Danish *spids*, Italian *spica* and Spanish *espiga*.

Spica and *espiga* come from Latin *spica* "ear of grain, spike", another derivative of the PIE **spei-* root. English has extensively borrowed from Romance languages to further supplement its stock of prickly sp- words. These include *spine* from Old French *espine* "thorn, prickle, backbone"; *spinney* from Old French *espinoi* "thorny thicket, copse" and *spigot* "plug, peg" from Old Provençal *espigot* "small ear of grain, core of a fruit" via French.

The ancient art of *spinning*, when undertaken by a human being rather than a *spider* (*spider* literally means "spinner"), is the craft of taking plant or animal fibres and then twisting them together to make yarn. Spinning is abundantly supplied with sp-words. In Stone Age times, hand spinning was done on a wooden *spike* named a hand *spindle*. This later became part of the much larger *spinning wheel*, which had internal bars or *spokes*. Spun yarn was then wrapped around bobbins or *spools*. The job of spinning was done by a male *spinner* or a female *spinster*. By the 17th century, *spinster* had also acquired the meaning of "unmarried woman". To this day, marriage certificates in the UK list the condition (marital status) of the bride-to-be as *spinster*, to the prospective groom's *bachelor*, which originally meant "youthful knight, squire". The males seem to have got the best deal here! *Spinster* later became an unflattering term used for those who were past the usual age for marrying, an alternative to the term *old maid*. The -ster ending derives from the Old English feminine suffix *-istre* /-estre* "woman who is, does or is associated with", the equivalent of the male suffix *-ere*, modern *-er*, the male occupational suffix found in *teacher*, *writer* etc. By the end of the Middle English period, *-ster* had become productive for both male and female workers, as attested by the numbers of *Baxters*, *Brewsters* and *Websters* in English speaking countries – bakers, brewers and weavers, respectively, not to mention contemporary *gangsters* and *hipsters*.

Spin comes from the PIE root **spen-* "draw out, stretch", presumably due to the drawn fibres being stretched taut before being twisted into thread. *Span* comes from the same root, as do *spanner*, *spasm* and *spastic*, the latter pair through the semantic idea of "drawing in, convulsing". Chips and shavings of wood are also long and flat, the notion that lies behind Old English *spon*, the predecessor of *spade* and *spoon*. Amusingly, it is likely that the humble *spud* also comes from this root. Although generally associated with a rounded rather dumpy tuber, *spud* is believed to come from the short, crude knife used for preparing the soil before the potatoes were planted. *Spud* is related to the Danish *spyd* "spear" but sometime in the 19th century, the name *spud* transferred from the digging tool to the potato itself. Latin also embraced the **spen-* root for stretched, drawn out objects, although the *s* was dropped, as with *pendere* "to hang", *pensare* "to weigh up, consider" and their multiple derivatives. Many of these words found their way into English in the medieval period – *pensive*, *compensation*, *spend*, *depend*, *suspend* and *pendulum* only scratch the surface, but let's not hang around!

Other long, stretched out objects endowed with the sp- cluster come from Greek σπάθη (*spáthē*), borrowed by Latin as *spatha* "broad blade of wood or metal". The Latin *spatha* was a long, flat, two-edged sword carried by Roman cavalry officers. French adopted a number of words from *spatha*. It kept a glamorous sword, the *espee*, now *épée*, as well as some snazzy *épaulettes* but was happy to pass on to English the slightly more prosaic *spay* and *spatula*. Blades and spades abound with the sp- cluster in Indo-European languages. A *sword* is *spada* in Italian and is *espada* in Portuguese; a *spatula* is *spaða* in Icelandic and *Spatel* in German. Slavic languages have borrowed the *Spatel* from German, so there is шпатель (*špátel'*) in Russian and *szpatułka* in Polish, for example. If you want to *call a spade* a *spade* in Dutch, Swedish, Norwegian or Danish, you will be easily understood as *spade* is "spade" in each of these languages. However, if you call a *spanner* a *Spanner* in German, you are calling it a "Peeping Tom"!

Another spiky source of sp- words is the PIE root **spere* "ankle". This led to Old English *spurnan* "kick" and the noun *spora* from which Modern English takes *spur*. If men performed great acts of valour, they were awarded with a knighthood and given gilded spurs, in recognition of their manifest *spunk*. Few men would *spurn* "kick away" such marks of respect. *Spur* also came to mean the sharp projections from the feet of various birds, such as a cockerel or indeed a lark: the *larkspur* plant gets its name from the resemblance of its spiky calyx and petals to the lark's hind claw. Sp- for a *spur* also spans Germanic and Latin languages: in Icelandic it is *spori* and in German *Sporn*, while the Portuguese and Italian equivalents are *esporão* and *sperone*. Old English also had the verb *spyrian* and the noun *spor* "trace, footprint". Its Dutch cognate *spor* was used by trekkers in South Africa as Afrikaans *spoor* "track, trace". *Spoor* was then reintegrated into English in the 19th century to mean "the footprints, droppings or scent of an animal.

One further interesting root, **spel-* "break off", is the source of *spoil* and *spill* and fits snugly into the volatile phonosemantic sp- category. The Latin ancestor of *spoil* is *spolio* "pillage, ruin" and the original meaning was "skin stripped from a killed animal", and as such, a valuable commodity. The word was initially used very much for "booty" in the *spoils of war* sense – stripping the slain on the battlefield of their belongings and depriving vanquished enemies of their possessions. If you were *spoiling for a fight*, you would spoil if you didn't get a good punch-up, which is very much in tune with the violent undertones of this word. One of the Proto-Germanic descendants of **spel-* is **spilþijan* "destroy, lay waste". This gave Old English *spillan* "destroy, kill", so the idea of Modern English *spill* "letting liquid fall" comes from the altogether less innocent concept of spilling blood. Cognates show the connection between *spoil* and *spill* with Icelandic *spilla* "corrupt, violate", French *gaspiller* "waste, squander" and Dutch *spillen* "use needlessly, waste" among many others.

10.   spl- splashing and splitting

When the ducks stood on their heads suddenly, as ducks will, he would dive down and tickle their necks, just under where their chins would be if ducks had chins, till they were forced to come to the surface again in a hurry, spluttering and angry and shaking their feathers at him, for it is impossible to say quite all you feel when your head is under water.

Kenneth Grahame: *The Wind in the Willows*

Spl- is a cluster which is wonderful in its expressiveness. The combination of sibilant /s/ with plosive /p/ and lateral /l/ moulds the mouth into a gloriously *splenetic splutter* of sound, with the mouth and lips working *splendidly* in tandem. Spl- clearly has a link to the sp- cluster but its liquids *splash* rather than *spurt* with the idea that spl- words *splatter* outwards on impact, rather than in a linear trajectory. They *split* or *splinter* off from their source, *splaying* outwards.

PIE **splei-* "splice, split" is our prime candidate for the ancient *splitting* source root. It is a variant of PIE **spel-* "break off" discussed in the last chapter under *spill* and *spoil*, but **splei-* is a *splitter*: it splashes outwards rather than gushing forwards. As well as being the source of *split* and *splice*, **splei-* is also the source of *splint* and its diminutive *splinter*. The close similarities in the descendants of **splei-* in Germanic languages reveal the durability of this root; many spl- words are essentially the same throughout the Germanic world, and outlining the differences would merely be *splitting hairs*. The idiom "to split hairs" was first recorded in the 17th century, and is one of our more transparent sayings, the idea being that attempting to split hairs (lengthways) would be a futile exercise and so a total waste of time. The metaphor when applied to people's arguments implies that needlessly fine distinctions are being made, and that the hairsplitter is a pedant of the first degree. So with all that said... *split* is *split* in German, Danish and Swedish, while in Dutch it is *spleet*. The verb *splice* is similarly recognisable in Germanic languages as can be seen by *splitsa* (Swedish), *spleise* (Norwegian) and *spleißen* (German).

Other spl- words survive in dialects of English, for instance, in the north-eastern English dialect word *spelk*, "splinter of wood", which comes from the Old English *spelc* and Old Norse *spelkur* both of which denote "surgical splint". While *spelk* is still going strong, a recent University of Cambridge study found that other British sp- and spl- dialect words for *splinter* are in the process of dying out, including *spill* (Yorkshire), *spool* (Manchester), *spile* (Lancashire), *speel* (parts of Cumbria and Lincolnshire), *spell* (Shropshire) and *splint* (Staffordshire and Cheshire). Another word which is probably related is *spline*, first attested as an East Anglian dialect word in the mid-18th century. A spline is a long, thin, flexible piece of wood or metal inserted into grooves to join points or curves together.

Grimm's Law is again in evidence with several Germanic words where (s)pl- has become fl- in the same way as we noted with PIE *pleu-* becoming *flow* in chapter 3. Hence, **splei-* is also the source root of a group of splitting fl- words, including *flense* "slice the skin or blubber from a whale carcass", *flint* (as well as *plinth*), *flinders* "fragments, splinters" cognate with Norwegian *flindra* "chip, thin piece of stone", and *flash* in the sense of "sudden rush of water" as preserved in *flash flood*. In this meaning, the etymology of *flash* is related to Middle Dutch *vlacke* "estuary, stagnant pool" and the French words *flaque* "puddle" and *flaquer* "splash", both of which were earlier borrowed from Germanic.

The explosive juiciness of the spl- cluster lends itself to onomatopoeic coinages, such as *splutter*, *splat* and *splodge* as well as new words introduced through *apophony*, that is, regular vowel gradation. Hence, we have *splish*, *splash*, *splosh* and *sploosh*, in which the splashing gets heavier and more liquid is displaced as the vowels are articulated from the front to the back of the mouth, so *sploosh* makes the biggest splash. Many linguists believe that *splash* is a variant of Middle English *plashe* "puddle", which still survives in some dialects as *plash*, a noun meaning "puddle" and a verb meaning "splash". If so, then *splash* is related to the German *platschen* "splash", its Norwegian equivalent *plaske* and Dutch *plas* "puddle, pool of water".

Lewis Carroll, a man attuned to the different resonances of sound symbolism, coined the term *portmanteau* in *Through the Looking-Glass* (1871). Portmanteau words are made up of two elements to create a new word, for example: *smoke + fog = smog, chuckle + snort = chortle*. In *Through the Looking-Glass*, Humpty Dumpty explains to Alice about the unusual words in *Jabberwocky*, where *slithy* means "lithe and slimy" and *mimsy* is "flimsy and miserable." Humpty says that "it's like a portmanteau – there are two meanings packed up into one word."

New portmanteau words are being coined all the time, in many different spheres. They are often dreamt up to be amusing, and may be shortlived – who knows how long *textpectation* "a feeling of anticipation waiting for a response to a text" and *nonversation* "completely worthless chat" will last? In the animal kingdom, portmanteaux are often used with animal hybrids or crosses, as in *labradoodle* (*labrador + poodle*), *liger* (progeny of a male *lion + tigress*) and *geep* (*goat + sheep*). The world of entertainment has given us *Brangelina* with the celebrity pairing of *Brad* Pitt and *Angelina* Jolie, *biopic* from *biography* and *picture*, and *televangelist* from *television* and *evangelist*. Among the hundreds of other twentieth century portmanteau coinages are *malware* (*malicious software*), *botox*, (from *botulism* and *toxin*), *Chunnel*, (from *Channel* and *tunnel*), and *bit* (from *binary* and *digit*).

There are also a large number of portmanteau words in English that begin with the spl- cluster. Spl- portmanteaux include *splake*, a hybrid of *speckled trout* and *lake trout*; *splatter*, a mix of *splash* and *spatter*; *splotch*, a blend of *spot* and either *blot* or *blotch*; *splurge*, from *splash (out)* and *surge;* and *splurt*, a combination of *splash* and *spurt*. Whereas if something *spurts* it comes out in a powerful stream, something that *splurts* will gush out in all directions. Another such word is *spliff*, a marijuana cigarette. This is said to be made up of *split* and *spiff*, meaning "well-dressed" or "smart".

Splay is an interesting word as it is actually a shortened form of *desplayen*, the Middle English ancestor of *display*. *Desplayen* had the meaning of "unfurl, spread out". This meaning has largely been maintained with modern *splay* "spread apart awkwardly", in line with the outward movement of other words with the spl- cluster. However, *display* has lost this sense with its Modern English meaning of "show, exhibit". More precisely, *splay* is an *aphetic* form of *display*, aphetic forms being words which have lost an initial unstressed vowel or syllable. Other examples include *cute* from *acute, mend* from *amend, squire* from *esquire* and *sample* from *example*. Continuing this digression a moment, the word *way* when used as an intensifier meaning "a great distance, very far" as in "this is *way* off topic" is an aphetic form of *away* and used to be written *'way* like *'pon* the aphetic form of *upon*.

Splashing *backwards* (the aphetic form of *abackwards*) to spl-, the onomatopoeic *splash* exists in several Germanic languages and many languages agree that splashing needs a combination of sibilant, plosive and lateral (see appendix), but not necessarily in the spl- order. Thus, although we have Welsh *sblash*, we also have Dutch *plons*, Bulgarian плясък (*plyasŭk*) and Danish *plask* while Spanish has *salpicadura* and Portuguese *salpico*, the latter two languages perhaps considering a splash as more of a slap! Other languages prefer spr- as the splashing cluster, so we can find German *Spritzen* and Italian *spruzzo* amongst others of this ilk. As we shall see in the next chapter, English spr- is rather different.

11.   spr- sprouting and sprinkling

And all I ask is a windy day with the white clouds flying,
And the flung spray and the blown spume, and the sea-gulls crying.

John Masefield: *Sea Fever*

Spr- spreads in all directions, radiating outwards from a single point of origin. Plants *sprout*, *sprinklers spray* and "love *spreads* her arms, waits there for the nails, I forgive you boy, I will prevail", as the *Stone Roses* sang in their somewhat controversial 1994 hit, *Love Spreads*, in which Jesus is portrayed as a black woman being crucified. Like sp- and spl-, the cluster spr- can describe a liquid that emanates from one point and ends up in another, but crucially, with spr- no impact is required for the *spread* that occurs. When pronouncing *spr-* the air hisses along the tongue on the *s*, the lips purse together on the *p* and then the air is pushed outwards from the mouth with the *r* – much like the water in a high-pressure *spray*. Indeed, it is inadvisable to practise this sound with your mouth full of food or drink, unless you want to share what you are eating with those around you! Not recommended in polite company.

Words with the spr- cluster are often connected with the idea of dynamic extrusion: mythical *sprites* flit around the river (as the *spirit* moves them, obviously), *spry* old people retain more vitality than jaded youths, who nonetheless may *sprawl* out, *spread-eagled* on their beds. A *sprained* ankle will swell up and out, while *sprockets* in engineering are projecting teeth radiating outwards from a wheel to engage with the links of a chain.

Spr- energises and reinvigorates. Of course, the season of the year most associated with the spread of new life is the *spring*, a word sprouting from the PIE root *sprengh* which is related to rapid movement. As a noun, *spring* first meant "place from which a stream rose up from the ground" and soon acquired the general meaning of "source of a river", and then "place from which new growth originated". This led to its adoption as the word for the season following winter, *spring* replacing the older term *Lent* by the sixteenth century. *Lent* is derived from *long*, referring to the lengthening of the days in spring and now mainly survives only in the context of the forty days before Easter when Christians fast. In the fourteenth century, *spring* was known as the *springing time*, the time of rising sap when plants *sprout* and extend their *sprigs*, spreading their tendrils in a *sprint* for growth. And it's *asparagus* season too, or *sparrowgrass* as the folk etymology has it.

Spring is ubiquitous in English with numerous *sprightly* derivatives *springing to mind*. Different meanings are linked to the vigorous central concept; dormant or coiled springs waiting for their time to jump up and suddenly extend, gush or indeed *spring out*. It's highly debatable whether mothers would agree that their *offspring sprang out*, but even here, the main spr- theme of emanating from a source holds true. Spring is also the season for *sprucing up* your house with a bit of *spring cleaning*, and the masses of idioms to do with *spring* – *full of the joys of spring*, *no spring chicken*, *spring fever* – all have the idea that *spring* is a time of energy and vigour, as does *springbok*, borrowed from Afrikaans.

Other Germanic languages have appropriately bouncy cognates, which *spring to attention*: German and Dutch have *springen* "jump", Danish has *springe* "skip, jump", Icelandic has *spretta* "spring forth" and Swedish has *springa* "run". Other Indo-European cognates include Russian прясть (*prjast'*) "spin", Ancient Greek σπερχω (*sperkhō*) "hasten, set in motion" and Sanskrit स्पृहयति (*spṛhayati*) "desire eagerly". English has even taken *spring roll* 春卷 (*chūnjuan*), as a calque from Mandarin Chinese. *Calques* or *loan translations* are words or phrases which are borrowed word-for-word by other languages, from the French word *calque* "close copy, tracing".

Calquing is a two-way street, and languages freely give, as well as take. If a word or phrase in one language is deemed to be suitably useful or evocative, it is liable to be translated word-for-word into another. Some language academies, such as *l'Académie française*, which fight the losing battle for linguistic purism and language regulation, find calques a more acceptable solution to naming new concepts than the wholesale borrowing of foreign terms. Hence, French has *le disque compacte*, and *les contre-vérités*, although many people say *le CD* and *les fake news*. English computing terms are in general use among young French software developers, web designers and programmers, but there are a number of calques which are preferred by *l'Académie française*. The techies may use *l'email*, *le web* or *le wifi*, but the academy prefers *le courriel, la toile* and the frankly unwieldy *connexion internet sans fil*. In this, as with most instances when an academy attempts to regulate what is already in common usage, it is a waste of time and effort – *like pissing in the wind*, for which the French have the excellent equivalent: *c'est comme si on pissait dans un violon*. However, the venerable members of *l'Académie* might muster up a wry smile should they consider the history of English *ready-to-wear*, which was calqued by French as *prêt-à-porter* after the Second World War. It was promptly reborrowed by English as the loan phrase *prêt-à-porter* and continues to coexist happily with its doublet *ready-to-wear* today.

In fact, English has calqued vast numbers of foreign words and phrases, on top of the multitude of *loanwords* (calque of German *Lehnwort*) simply copied from the source language. (The French word *calque* is itself a borrowing in English rather than a calque, lifted in the seventeenth century as *calk* "trace a chalk drawing"). From French, English has taken *flea market* (*marché aux puces*), *Adam's Apple* (*pomme d'Adam*) and *that goes without saying* (*cela va sans dire*). English is actually a globetrotter in this respect. Other calques include *rainforest* (German *Regenwald*), *earworm* (German *Ohrwurm*), *masterpiece* (Dutch *meesterstuk*), *moment of truth* (Spanish *el momento de la verdad*, used for the final sword thrust in a bullfight), *Milky Way* (Latin *via lactea*), and *little emperor* (Chinese 小皇帝) "spoilt child", said to be the result of the Chinese state's one-child policy.

The Proto-Indo-European root **spreg* "jerk, scatter" is the source of many of the other springy spr- words in English, including *spark*, *sprinkle* and the dialectal English term *sprack* "lively". This root also gave Latin *spargo* "scatter" which is the source of a number of later borrowings into English (often via French), such as *sparse*, *disperse*, and *aspersion*, which in its original theological sense referred to the shedding of Christ's blood, before taking on the meaning of "sprinkling holy water" in the Catholic ritual of *Asperges* and then "slanderous rumours". PIE **spreg-* also led to a variety of interesting Indo-European cognates, including the Lithuanian verb *sprogti* "shoot forth, germinate", Persian پراكندن (*parâkandan*) "scatter, spread" and Sanskrit पर्जन्य (parjánya) "rain god, rain". **Spreg-* is believed to be related to the PIE root **sper-* "strew", which was briefly introduced in chapter 9 as the source of *spore* and *sperm*. It is also the ultimate ancestor of *sporadic*, *spread*, *sprawl*, *sprout*, *spurt*, *spray* and probably even *sprat*. As can be seen from this list, metathesis has shifted the position of the *r* to before the first vowel in many of these words.

Spr- has spread its wings to encompass the Indo-European world with its zest for life. Here's hoping your weekend is more *spritzers* than *sprouts*. And more to the point, mine! *Hope springs eternal.*

12.   cr- crooks and cracks

There was a crooked man, and he walked a crooked mile.
He found a crooked sixpence upon a crooked stile.
He bought a crooked cat, which caught a crooked mouse,
And they all lived together in a little crooked house.

Traditional nursery rhyme

Cr- is the cluster of the *crippled* and the *crooked*, a home for *crocks* on *crutches* as well as *crafty criminals* with their dubious ethics and underhand practices. The cr- combination indicates objects that are *crooked, crossed* or misshapen. Cr- often demonstrates how the straight and true can be bent or otherwise disfigured, and as such, it is often the shifty counterpart of the strong and loyal str- cluster (see chapter 21). Cr- may involve minor distortion, as with *crimping* and *crinkling*, or a more serious mutilation caused by *cracking* or *crippling*. As well as being bent out of shape, cr- words can also indicate compression. Things get *crumpled up, curbed* or *crushed* to be *crammed* into nooks, *crannies* and *corners.*

The *crooked man* of the nursery rhyme above is thought to be Alexander Leslie, 1st Earl of Leven (1582–1661). Leslie fought with distinction for the Swedes in the Thirty Years War (1618–1648), reaching the rank of Field Marshal and being knighted by the Swedish king. He returned to a turbulent Scotland in 1637, and his many switches of allegiance in the years that followed earned him the epithet "crooked man". He took Edinburgh Castle from forces loyal to Charles I in 1639, and the following year, crossed the border, the *crooked mile*, and defeated the king at the Battle of Newburn. Charles then brought Leslie over to the Royalist side naming him Earl of Leven and Lord Balgonie, enabling him to amass a lot of money in consequence – his *crooked sixpence*. Leslie soon changed sides again though, becoming a commander in the army of the Solemn League and Covenant on the side of the Parliamentarians against the Royalist forces in the English Civil Wars. After the Parliamentary forces had captured York and Newcastle, Charles surrendered to the Scots, in the misguided belief that he would be safe in their hands. *Crooked man* Leslie handed Charles over to the English Parliament, who eventually executed him. The Anglo-Scottish alliance held firm for some time after this, as they all lived together in their *little crooked house*.

Proto-Indo-European **ger-* "turn, wind" is believed to be the source root for many of our contemporary crooked words. Grimm's Law turns **ger-* into the kr- of a number of different Proto-Germanic words. These words are the predecessors of many of the cr- words in English and their kr- counterparts in other Germanic languages. One reconstructed Proto-Germanic root is the form **krokaz* "hook, corner, bent thing". This led to Old English *croc* which is our modern *crook*, and Old Norse *krokr* "hook, bend", the latter being the source for English *crouch*, not to mention the very familiar-sounding Danish *kroget* "crooked". Other crooked cr-words that came to English from Old Norse include *creek* and *crawl*.

Old Norse *krokr* was also borrowed by French as *croc* "hook", possibly via Frankish. This then gave French *crochet* "small hook", which then lent its name to the practice of creating fabric with a hooked needle, the crochet hook. The quarter note or *crotchet* also comes from this root as there used to be a small hook on the stem of the note in black musical notation. Confusingly, this hook is no longer on the crotchet, but has been on the stem of the eighth note or quaver since the 15th century when white notation was adopted and scribes began using hollow note shapes for the longer notes. Even more confusingly, French calls the quaver *une croche*, as it still proudly carries a hook, and the crotchet *une noire* "a black", as it is the longest of the wholly black notes. The sport of *croquet* also came to English via Old French *croc* and several other words have gone from Germanic to French and back to English in this way. These include *cramp*, *crampon*, *crotch* "place where the body forks", *encroach* from *encrochier* "seize, grab with a hook", *lacrosse* from French *jeu de la crosse* "game of the hooked sticks" and possibly even the most quintessentially English sport of *cricket*, from French *criquet* "stick, goalpost".

PIE **ger-* has given English other bent and deformed cr- words. Old English had the word *crump* "crooked", which survives dialectically to mean "crunch" and is sometimes used onomatopoeically as the sound made when walking over snow or to describe the sound of an exploding shell or bomb. Its frequentative (see chapter 7) *crumple* is, of course, still in common use. Other related contemporary words include *crumpet*, *crumb* and its frequentative *crumble*. Germanic languages maintain close cognates with Dutch *krom* "bent", German *krumm* "crooked, hunched" and Danish *krum* "curved, bent".

On *Radiohead's* breakthrough 1992 single *Creep*, professional miserabilist Thom Yorke sings, "I'm a creep, I'm a weirdo. What the hell am I doing here? I don't belong here". On a personal level, the doom-laden lead singer may be right, but from a phonosemantic perspective, *creeps* fit perfectly into the cr- category along with other *crooks*, *cranks* and *crackpots*. Disappointingly though, people with the surname *Crook* or *Crooks* are not descended from master criminals, but from those who lived by a bend in the road or river, or even more prosaically, from people who sold hooks. Proto-Germanic **krank-* "bend, curl up, yield" produces English *crank*, *crinkle* and *cringe*. It is also the source of German *Krank* "sick", and poorly Germans need to seek treatment in the *Krankenhaus* "hospital", along with the other *crocks*. The curling notion of *krank-* also gave Old Norse *kringr* and Dutch *kring*, both of which mean "circle".

While the "turning" and "winding" senses of the cr-cluster often end up producing words with negative connotations, such as *creep*, *cripple* and *crutch*, other cr- words have more positive associations. For example, *cranking something up* will give it drive and energy. Similarly, Proto-Germanic *kraftaz-* "power", gave Old English *cræft* "physical strength, power, art, science". This led to *craft* as a skilful noun in itself, and as a suffix for vehicles produced by master *craftsmen* – *hovercraft*, *aircraft*, *spacecraft* – and activities requiring skilful handling – *stagecraft*, *statecraft* and, of course, *witchcraft*, with its *crafty* sorceresses. Germanic cognates remain closer to the original sense of *kraftaz-*, with for example, Old Norse *kraptr* "strength, virtue", West Frisian *krêft* "strength, power" and German *Kraft* "force".

Ger- was also the base root of a descendant PIE form, reconstructed as *gerbh-* "clump, bunch" which is the source of objects which have been *crafted* or carefully put together. On the one hand, this gives us words such as *crib* and *crèche*, (which originally described the Christmas manger scene from Old French *cresche* "manger, crib") alongside German *Krippe* "rack, crib" and Icelandic *krubba* "crib". On the other hand, *gerbh-* also meant "carve" and is the ancestor of *graph*, *grammar* and the common suffixes *-gram* and *-graphy* via Greek γράφω (*gráphō*), as well as that famous scratcher, the *crab* (see chapter 26 for more on this).

Another posited meaning of PIE *ger-* is "to cry hoarsely". It is the root of the word for "crane" in most Indo-European languages, probably an echo of this bird's harsh, discordant cry. This can be seen in Welsh *garan*, Latin *grus* and German *Kranich*, all of which mean "crane". *Crane* plus *berry* equals *cranberry* and it is thought that this plant got its name from the resemblance of its stamen to a crane's beak. Similarly, the native English name for the geranium

94

flower was *cranesbill* until it was largely displaced by *geranium*. *Geranium* comes from the Ancient Greek γέρανος (*géranos*), which once again means "crane", plus the Latin suffix *-ium*. This time it is the seed pods of the flower that are said to resemble a crane's beak.

Other words carrying the cr- cluster are also related to its rather harsh *cracking* sound and so are probably imitative. Hence, *crack*, its frequentative *crackle*, *crash* and *croak* are all believed to be closely related and to a large degree onomatopoeic. The same applies in many contemporary European languages: Spaniards *creak*, *crackle* and *crunch* with the verb *crujir*, Romanians follow suit with *crănţăi*, the Dutch have *kraken*, while a Croat equivalent is *krskati*. French cognates are *craquer* "crash" and its variant *croquer* "crunch", the latter being the base of those tasty French snacks *croque-monsieurs* – toasted ham and cheese sandwiches – and *croque-madames* – the same with a fried egg on top. *Croquer* is also the source of the French idiom *croquer la pomme*, literally "crunch the apple", but in fact, a saucy euphemism for "make love". Typically, the word English adopted from this fertile source was the rather more prosaic *croquette*, which, with its bland spudness, only rarely reaches the exciting heights of crunchiness.

The *crunch* of the cr- cluster is used liberally in French advertising where many *crispy* products are labelled as *croquant*, including a delicious dessert of caramelised sugar and almonds similar to nut brittle. However, *croquant* also means "yokel" and the croquant rebellions – *Jacquerie des croquants* – were violent uprisings in 16th and 17th century France against excessive taxation. The peasant farmers were labelled *croquants* "crispies" by the nobles and wealthy classes who were "chewing up" their lands and devouring them as "snacks". This pejorative cr- has its English echo in the derisive term *crusty* for a tramp or unkempt person, and in *cruddy*, *crusty*, *crummy* and *crap*.

Crap was liberally thrown around northern Europe in the Middle Ages. The Modern English word descends from Middle English *crappe* "chaff, buckwheat" from the same word with the same meaning in Old French, and/or Old Dutch *krappen* "pluck, cut off". From this notion of "casting off what was worthless" comes the current sense of *crap* as "junk", and also "excrement". The French, however, continue to associate *crap* with the crunchiness of grain. This led to one of a number of unfortunately named onomatopoeically-inspired products on French shelves which I delighted in when we went to France on family holidays in the 1980s. The product *Crap's*, with what seems to be an utterly random and un-French apostrophe, was *chocolat au lait superieur au riz* – milk chocolate with crunchy rice – at that time. One of its counterparts on the shelves was Perrier's lemonade brand *Pschitt*. This supposedly represented the sound of escaping carbon dioxide when the bottle was opened, but pronounced with a silent *p* was enough to reduce me to helpless laughter. More often than strictly necessary, I would go to the supermarket to say "j'achète *Pschitt* and *Crap's*". At the time of writing, the *Crap's* has long since gone to the wall, but the *Pschitt* is still to hit the fan, and remains a popular beverage throughout France.

As well as *ger-*, another reconstructed PIE root, *ker-* is imitative of harsh and grating sounds. *Ker-* is surmised to be one of the source roots for *cawing* birds of the *crow* family. Latin *cornix* "crow" and *corvus* "raven", Ancient Greek κορώνη (*korōnē*) "rook, shearwater, crow", Modern Greek κοράκι (*koraki*) "crow", and κόρακας (*kórakas*) "raven", Norwegian *kråke* "crow", Lithuanian *kranklys* "raven" and Polish *kruk* "raven" can all be traced back to the same PIE root. This is very similar to Slavic words for "neck" or "throat", from where the cawing originates. Examples include Czech *krk* "throat, neck", Polish *kark* "nape, neck" as well as the Estonian borrowing *kurk* "throat".

Along with "rook", Ancient Greek κορώνη (*korōnē*) meant "crown", "wreath" or "garland" and more generally, "anything curved". Latin took this as *corona*, "wreath, crown", which was in turn borrowed by Old English for "crown". It wasn't until Norman times that *crown* supplanted *corona* as a monarch's royal headpiece, influenced by Old French *coronne*. *Corona* kept being borrowed and used as a source for other loan words, however. Apart from the aura of plasma wreathing the sun, *corona* is the source of *coronet* and *coronation*. Other close words have more interesting backstories. *Corollary* originally meant "money taken to pay for a garland" – its sense evolution then went from "gift", via "something extra" to "deduction" and then arrived at "natural consequence"; a *coroner's* work used to be to protect the property of the Crown rather than to determine the cause of death; *coronary*, referring to the heart, initially meant "suitable for garlands", but took its anatomical use from the arteries that surround the heart and resemble a crown. The diminutive of *corona* is *corolla*: this pertains to the petals which, taken as a whole, "crown" a flower.

Ker- also gave Latin *crepo* "crack, creak, prate", which spawned a number of *creaking*, *cracked* or *curved* descendants, and so another source for the *crooked*, *crackly* cr- phonesthemes. These have since been borrowed at various times by English, and the cr-cluster has gone from strength to strength. Among contemporary words, there are *decrepit*, *crevice*, *crevasse*, *crease*, *crest*, *crisp* and *crinoline*, all of which have entered English either directly from Latin derivatives of *crepo*, or by some more convoluted route. The name *Crispin* "curly-haired", is another descendant, a variation of which is *Crippen*, as in the notorious wife-murdering Doctor.

13.   squ- squeezing and squashing

I don't go out there to love my enemy. I go out there to squash him.

Jimmy Connors

Squ- *squatly* refuses to stand up straight, it is *squeezed* and *squashed* into smaller forms, often with a *squelching* sound. Squ- indicates compression, and as we compress and squeeze the lips together when producing this sound, there is a pleasing symmetry here: another example of echoic onomatopoeia. The squ- cluster is also good supporting evidence for proponents of the theory of phonosemantics: words that denote compression come from a number of different origins, but have come together in settling on a squ- form in contemporary English. They have been influenced by sound symbolism and are imitative of each other, resulting in a large number of *squirming* near synonyms.

The verb *squash* comes from the Latin verb ex*quassare* made up of the prefix ex- "out" and *quassare* "shake, shatter". This entered French as *esquasser* and *escasser* "crush, break" before being taken into Middle English as the recognisable *squachen*, the e- having been lost through *aphesis* – the loss of an unstressed vowel at the start of a word – *esquire* becoming *squire* is another example (see chapter 10 for more on this). The sport of *squash* is named after the *squashable* ball used, but the soft, *squishy squash* fruits arrived in English from a different source, namely the Algonquian language of the Narragansett people of what is now the American state of Rhode Island. *Squash* here is a shortened form of *askutasquash* "vegetable eaten green or raw". *Squat* is another aphetic form, coming into Middle English as *squatten* from Old French *esquatir*, as outlined by Captain John Smith, (c.1580-1631)

Admiral of New England, colonist, explorer and soldier and another who had contact with Algonquian tribes. Here he writes of the Indians of Virginia:

> ...take they ther bowes and arrows and hauinge made ridie to shoot they softly steale toward ther enimies, Sumtime squattinge doune and priinge if they can spie any to shoot at...

(from *Travels and Works of Captain John Smith*)

It is not only by aphesis that the consonant cluster squ- has appeared. In fact, some words have actually added the s- to an older word as an intensifier, turning qu- into squ-. One such word is *squeeze*, which descends from Middle English *quease* and Old English *cwysan* "crush, squeeze". Similarly, *quench* has the rarer emphatic form *squench*. The same phenomenon of s- as intensifier has occurred with other clusters beginning with voiceless stops (see appendix), for example *plash* has become *splash* and *crunch* has the more emphatic *scrunch* variant.

Other words have adopted the squ- cluster for compression by imitation of existing words or by blending. Hence, we have *squirm* influenced by the movements of a *worm*, *squiggle*, which is probably a blend of *squirm* and either *wiggle* or *wriggle* and the colloquial *squits* "diarrhoea" which is graphically reminiscent of *squirt*, and indeed Swedish *skvätta* "splash".

John Smith had a remarkably colourful life. Born in a sleepy village in Lincolnshire, he decided at the age of sixteen to embark upon a military life and to work as a mercenary abroad. He first served in the army of Henri IV of France, and then fought against the Spaniards in the cause of Dutch independence. In 1600, he was shipwrecked on an island near Cannes and was rescued by the crew of a French pirate ship who had come ashore for fresh water. Impressed by their leader, a certain Captain La Roche, he joined their number. He soon found himself plundering a

Venetian ship whose cargo was so valuable that Smith's share of the spoils made him a rich man.

His adventures continued when he decided to turn again to the military life as what is rather generously called "a soldier of fortune", this time for the Habsburgs against the Ottoman Turks in Hungary and Wallachia. Smith is said to have killed and beheaded three Turkish opponents in single combat duels, a feat for which he was knighted by the Prince of Transylvania, given a horse and awarded a coat of arms showing three Turks' heads. In 1602, Smith's luck ran out when he was wounded fighting the Tartars. He was captured and sent to Constantinople, where he was sold as a slave. However, he managed to escape by killing his master, hiding his body and stealing his clothes and horse. He returned to England and joined an expedition aiming to colonise Virginia. Not one for a quiet life, Smith was arrested mid-voyage for mutiny and arrived in America in chains. Despite this, Smith was designated as one of the leaders of the new colony and released to help in the building of Jamestown.

In late 1607, Smith was captured by a native American band and taken before Wahunsonacock, chief of the Powhatan tribe. Smith recounted that he feared for his life, but was saved by the actions of Wahunsonacock's daughter, Pocahontas – yes, that one – who pleaded for his life and secured his release. Relations between the Indians and the colonists improved for a time, although conflict would arise again with the colony's further expansion into the tribes' ancestral land. Still not 30, Smith was forced to return to England in 1609 because of the severe burns he suffered in an accident when handling gunpowder.

Appearances are important to squ- too. If we look *askew*, we *squint*, while objects which look soft and *squishy* also take the squ- cluster: *squeegees* are soft and *squidgy*, a fat young bird is a *squab*, and a rubbery cephalopod is a *squid*, although it has even been suggested that the squid was named by sailors who observed the way it *squirted* its "ink".

The onomatopoeia and imitation are especially evident with the high-pitched noises that are made when pressure is applied. This can be seen with the verbs *squall* (or its alternative version *squawl*) "cry out loudly" and *squeal* and the parallel pair of *squawk* and *squeak*. The latter pair may also be blends, *squawk* coming from *squeak* and *bawl* and *squeak* itself the result of *squeal* and *shriek*. The source for all of these squ- verbs is probably Old Norse *skvala* "cry out, shriek", while the related noun of *squall* "sudden storm, violent gust of wind" is also from a Scandinavian source, *skval* being Norwegian for "sudden gush" and Swedish for "drenching". The evocative nature of *skval* has led to it being widely borrowed, not only by English, but also by Balto-Slavic languages, such as Lithuanian *škvalas*, Russian шквал (*škval*) and Polish *szkwał*.

14.   tw- twists and twins

I went to Cambridge and thought I would stay there. I thought I would quietly grow tweed in a corner somewhere and become a Don or something.

Stephen Fry

Tw- has a dual focus: it is a *twanger* and a *twin*. A number of tw- words are related to *tweaking* - spinning, pulling or plucking – while most of the others are connected with the number *two*. Both themes go back to Proto-Indo-European, in **terkw-* "twist, wind" and **duwo-* "two", so are obviously very old indeed. The *tweaking* tw- words have a Proto-Germanic ancestor **twikkijana* "pin, pinch, nip", which gave Old English *twiccian* "pluck" and Low German *twicken* "pinch". Modern cognates of *tweak* include *twitch*, and its nasalised form *twinge*, while German has *zwicken* "pinch". Probable blends add to the stock of tw- words, with *twirl* seemingly a blend of *twist* and *whirl*, and *twirl* itself combining with *fiddle* to make *twiddle*.

Quite often, the two senses of tw- coincide, as with the word *twist*. In Old English, *twist* meant "spin two threads together to make *twine*" – double-thread or yarn. Obviously, the more threads that *intertwine*, the stronger the resulting cord, so you might have ended up with Old English *candeltwist* "wick" or *mæsttwist* "rope" depending on how much string was twisted together. The names of the cloths *twill* and *tweed* are both derived from *twine*. *Twill* is a cloth that produces a pattern of diagonal lines by weaving the weft (horizontal) thread over one and then under two warp (vertical) threads. *Twill* is associated with the upper crust and cavalrymen's trousers. *Tweed* is a rough, woollen cloth originally from the River

102

Tweed in the Scottish Borders area. It uses twill weaves in the making of suits, hats and skirts. Tweed is likewise associated with the upper crust, specifically the country gentleman in his hunting and shooting of defenceless animals apparel. The eclectic tweed is also associated with the Prince of Wales, Sherlock Holmes, dusty academics and Mr Toad.

In practice, there is little difference between the *Tweedledum* of *twill* and the *Tweedledee* of *tweed* – they are twins from the same stock. Made famous in *Through the Looking-Glass* (1871), Tweedledum and Tweedledee are not actually creations of Lewis Carroll. In fact, they are the invention of the poet John Byrom (1692-1763), who used the terms to mock the composers Handel and Bononcini in 1725. The furious rivalry between the composers had become a cause célèbre in 1720s London with the Whig Party favouring Handel, and the Tories preferring Bononcini. However, for many, including Byrom, there was little to choose between them, as he outlined in his satirical poem *On the Feud Between Handel and Bononcini*:

Some say, compar'd to Bononcini,
That Mynheer Handel's but a Ninny
Others aver, that he to Handel
Is scarcely fit to hold a Candle
Strange all this Difference should be
'Twixt Tweedle-dum and Tweedle-dee!

It is tempting to speculate that many other tweaking tw-s are *twinned* with the double tw-s from sometime back in Proto-Indo-European, as the crossover between the two categories is there when you look for it. This is as true for more recent words as for words which can be traced back deep into history. Should you *twang* a stringed instrument or *tweak* someone's ear, you are likely to use two fingers; *tweezers* are made up of two parts; the strangely fascinating contemporary craze for *twerking* involves jerking both buttocks in defiance of the laws of physics. Meanwhile, *twizzling* is spinning, twirling and twisting, but actually comes from an alteration of Middle English *twissel* "double, twofold" from Old English *twisel* "forked". Modern German *Zwiesel* "fork" goes back by the same twisted path to Proto-Germanic **twisila* "fork, junction", which in turn stems from Proto-Indo-European **dwis-* "twice, in two" and ultimately from the PIE **duwo-* "two" ancestral root.

The same goes for *twigs*, which would be ideal instruments for prodding, tweaking or twanging, but again can be traced back as far as **duwo-* via Proto-Germanic *twigga* "fork, point of division". Cognates exist across Indo-European languages with Old Church Slavonic двигъ (*dvigŭ*) "branch", Albanian *degë* "branch" and, closer to home, Dutch *twijg* "twig" and German *Zweig* "branch, twig". The most likely explanation regarding the derivation of the secondary meaning of *twig*, "realise, comprehend" is that it is totally unrelated to *twig* as in "stick, forked branch" but has instead been borrowed from Scottish and Irish Gaelic *tuig* "understand".

Two was spelt *twa* in its neuter form in Old English and pronounced [twa:], which explains its seemingly superfluous *w*. Its close relatives also begin with the tw- cluster. The most obvious are clearly the cardinal numbers *two*, *twelve* and *twenty*, along with *twice* and *twin*. Then of course, we have *betwixt* and *between* and "never the *twain* shall meet", the *twain* in question being an archaic masculine form of *two*. The *twi-* of *twilight* is that of "half" or "between" rather than "double" or "twofold", with dusk being the juncture between day and night and a clear dividing point. This can also be seen in German *Zwielicht*, a descendant of Middle High German *zwischerliecht*, literally "tweenlight." Marketing executives at *Mars* also jumped on the "tw- for two" bandwagon when coining the name of the popular chocolate bar *Twix*. It is either a portmanteau (see chapter 10) of *twin* and *bix* as it comes in a two biscuit-bar pack, or even more wretchedly, because it refers to the caramel 'twixt the chocolate and biscuit. Whatever, "a twin Twix pack is the longer-lasting snack", or at least it was back in the 1980s when it weighed in at a princely 60g, rather than its measly current 50g microweight.

When comparative linguistics was in its infancy, the striking similarities in words denoting the number *two* helped persuade linguists that the case for a Proto-Indo-European ancestor language was strong. Greek and Latin have *duo*, Sanskrit has द्व (*dvá*) and the Avestan pronunciation of "two" is also [dva]. The Slavic languages also tend to keep the dv- combination, with Bulgarian две (*dve*), Czech *dvě* etc. The High German Consonant Shift (aka the Second Germanic Consonant Shift – keep up!) was responsible for the original Germanic *t* of Old English, Gothic etc, morphing into a *z* in German, representing the sound /ts/. This is in evidence in *zwei* "two", *zwischen* "between", *Zwirne* "twine" and *Zwilling* "twin". Scandinavian languages often have a tv- cluster: Icelandic has *tveir*, *tvö* and *tvær* for *two* and Swedish has *två*. Dutch and Frisian maintain the tw- spelling of Old English *twa* with *twee* and *twa* respectively, although in both cases the *w* is pronounced nearer to /v/. Modern English shares the erosion of the /w/ of *two* with Norwegian and Danish, where *two* has become *to*.

Twice (literally "of two"), along with its bedfellows *once* and *thrice*, is an *adverbial genitive*, a relic form from a time when the genitive (possessive) case was still productive in Old and Middle English. Nouns and adjectives declined in the genitive case fall into the adverbial genitive category when they are used as adverbs. The *-ce* ending of *once*, *twice* and *thrice* is derived from the Middle English adverbial genitive *-es/-se* form of *ones*, *twise* and *thries* "of one", "of two", "of three" and thus "one time", "two times", "three times". The *-ce* spelling came about because it better indicated the voiceless /s/ pronunciation of the adverbial genitive, rather than a voiced /z/ – compare the pronunciation of *once* and *ones*. For the same reason, *since*, from ME *sithens*, developed the *-ce* ending. Hence, *thence* and *whence* from the roots of *here*, *there* and *where* also take this form.

The genitive case in Middle English had a final -s case marker on all noun forms by the 16th century. This is reflected in the so-called *Saxon genitive* of English possessives – the *'s* clitic being a remnant form. Compounds with *-way* had the adverbial genitive appended to give us *always, sideways, lengthways*, and so on. Similarly, the directional suffix *–ward* "turned toward" (from PIE **wert-* "turn, wind"), which was originally attached to adjectives, had the -s tacked on to create adverbs like *northwards, forwards, backwards* and *afterwards*. Other common adverbial genitive forms include *unawares, nowadays, sometimes, needs* (of *needs must*), *indoors* and *outdoors*. There is also a small group which has adopted the adverbial genitive along with a parasitic *t* to make the -st suffix of *whilst, midst* and *amongst*, as well as the variant *betwixt*.

The adverbial genitive is still a common feature in other Germanic languages. German, for example, has expressions such as *eines Tages* and *eines Nachts* which do not refer to one specific day or night, but rather "in the day", "at night", as well as *morgens, abends* etc. This kind of adverbial has been phrased in English with "mornings" and "evenings" and the more overtly genitive structure "of a morning", "of an evening" to report routine actions. Similarly, anyone arriving in Britain from the European mainland will see signs instructing drivers to *"links fahren"*, so that German speakers know to "drive leftwards", that is, "on the left", the adverbial genitive *–s* of *links* clearly in evidence.

One recent arrival to the phonosemantic tw- party is the group of tw- words which relate to fools and those who can easily be dismissed as *twits, twerps* and *twonks* who speak *twaddle*. The more offensive *twat* also fits into this group without difficulty and gives me the chance to retell the story of Robert Browning, who in his poem *Pippa Passes* (1841), somewhat *twittishly* writes:

> Then, owls and bats, cowls and *twats*,
> Monks and nuns, in a cloister's moods,
> Adjourn to the oak-stump pantry!

Apparently, Browning had mistaken *twat* for part of a nun's habit, pairing it with a priest's cowl. This error was based on his misunderstanding of a poem from 1660, *Vanity of Vanities*, containing the lines:

> They'd talk't of his having a Cardinalls Hat
> They'd send him as soon an Old Nuns Twat.

Oh Robert! This demonstrates the importance of checking the meanings of unfamiliar words, not to mention the veracity of purported "translations". Here's hoping that nobody has been mischievous in translating Sanskrit or Avestan!

15.   sc- / sk- scarves, scales and skin

Then gently scan your brother man,
Still gentler sister woman;
Tho' they may gang a kennin wrang,
To step aside is human.

Robert Burns, *Address to the Unco Guid, or the Rigidly Righteous*

The sound /sk/ can be written both as **sk-** or **sc-** in English, but both spellings have the same phonosemantic themes. Following Lawler (1990), it seems clear that the main idea of the /sk/ sound is of extending something that is flat or two-dimensional horizontally. This often involves cutting or knitting something into a long, thin strip of material. If we think of *skirts* and *scarves*, they are basically flat pieces of cloth which have been stretched out to form items of clothing. When children *sketch* the *sky*, it is usually with extended horizontal brush strokes on paper and historically, the sky as a concept has been difficult for people to imagine as a three-dimensional space. In addition, if we look at verbs describing extended horizontal movement, /sk/ is very well-represented. *Skating*, *skimming*, *scampering*, *scanning* and *scouring* are all variations on this theme. Even with *scalding*, *scuffing* and *scorching*, there is a starting point which is then rapidly extended upon contact with the 2D surface of the *skin* or the ground. The friction or tearing involved here may well result in *scabs*, *scars* and *scratches* – the related cluster scr- will be dealt with in the next chapter.

Despite the Old English sc- spelling, Proto-Germanic /sk/ was palatalised in the Early Old English period to /ʃ/, so *scead* "shade", *sculdor* "shoulder" and *sceaft* "shaft" all began with the /ʃ/ sound that is still there today. The former /sk/ pronunciation is found in their Proto-Germanic forebears: *skadwaz, *skuldro and *skaftaz respectively. With the arrival of Viking settlers from the 9th to 11th centuries, unpalatalised /sk/ returned to Britain. Dialectal sk- words of Old Norse origin are common in areas of Britain where there was the greatest concentration of Viking settlement e.g. North-East English *skeg* "glance", Yorkshire *skell* "bent out of shape, upset".

Sk- place names also bear witness to the impact of Old Norse, as demonstrated by *Skegness*, Lincolnshire, which is either "Skeggi's headland" or "the bearded one's headland" and *Scarborough*, North Yorkshire, ON *Skarðaborg* – "the town of (Viking raider) Thorgils Skarthi". I was brought up in the sprawling metropolis of Marske-by-the-Sea, Cleveland, pronounced [mask] by the locals, and named after a *marsh* by the sea – Danish *marsk*. The greatest evidence for the reintroduction of sk- is found in the Northern Isles of Shetland and Orkney, which made up the Norse province of Norðreyjar from the 9th to 14th century. In fact, the Norn dialect of Old Norse was spoken here for hundreds of years, so almost every place name has a Norse origin. *Scapa Flow*, Orkney, ON *Skalpaflói* – "the bay of the long isthmus"; and *Scalloway*, Shetland, ON *Skálavágr* – "the bay with the large house(s}" illustrate this Scandinavian influence, as well as the characteristic unpalatalised /sk/ of the Viking settlers.

Norse influence also resulted in a number of doublets in English e.g. *shirt/skirt*, *dish/disc*, *shabby/scabby*, *shatter/scatter* and possibly *shell/skull*. Later spelling changes would reflect pronunciation, so palatalised /ʃ/ became sh- and unpalatalised /sk/ as either sc- (usually before a back vowel or consonant) or sk- (usually before a front vowel). Sc-/sk- words borrowed from Old Norse or from other languages at a later date were not palatalised, as we can see in the difference between *ship* (from palatalised OE *scip*), and *skipper* (borrowed from unpalatalised Middle Dutch *scipper*) and *skiff* (from Middle French *esquif*). Obviously, this means that there are strong phonosemantic connections between words beginning with sc-/sk- and those which now begin with sh-. Even today, there is not always a definitive consensus on pronunciation, as the heated debate over how to say "schedule" illustrates. We will see further evidence of these close links between /ʃ/ and /sk/ in chapters 16 and 27.

One of the sources for many of the sc- and sk- words in contemporary English (as well as the related items spelt with sh-) is the Proto-Indo-European root *(s)ker-* "cut". The underlying idea here seems to be that things are cut to a length, and *shorn* from the whole – *scieran* is the Old English predecessor of *shear*, a word with a multitude of Indo-European cognates: Dutch and German *scheran*, Danish *skære*, along with Lithuanian *skirti* "separate" and Croatian *škare* "scissors". Cutting through coarse material will obviously require some *sharp* tool so material can be cut to make *skirts*, *shirts* or *shorts*: Old English has *scearp* "sharp", *scyrte* "skirt, apron", *scafan* "shave" and *sceort* "short".

To avoid a self-inflicted cut, it is wise to put your sword in a *scabbard*. However, if you want to get your cut, you wish to take hold of your *share* (OE *scearu*). For complex calculations, you may be required to count larger numbers and keep *score*. Drovers used to make a notch in a tally stick when a *score* of sheep, i.e. twenty, passed through a tollgate. The Proto-Germanic word for "score",*skura-* (again from PIE *(s)ker-*), probably meant "line drawn by a sharp instrument" and the sense moved to include "marks made to keep count of a customer's drinks in a tavern" to "number of points, goals etc. in a game".

Counting with twenty as a base, or *vigesimalism*, seems to have been very common in early agricultural societies. Celtic languages still have twenty as a base for numbers 20-100, as exemplified by these words for "seventy": Breton *dec ha tri uéguend* and Welsh *deg a thrigain* (both "ten and three twenty"), and Manx *three-feed as jeih* and Scottish Gaelic *tri fichead 's a deich* (both "three twenty and ten"). In Old French, *vint* "twenty" or a multiple of it could be used as a base as in "fifty" *dous vinz et diz*, literally "two twenties and ten" and 120 *six vinz*. The importance of twenty remains current in Modern French with numbers such as quatre-vingt "eighty" i.e. "four twenties". However, the European language with the most impressive examples of vigesimalism is Danish, which has these beauties: *otteoghalvfierdsindstyve* "seventy-eight" – "eight and three score plus half of the fourth score" and *halvfemsindstyve* "ninety" – "four score plus half of the fifth score".

Remains of a vigesimal system live on in English. The word *score* was used frequently in the bible, most famously in Psalm 90, which states that "the days of our years are threescore years and ten". In many rural Northern English communities, a vigesimal system of counting sheep was widespread until the early 20th century, and still exists in the most isolated pockets of Yorkshire and Lancashire. The numbers used are from a Brythonic Celtic language such as Cumbric, with variations of *yan tan tethera* for *one, two* and *three* up to *jiggit* "twenty", when the shepherd would *score* a mark on the ground, drop a stone into his pocket or move his hand to another notch on his crook. This dialectal numbering system is also attested in knitting songs and in children's games and nursery rhymes.

Cutting and *sculpting* tools were often made of *shards* of sharp stone to ensure a clean cut. A *shard* (OE *sceard*) might be easier to find on *sheer*, exposed *scarp* slopes, or possibly on *skerries* – small rocky islands. *(S)ker-* was also the ancestor of Ancient Greek σκύρος (*skûros*) "stone chippings" (which may be familiar from the Greek island of Σκῦρος – English *Skyros* – one of the Spirades islands), and Latin *scrupus* "sharp stone". *Scrupus* gives English *scruples*, when the conscience digs in to cause doubt and anxiety. A different root, PIE *(s)kep-* "cut, dig out" is thought to be the source of /sk/ words for the digging, scraping process itself, such as *scoop, shovel, scuff, scupper* and *shuffle*, as well as *scapula*, the shoulder blade. Early spades were often made from animal shoulder blades.

Another PIE root that also contains the cutting and dividing theme of sc-/sk- is *skei- "split". This is thought to be the source of Old English *scadan*, the forerunner of Modern English *shed*, as in "cast off, separate", and has descendants throughout the Indo-European world, including Sanskrit च्यति (*chyáti*) "he cuts off", Irish *scian* "knife", German *scheiden* "part, separate" and Lithuanian *skedzu* "skim off, make thin, divide". It is also the root of Latin verbs *scire* "know", which probably originally meant "separate one thing from another, distinguish" and is the source of *science, conscience, and conscious*; and *scindere* "split, cut", from which English later borrowed *rescind*. The same PIE root is responsible for the Greek root σχίζ- (*schiz-*), source of σχίζω (*schizo*) "sliver, splinter" and σχίσμα (*schisma*) "division". This root gave English *schism, schist, schedule* (via Latin) and later the new coinage *schizophrenia*. Various Germanic sources were also conduits for a large number of contemporary English descendants of *skei-*. These include *shiver* "break into bits, splinter", *skewer, shin, ski, skid* and *shit* – the latter going back to the notion of "separation" from the body. *Skin* (Old English *scinn* and Old Norse *skinn*) also comes from *skei-*, as does *skint*, which is in fact a slangy variant of *skinned* – possibly in the sense of *fleeced*, "swindled", or else *broke*, as in "broken" – either by creditors or by the proprietor of the gaming tables to whom you've lost all your money – you've *broken the bank*.

Extending or stretching out material in swathes will also lead to objects being hidden or *screened*, a concept which is at the heart of the PIE root *(s)keu- "cover, conceal". The Proto-Germanic descendant of this has been reconstructed as *skeuja-*, the source of Old Norse *sky* "cloud", Old English *scua* "shadow" and *sceo* "cloud" as well as Latin *obscurus* "dark, shadowy". Modern English has several /sk/ or /ʃ/ words arising from these roots, including *sky, obscure, skim, scum, shoe* (in which you hide your foot), and *shame*. Descendants of *(s)keu- where the s- has been dropped maintain the notion of covering and concealment. Among their number are *house*, *hose*, *hoard*, *hut*, *huddle* and *hide*, the latter of course, meaning "conceal", but also "skin".

The word *scale* is interesting in that its numerous meanings seem to encompass the different phonosemantic meanings inherent in the sc-/sk- cluster: *scale* in the mathematical sense, representing extended distance, weight, temperature etc. comes from Latin *scala* "ladder, step", from *scandere* "climb", which will be what you do if you *scale* a cliff; playing *scales* on a piano involves the fingers moving in horizontal steps across the keyboard; *scales* are also flattened plates covering the skin of fish and reptiles; *scaling* a fish in cooking preparation involves making horizontal sweeping movements across the surface of the fish's skin to separate the fish from the scales; the thin layer of calcium at the bottom of your kettle or boiler is *limescale*, which will of course necessitate *descaling* to get rid of the *scaly* layer of *scum*.

Scandinavian languages remain fond of the /sk/ cluster for extended two-dimensional space: "scab" is *skorper* in Norwegian and Danish; "skim" is *skumma* in Swedish and *skimme* in Danish; "scum" in Norwegian and Swedish is *avskum*, while in Danish it is *udskud*. Even here in the Viking heartlands, there is a mix of /sk/ and /ʃ/ sounds, though, notwithstanding spelling. For example, "ship" is unpalatalised *skip* [skɪ:p] in Icelandic and *skib* [ski:b] in Danish, but palatalised *skip* [ʃi:p] in Faroese and Norwegian. Although /sk/ does appear in the West Germanic languages – *skalp* and *skaten* occur in German, for example – it is much rarer here. German prefers a /ʃ/ for this cluster, while Dutch combines the /s/ sound with the voiceless velar fricative (see appendix) of Scottish *loch* /x/, the /sk/ to /sx/ change here happening in the Middle Dutch period c.1150 1500. Hence, *scoop* is *schep* in both languages but pronounced [ʃep] in German and [sxep] in Dutch. Similarly, *scour* is *scheuern* [ʃɔɪern] in German but *schuren* [sxu:ren] in Dutch.

16.   scr- scratching and scraps

He was his own leftover, the spat-out scrag.
He was what his brain could make nothing of.

Ted Hughes, *Crow's Playmates*

Scr- *scrambles* through life: it is a *scrunched-up scrag* of a cluster *scrabbling* through the trash. It is related to the sc-/sk-cluster and often seems phonosemantically similar, but an extra layer of meaning is usually added. **Scr-** often combines extended two-dimensional space with further lateral or *scrambled* movement across it. Movements are made on a surface, which could be *scratched* or *scribbled* on, but the marks that are left will be superficial and lacking in depth – the two-dimensional object will remain fundamentally intact, once the marks have been *scrubbed* out. A *scribe* will roll out a *scroll* and proceed to *scratch* its surface with the nib of a pen. Of course, work should be done neatly so the *manuscript* is pleasant to look at rather than an unsightly *scrawl*. Frequently, words with scr- also come with a grating sound or impact, as in the onomatopoeic *scringe* "make a harsh grinding or creaking sound".

The PIE root **(s)ker-* "cut" encountered in the previous chapter, is again at the heart of the scr- cluster, this time through its extended form **skerb-* "engrave, scratch", the source of the majority of the scr- words we will meet in this chapter. As seems to often be the way in English, the root existed in several Old English words, but over time more and more scr- words were absorbed from other Germanic languages, as well as French and Latin. This has boosted our stock of scr- words, reinforcing and supplementing the underlying phonesthemes of the scr- cluster.

It is Latin *scribo* "write" and its derived forms that have given a vast number of the more sophisticated scr- items to the English lexicon. The base root gives us *scribe* and its French influenced version *scrivener*, as well as *script, scribble* and *scripture*. Various prefixes were added to the Latin root and borrowed indiscriminately by English, usually via other Romance languages. Hence, we have *inscribe, ascribe, describe, circumscribe, transcribe, prescribe, proscribe* etc. *Scribo's* influence is felt throughout Romance and Germanic languages, as witnessed by different words for *write*, such as Italian *scrivere*, Spanish *escribir*, German *schreiben* and Icelandic *skrifa*. For the hasty *scribblers*, Italian has *scarabocchiare* "scribble, doodle", while Portuguese has *escrevinhar* "scrawl" and Croatian, Bosnian and Slovenian have *škrabati* "scribble, scrabble".

The Old English verb for "write" was *scrifan*, a word whose meaning expanded to mean "decree, impose penance" and then "hear confession". *Shrove Tuesday* was not initially an excuse to stuff your face with pancakes, but was a day of merrymaking followed by a visit to the priest who would hear your *shrift* "confession" at the beginning of Lent. Prisoners condemned to die would be given *short shrift*, that is, a rushed sacrament of confession in the brief time before they were to be executed, rather than a high-handed and thoughtless rejection.

A second set of scr- words shows another relationship with the parent sc-/sk- cluster focusing on what is cut off or withered. Here the cluster is closely related to the shr- cluster which we shall examine in chapter 27. Whereas sc- concentrates on the *skirt* or *scarf* carefully and deliberately cut out of the fabric, scr- looks at the useless *scraps* and *shreds* of material that are left to be *scrunched* up and thrown away. Sc- words have *scope* and *scale*; scr- words *scrabble* around in the cast-offs, *scraping* the bottom of the barrel. *Scrutiny* may come from the notion of "rooting through rubbish" and comes from Latin *scruta* "shreds, rags, trash". Related to this is the Northern English dialectal *scran* "food", believed to come from Old Norse (and Modern Icelandic) *skran* – "rubbish, junk", as *scran* was originally the *scraps* of food, the leftovers that the better-off did not deign to eat.

(S)ker- gives Latin *scortum* "hide" and *corium* "hide, bark, crust, shell" not to mention *scrotum* and *scrofa* – literally "digger, rooter" but also "breeding sow". The diminutive of *scrofa* is *scrofula* "swelling of the neck glands" a disease which got its name either due to it being thought to afflict piglets or from the somewhat whimsical notion that the glandular swellings resembled young pigs or sows. *Screw* also comes from *(s)ker-*, although how it ended up in its present form from the PIE root is disputed. Many experts affirm that it also came from *scrofa* via Old French *escroue* "screwhole, nut", which aligns it with Spanish *puerca* and Portuguese *porca*, both of which mean "sow" but also "screwhole". Apparently, this is due to the boar's penis having a screw-like tip, so the sow's vulva is a screwhole by a less than charming analogy. *Screw* also has many similar sounding Germanic cognates, e.g. Dutch *schroef*, Swedish *skruv*, Danish *skrue*, so a more humdrum possibility is that it acquired its present form by conflation with these words.

The extended root *skerb-* provides a number of earthy, *scruffy* elements which arrived in English via Proto-Germanic *skurf* "gnaw". Such words include *scruff*, *scurf* "dandruff, crust", and *scurvy*. *Scruff* in the sense of "nape of the neck" is related to North Frisian *skuft* "back of a horse's neck", Old Norse *skopt* "hair of the head" and Dutch *schoft*, which means "withers of a horse" but also, in keeping with the rather coarse elements of this cluster, "bastard", "low-life trash". A similar scr- phonestheme is found in many European languages for undesirable characteristics: Italian has *scrocco* "scrounging", French has *escroc* "crook", and German has *Schurke* "villain, rascal", which is cognate to *shirk*, and thought to be the source for English *shark* – by semantic extension a "scoundrelfish".

Scurvy is caused by a vitamin C deficiency which causes spongy gums, loosening of the teeth and bleeding from the gums and mucus membranes. It occurs in humans as well as in simians, birds, bats and guinea pigs, all animals which are unable to synthesise their own vitamin C. Instead, humans need to consume vitamin C, usually in the form of *ascorbic* (literally "away from scurvy") acid as part of their diet. Scurvy was first documented by the Ancient Egyptians, and was also recorded as a disease by Hippocrates, yet its treatment was not well-understood. Sailors who went without fresh fruit and vegetables for months on end were particularly prone to scurvy, but its prevention through the consumption of citrus fruits and lemon juice only really became widespread towards the end of the eighteenth century.

In cases where citrus fruits are not at hand, fresh meat from animals that make their own vitamin C has been used to prevent scurvy. Hence, in Arctic climates the Inuit have long consumed muktuk (whale skin), Scott's 1901-4 expedition to the Antarctic used lightly-fried seal meat and seal liver and French soldiers famously ate fresh horse meat. This came about on the recommendation of Napoleon's surgeon-in-chief, Baron Dominique-Jean Larrey, who had noticed that wounded soldiers who ate horse meat scavenged from the battlefield recovered more quickly and became immune to scurvy. He gave orders for horse meat soup to be served in hospitals. Horse meat was also eaten in large quantities during the 1870 Siege of Paris.

The Merchant Shipping Act of 1867 required all Royal Navy and Merchant Navy ships to serve their sailors with a daily lime ration to ward off scurvy. From this, British sailors came to be known as *limeys*, which was originally quite a derogatory term. *Limey* soon spread to be applied to British immigrants to the former English colonies of America, South Africa, Australia and New Zealand and then, in American slang, to refer to British people in general.

If you are a cider buff, you will be familiar with the scr- cluster. *Scrumps* "withered apples" produce *scrumpy* cider, a drink which was originally considered to be "rough", because it was made of unselected apples. The scrumpy apples may not have been top quality because the best apples were sold as fruit, but another possibility was that they were gathered by *scrumpers*, apple thieves, who had *scrumped* the apples indiscriminately from someone else's orchard or garden. Cider apples need to be "prepared" before they are pressed. Essentially, this means they need to be battered to a pulp, and this is usually accomplished with a *scratter*, or apple mill. The chunks of apple that have been through the mill are known as *scrattings*.

Other withered scr- words include *scrawny, scrag, scraggly, scrod* "young cod, which is split and cooked", from Middle Dutch *scrode* "piece cut off, shred" and Scottish dialectal *scrog* "stunted bush" or "crab-apple tree". Similarly, **skerb-* is easy to detect in the barely altered English words *scrub* and *shrub*, both of which show the link between stunted, woody plants and the brooms which were made from them. Close cognates remain in other Germanic languages, for instance, Danish *skrub* "brushwood," Norwegian *skrubba* "dwarf tree" and North Frisian *skrobb* "broom plant, brushwood".

The verb *scrimp* "make too small; be frugal" (first attested as an adjective meaning "scant, meagre") is also a descendant of **skerb-* and has close Scandinavian cognates such as Swedish *skrumpna* or Norwegian *skrumpe*, both meaning "shrivel". *Scrimp* is related to *shrimp, skimpy* and *scrounge*, all of which are pejorative and carry the notion of "a lack". Pejorative scr- overtones occur throughout Germanic, as in Swedish *skral* "poor, inferior", Norwegian *skrike* "scream, screech", Dutch *schruk* "blackguard", and Icelandic *skratti* "demon".

The unprepossessing associations of scr- were undoubtedly in Charles Dickens's mind when he decided to call his famous miser Ebenezer *Scrooge* (see chapter 6). Dickens was well aware of the connotations which came with his names and it is usually easy to tell whether his characters will have positive or negative attributes. Thus, we have the positive Reverend Crisparkle in *The Mystery of Edwin Drood*, the snooty Lady Snuphanuph in *The Pickwick Papers*, the benevolent Cheeryble brothers in *Nicholas Nickleby* and the grim and unemotional Thomas Gradgrind in *Hard Times*, among many, many more evocative names.

Scr- also has its suspected blends, with *scrawl* a possible combination of *sprawl* and *crawl*, or else an alteration of one of the two and *scratch* being a blend of two Middle English words for "scratch": *scratten* and *crachen*. Scr- also gives rise to *skyscraper*, one of the most widely-used calques in the world (see chapter 11). French has *gratte-ciel,* Russian has небоскрёб (*neboskrjob*), Italian has *grattacielo* and Swedish has the eminently translatable *skyskrapa*.

17.　　sl- slippery slime

Beware the sauce! Where food comes beslobbered with an elegant slime you may well suspect the integrity of the basic ingredients.

Edward Abbey, *The Fool's Progress*

The consonant cluster **sl-** has two connected themes. One refers to "where solid meets liquid". At this smooth and *slippery* juncture, things start to *slide*, snow turns to *sleet* and you could end up *sloshing* around in the *slush*. On slippery snow and ice, pedestrians need to *slow* down and the transport needs to slide too, so as to get us from A to B. Hence, *sleds*, *sledges* and *sleighs* all have smooth runners to minimise friction. This in-between state is characterised by inconstancy, which leads on to the second major theme of sl-, which is basically pejorative. A lot of sl- words have very negative connotations. A *slick* presentation may be admirable, but there is still a hint of the oleaginous side parting about it. Other words with the sl- cluster are more overtly critical, especially towards those we perceive to have *slack* morals and living lives that are on the *slippery slope*. We *slam* people we perceive to be *sleazy*, *slothful* or *slutty*. From our high horses, we *slag off slappers*, castigate the *slovenly* and ridicule the *slobbering* masses *slouched* in front of the TV with their *sloppy* manners and *slavish* addiction to the cult of celebrity, *slushy* films, and mindless TV *slop*.

The different strands of the sl- cluster are exemplified by the different meanings of the word *slip*. Everything is either smooth or greasy. *Slipping* clothes on and off is smooth and easy, while taking a *slip road* will give you easy access to the motorway. On the greasy side, slipping over is a real possibility with a slippery surface. *Slip* as an uncountable noun is the mixture of fine clay and water used by potters in the casting of ceramics. The *cowslip*, (*primula veris*), is a common flower of the primrose family, which gets its name because it is often found growing in cow dung, or *cow slop*.

There are several reconstructed Proto-Indo-European roots which seem to have contributed to English words with the sl- cluster, though the dividing line between them is not clear and they may well have developed by analogy with each other. One such root is PIE **(s)lei-* "slimy, sticky" which is the leading candidate for the descendants *slop, slip, slipper, schlep, slapper, sleeve, slough, slope* and *slipshod* among others. *Slipshod* derives from the idea that only the careless, slovenly or down-at-heel would go outside shod in slippers. How *slapdash*! **(S)lei-* is also the source of Latin *limus* "mud" and Old English *lim "mud"* from where we have *lime* for "calcium", Danish has *lim* for "birdlime" and Dutch takes *lijm* for "glue". Another descendant of PIE **(s)lei-* became **slima-* in Proto-Germanic, whence German took *Schleim* "mucus, slime", Dutch *slijm* and Old English *slim*, our modern *slime*. *Slugs*, too *slime along* with sl- across Europe. In Dutch, *slug* is *naaktslak*, while in Czech and Polish it is *slimák*. Many Slavic languages focus on the *sliminess* of spittle rather than its expulsion from the mouth, so Russian has слюна (*sljuna*) and Slovak has *slina*, as does Ukrainian with слина (*slina*), all practically unchanged from the Proto-Slavic *slina* "saliva".

The contemporary word *slim* has an interesting history, as up until very recently it accorded perfectly with the overall pejorative connotations carried by the sl- cluster. It is derived from either West Frisian *slim* "bad, dire" or more probably from the same word in Dutch, where *slim* used to mean "bad, sly,", but has since had as successful a facelift as its English cognate, and now means "intelligent, smart, bright". Similarly, *slight* meant "poor quality, bad" as well as "smooth, level" in its Middle English incarnation, and was a cognate of German *schlecht*, Dutch *slecht* and Danish *slet*, all of which now mean "bad". Both *slim* and *slight* come from **sleig-*

121

"to glide, smooth, spread", which is a collateral form (i.e. synonymous, but not identical form) of PIE *(s)lei-. *Sleig- is thought to be the forerunner of Proto-Germanic *slikana, "creep, crawl", in turn the source of English slick, sleek, slender, slinky, sling and probably slather.

Another PIE root which has influenced English is the root sleidh- "slip, slide". As well as slide, and its frequentative slither, this root has given us sled and sledge, and more surprisingly, sleuth and slot. Things that slide leave tracks, and this idea can be seen in many of the words in contemporary languages that stem from *sleidh-. Bulgarian has следа (sleda) "trace, track" and следвам (sledvam) "follow" while the Polish equivalents are ślad and śledzić. Old Norse (and its close relative Icelandic) have slóð for "trace, track" from which English took sleuth-hound, a kind of bloodhound, which was shortened to sleuth for "detective". The track of a deer is known as a slot, which came into English via French esclot "hoofprint of a deer or horse", again from Old Norse slóð. The meaning of slot broadened to describe "the hollow above the breastbone and below the throat", then to "narrow aperture" and then "position in a list".

A suspiciously similar reconstructed PIE root is *sleibh-, also meaning "slip, slide", which appears as *slup- in Proto-Germanic. English descendants include slattern, slut and sloven, i.e. those women whose personal hygiene or moral behaviour has slipped in the eyes of (usually male) guardians of public decency; and sludge, slurry, slush and sleet, all of which you can easily slip on or in. Neighbouring languages have similar sl- words. In Swedish, a "slut" is slampa or slyna, a "slattern" is slarva, and slinka means "wench". German has Schlampe for "slut, slag or slattern", while Dutch has slet and slons for these highly unflattering terms. Sl- for "slush" is also widespread, with Irish slab "mud, mire dirt", Danish slus "sleet, mud" and Icelandic slabb "mud, sludge". Middle English also had *slosh* "muddy place", which evolved to mean "a watery mess" and then the familiar verb. The "watery mess" is also encapsulated in the related drool of *slobber*, *slaver* and *slurp*.

Sleaze may well be associated with slippery politicians (the Conservative Education Minister Kenneth Baker was portrayed as a *slug* by the satirical TV puppet show *Spitting Image*, and our parliamentary representatives are routinely described as "sleazy" or "slimy"), but *sleaze* seems to have come into English relatively recently. One theory is that it is a corrupted form of *Silesia*, which was an important centre for the production of thin cloth for export. This *sleazy* cloth was considered flimsy and soon became a synonym for low quality fabric.

Slime and slipperiness will also lead to *slowness* and a paucity of effort. *Sloth*, as in "idleness" and the notoriously lazy mammal is actually an earlier noun from *slow*, with the abstract nominal suffix –*th* forming nouns from adjectives, as in the familiar *length*, *width*, *youth*, *depth* etc. and the less immediately obvious *filth* from OE *ful* "foul", *wealth* from "well" and *mirth* from "merry". A number of PIE roots have been suggested as the ancestors of *slug*, *slack*, *slake*, *slouch*, *slurred* and *slow*, the most prominent being PIE **(s)leg-* "slack", which is also thought to be the forebear of *lazy*, *lax* and *lush*. All of these words are likely to be related to the main corpus of sl- words and certainly none of them are exactly dynamic. The PIE root **sleb-* "to be weak, sleep" may be a parallel root. It has given rise to many Indo-European cognates, including Polish *słaby* "weak", Ukrainian *слабкий* (*slabkyy*) "weak", Lithuanian *silpnas* "weak" and on the West Germanic side, Dutch *slapen*, German *schlafen* and Frisian *sliepe*, all equating to English *sleep*.

Two PIE roots which buck the trend of stickiness, sloth and inconstancy are the markedly more decisive **sled* "rend, injure" and **slak-* "strike". **Sled-* is the forerunner of Proto-Germanic **slitan-* "rend, tear", whose descendants may include *slit*, *slash*, *slice, sliver, slat* and *slate*. **Slak-* is the origin of Proto-Germanic **slahan* "fight, strike" and produced a host of Germanic words for "strike", including Old Frisian *sla*, German *schlagen* and Old English *slean* "smite, strike, kill with a weapon", which became Modern English *slay*. Yet, *slean* also had an almost limitless range of wider meanings in Old English times, and could also be used for "forge", "stamp", "sting", "throw", "pitch a tent", "play the harp" and "come quickly". Interestingly, *sly* and *sleight* also come from **slahan*. The word *sly* used to have more positive connotations, the idea being that sly people were skilful and clever, knowing exactly when and how to strike, while *sleight of hand* requires similar dexterity and shrewdness. *Slag*, (coal) *slack, slaughter, onslaught, slog, slug* "hit" and *sledgehammer* are other words deriving from the same root, the *sledge* of the latter coming from Old English *slecg* "hammer, mallet", making *sledgehammer* a *pleonastic* "hammerhammer" (see boxed text).

Pleonasm, from Greek πλεονασμός (*pleonasmós*), from πλέον (*pléon*) meaning "more, too much" is the use of more words than necessary to define or express an idea. Examples include *burning fire, safe haven, a free gift, a true fact, killed dead, at this moment in time, a rate of speed, each and every,* and *people's democracy*. Legal English has a particular fondness for these pleonastic doublets, and they are easy to find in most legal documents of any size. Some common examples are *terms and conditions, null and void, cease and desist, have and hold, aid and abet*, and *last will and testament*. Pleonasm is often used for emphasis or to enhance literary style. Even great writers have used it for this purpose, as with Shakespeare's *most unkindest cut of all*.

A common use of pleonasm is to aid communication and to avoid ambiguity, even though this often results in apparently needless repetition. This happens in several different instances in English. Wits have labelled one of these types *RAS syndrome* (Redundant Acronym Syndrome syndrome), which often occurs after an acronym when the elements of the acronym may not be familiar. Examples include *PIN*

---

number, HIV virus, scuba apparatus and *ATM machine.* Another use is with phrases containing foreign words – *the La Brea tar pits* (the the tar tar pits), *the Schwarzwald Forest* (the Black Forest forest), *the Sahara Desert* (the Deserts desert) – although again this is sometimes done for humorous effect: it's like *déjà vu* all over again. Finally, Britain is awash with pleonastic placenames, largely because the different peoples who have lived in the same place have added to existing names with words from their own languages that had the same meaning. Hence, we can find several different rivers named the *River Ouse,* (River River – from Brythonic *usa* "water, river"); *Eas Fors Waterfall* on the island of Mull in Scotland, (Waterfall, Waterfall, Waterfall – from Scottish Gaelic *eas* and Norse *fors*, both meaning "waterfall"); and *Napton-on-the-Hill* in Warwickshire (Hilltop Settlement on the Hill – from *cnaepp* Old English "hilltop" and *tun* OE "settlement"). Hills give particularly brilliant examples of pleonasm. England has two hills named "Hill Hill Hill" – Pendle Hill in Lancashire (Cumbric *pen* and OE *hyll* combined to make *Pennul* before *Hill* was added) and Bredon Hill in Worcestershire (Celtic *bre* and OE *don*). But the Daddy of them all is supposedly Torpenhow Hill, in Cumbria (Saxon *tor*, Brythonic *pen*, and *how* from Old Norse *haugr*) rejoicing in the name of "Hill Hill Hill Hill". Unfortunately, spoilsport experts have debunked this as a nineteenth century invention – the village of Torpenhow does indeed stand on a hill, but there is no Torpenhow Hill as such. On the other hand, in the land of our glorious Brexit we can ignore and denigrate so-called "experts", believe whatever nonsense we want, and even paint such "alternative facts" on the side of a bus. Therefore, let me declare that Torpenhow Hill *does* exist!

18.   sw- swinging and swaggering

Some folks look at me and see a certain swagger, which in Texas is called 'walking'.

George W Bush

The consonant cluster **sw-** makes an entrance by *swishing in*, *swerving* round the autograph hunters and the paparazzi and *swinging* its tush around the consonant cluster dancefloor. From the *swanky* in-crowd strutting their stuff, to snake-hipped *swaggerers* from the *swinging sixties*, this cluster often shows *sweeping*, oscillating motion. The *suave*, swinging gait of those who are *swelling* with pride is likely to be the cause of the considerable number of sw- words to do with *swaggering*, *swaying* and generally *swanning about*. Confidence is, of course, vitally important for those in showbiz. Pop star Justin Bieber even hired a "swagger coach" to help him with his image and style, and to teach him "different *swaggerific* things to do". How is he doing now? *Swell*, thanks very much.

PIE *sweng- "flog, strike, swing, turn" is the source of *swing* and many other sw- forms. The Old English descendant verb was *swingan* "beat, flog, fling oneself", while the noun *swinge* meant "blow, chastisement". For much of the intervening time, the emphasis was definitely on the "beating, whipping" element of this verb. A *swingle* was an instrument for beating flax to extract the fibres from the stalks, an action which resulted in a clearly onomatopoeic *swish* or *swoosh* with the rush of air. This "lashing" sense is maintained in the form *swinge* "beat, flog, punish", often found in the modern collocation *swingeing cuts*. It wasn't until the sixteenth century that the notion of "moving back and forth"

126

started to become prominent in the word *swing*, and the noun for "seat suspended on ropes" isn't recorded until over a hundred years later. *Swat* is another striking sw- form, as is *swap*, which originally carried the idea of an "exchange of blows".

Nevertheless, other Middle English sw- words from the PIE *sweng-* root did deal with the idea of oscillation. One such word was *swey* "fall, swoon", which later became Modern English *sway*. Cognates include Dutch *zwaaien* "sway, wave", Danish *svaje* "sway" and Lithuanian *svaigti* "swim, become dizzy, swirl". Another example is the word *swag*, which at that time was most commonly used as a verb meaning "sag" or "cause to sway". This latter meaning was expanded with the development of the frequentative verb *swagger* meaning "walk with a swaying motion" and by extension "walk or act in a pompous manner" and "boast, brag". *Swag* as a noun originally had the sense of "bulging, round bag", and by the early 19th century the word had been adopted in the slang of British thieves to mean "stolen goods". It is with this sense that we can find the cartoon staple of the masked, stripy-jumpered burglar, making off with a sack of booty, with SWAG less than discreetly scrawled on it.

In the penal colony of Australia, convicts initially used *swag* in the same way, but soon the term came to mean "possessions carried by a bushman" and it is this idea that is famously present in the "jolly swagman" hero of *Waltzing Matilda*. A *swagman* was essentially an itinerant labourer who carried his belongings in a *swag* – a bedroll or canvas bag *swung* over the shoulder. In fact, *matilda* is a romantic term for the swagman's bundle, and to *waltz matilda* was to travel with a swag, *waltz* coming from the German *auf der Walz sein* "travel on foot from town to town for work". In the German journeyman tradition, this would happen after a craftsman had completed his apprenticeship, whereupon he would go *auf der Walz* for three years and one day.

The *swollen-headed* sw- of *swagger* is echoed in the extravagance of the *swashbuckler*, whose character matches the brashness of the alpha males of the br- cluster outlined in chapter 5. Some of the many meanings of *swash* are "fall of a blow", "blustering noise" and "swaggering behaviour". This is combined with *buckler*, a small round shield. The original swashbucklers would beat their shields in a showy, menacing fashion to intimidate their opponents. Another dizzying sw- is in *swindler*, borrowed from German *Schwindler*, originally a "giddy person". The sense developed to "person with fanciful ideas" through "schemer" to "cheat, fraudster".

Another root in swing with sw- is PIE **swei-* "bend, turn, swing". One of the Old English descendants of this root is *swapan* "sweep", which produced *sweep*, *swipe* and *swoop*. **Swei-* also gave us the word *switch*, originally used in English in the sense of "whip, pliant wand", and thus another sw- object that could be swung with a swiping motion. It is probably a borrowing from another Germanic language – Middle Dutch *swijch* "twig", or Low German *swutsche* "long thin stick" are the most likely contenders. *Switch* is also a cognate of German *Zweck* "purpose, intention", which is derived from the idea of using a wooden peg as a target. Another OE descendant of **swei-* is *swifan* "move in a course, revolve, sweep", which gave us *swivel*, *swift* and *swive*. *Swift* may well have originally meant "turn quickly" before acquiring its current meaning. *Swive* was widely used in the Middle English period as a slang verb for "have sexual intercourse with", presumably from the "moving in a course" sense of *swifan*. However, *swive* was also used in some dialects for "cut a crop with a sweeping motion", and in this way is similar to another **swei-*descendant, *swath*, the track cut out by a scythe in mowing. Rather neatly, the idiom *cut a wide swath* means "show off, behave in an ostentatious, showy manner", which brings us back to the idea of bragging.

The OE ancestor of *swath* is *swaðu* "track, scar, trace", and has cognates in Dutch *zwade* "heavy scythe" and German *Schwad* "swath, strip of cut grass", which is reminiscent of *sward*. This idea of a cut strip is also found in *swathe*, another variant of *swaðu*, and its alternative (and probably frequentative) form *swaddle* "bind in bandages, wrap up in fabric". This leads us to the age-old practice of *swaddling* babies in a misguided attempt to make their limbs grow straight, and so on to the gospel of Luke which tells us (and some discombobulated shepherds), that the baby Jesus is to be found "wrapped in *swaddling clothes*, lying in a manger".

Another root that has semantic links to the main body of sw-words in English is PIE *swel-* "eat, drink, devour". This is the source of English *swallow* as well as a number of Germanic cognates including German *schwelgen* "revel, indulge in", Dutch *zwelgen* "revel, carouse, guzzle", and Swedish *svälja* "swallow, gulp". These roots are also related to Old Norse *svelgr*, which as well as "devourer, swallower" was also used for "whirlpool". This Norse root is also the source for the extremely rapid tidal race in the Pentland Firth between the Scottish mainland and the Orkney Islands known as the *Swelkie*. According to Viking legend, the whirlpools of the Swelkie were caused by a sea-witch, turning mill wheels to grind the salt so as to keep the seas salty. Related terms include *swill*, *swirl*, *swash* (in the senses "narrow sound between a sandbank and the shore" and "water washed up by an incoming wave"), and possibly *swig*.

Although there is no definite connection between the aforementioned PIE roots and *swim*, the phonosemantic idea of sw-for sweeping, rolling motion seems very close. *Swim* comes from PIE *swem-* "to be in motion, swim", and Germanic languages have not strayed far from this root in their words for *swim*, all of which carry their equivalents of the sw- cluster: German *schwimmen*, Dutch *zwemmen*, Norwegian and Danish *svømme* etc. *Swim* is etymologically related to watery places such as *sump*, *swamp* and *sound* "strait, channel" and its Old English and Old Norse equivalent *sund* "swimming; sea, strait". Numerous coastal places, such as *Plymouth Sound*, Devon, *Ålesund*, Norway, and *Sundsvall*, Sweden preserve this idea in their names.

The sw- cluster for swinging, swaying and swaggering seems to be unique to Germanic languages, which freely employ their versions of sw- for words to do with oscillating motion. German has *schwingen*, *schwenken* and *schwanken* as it swings, swivels and sways, whilst Frisian has the very recognisable *swaaie*. The enlightened people of the Nordic countries use sv- for their liberated swinging. The Swedes have *svinga* and *svänga*, the Norwegians and the Danes prefer to *svinge* and the Icelanders have chosen to *sveifla*.

Let's end this chapter with a brief *swansong* – the English word is a direct translation of German *Schwanengesang*. Three of Britain's most recognisable bird species carry the initial sw- cluster – *swifts*, *swallows* and *swans* – but they do not appear to be directly related to each other, either genetically or etymologically. The swift, with its rapid, swirling flight, is closest to the main corpus of the swinging sw- cluster, taking its name from the adjective *swift* mentioned above. The name of the swallow is assumed to be from PIE **swol-wi-* which became *swealwe* in Old English. It has interesting Indo-European cognates: while Germanic swallows are very similar – Dutch *zwaluw*, German *Schwalbe*, Danish *svale* and Swedish *svala* – the same root may also be responsible for a totally different bird species in the Slavic world, as Russian соловей (*solovéj*) Slovak *slavik* and Bulgarian славей (*slávej*) all mean "nightingale".

Swan comes from the PIE root **swen-* "sing, create sound", the source of Latin *sonus* "sound", Russian звук (*zvuk*) "sound" and Old English *geswin* "melody, song". This is connected to the ancient belief that the swan is "the singing bird", which may come as a surprise to those who have heard its cacophonous honking, hissing and grunting. However, in antiquity, the idea of the *swansong* took hold, i.e. that swans would sing beautifully in the moments before their deaths. This idea is mentioned by some of the giants of western civilisation, including Aristotle, Virgil, Ovid, Chaucer, da Vinci and Shakespeare. It transpires that there is actually some basis for this legend, because certain species of swan have an additional elongated tracheal loop. This feature causes a long, drawn-out series of notes to be produced when the swan's lungs expel excess air as it collapses and dies.

19.   pl- plains and plates

I remain just one thing, and one thing only, and that is a clown. It places me on a far higher plane than any politician.

Charlie Chaplin

Pl- had everything handed to it on a silver *platter*. Although it is a cluster that is used in thousands of different English words and so has many different meanings, one of its major elements is describing flatness, smoothness and thickness. It is often *applied* to layered and deliberate design, as objects are folded and levelled out: *plaited*, *plated* and *plastered*. We also commonly see pl- in words denoting the *planet's* flat, two-dimensional *places*, such as *plains* and *plateaux*, and in flat objects, such as *plates*, *plaques* and *placentas*. There is also a rich fullness to the pl- cluster – it is not a cluster that is frugal or thrifty – layers are accumulated and comfort is gained. It takes a certain degree of *plenty* to acquire *plush* furnishings, a *plummy* accent and a smugly *plump* stomach, whether this is a consequence of hard work and dedication, or being born into the privileged classes. In the latter case, even being *as thick as two short planks* may not be a barrier to a *gold-plated*, *pleasurable* existence.

As is usual when we look at ancient Proto-Indo-European roots, we have to make our way through a tangled forest of interlocking and related word origins. With the pl- cluster, this is compounded by the variety of similar forms that linguists have reconstructed. One such root, **pele-* has two related meanings: **pele-* (1) is concerned with fullness, while **pele-* (2) is concerned with flatness, but sometimes the distinction between the two is rather blurred.

We shall look at *pele-* (2) first as it seems to have more influence on Modern English and perhaps has a stronger claim to be at the heart of the phonosemantic meaning of pl-.

Pele- (2) "spread out; broad, flat" has a number of reconstructed PIE daughter roots, including *plak-* "to be flat", and *plat-* "flat". These become more familiar with Ancient Greek πλατύς (*platús*) "broad, flat", Latin *planus* "flat, level, spread out", and French *plat* "flat", which are direct descendants (not to mention *flat* itself – for more see chapter 3). Their derivatives have been borrowed on numerous occasions into English, resulting in our *multiplicity* of pl- forms. For example, we have *plan* "ground plot of a building" and at least six words *plane* – "flat geometric surface", "level of existence", "tool for smoothing wood", "aeroplane", "soar, glide" and "plane tree". Close relatives include several *plains* and *explain*, which literally means "flatten, make level", much as French *expliquer* means "explain", but is literally "unfold". *Explain* and *expliquer explicate* by smoothing something out and laying it bare – if it can't be unfolded, it's *inexplicable*.

The word *plate* first entered English in the early Middle Ages in the sense of "flat sheet of metal" from Medieval Latin *plata* via Old French *plate*, also the source of *platter*. Similarly, French *plaquer* "to plate", itself a borrowing from Middle Dutch *placken* "to patch, beat metal into a plate" gave us *plaque* and *placard*. Spanish for "silver plate" was *plata d'argento*, but while French and Italian retain *argent* and *argento* respectively for "silver", Spanish silver is *plata* and in Portuguese it's *prata*. *Argent* is also the French word for "money", reflecting the main use of silver plate for coinage from the medieval period onward. The *Rio de la Plata* or "Silver River" is the widest river in the world and separates Uruguay from Argentina; its anglicised form, *River Plate*, is the name of Argentina's most successful football team. The metal *platinum* takes its name from the Spanish diminutive *platina* "little silver" as miners used to find this element as an apparent impurity with silver in the Spanish colonies of Latin America.

Old French *plat* "flat, stretched out" is the source of Modern French *plafond* "flat base", and thus "ceiling". It has also influenced English *plot* "piece of ground", *platform*, literally a "flat form", *plateau* "small plate, tray" and thus "flat area of high ground, tableland" and *platitude* "dullness, flatness", which gave rise to the sense of "trite, unoriginal remark". The Latin form *planus* gave Italian *piano* "smooth, soft, calm" from which we have taken the name of that soft-loud instrument, the *pianoforte*.

Place is also connected to flatness and width, (as is its fishy counterpart *plaice*), as it derives from the Greek πλατεῖα ὁδός (*plateîa hodós*) "broad way" via the abbreviated Latin form *platea* "open space, broad way". *Place* supplanted earlier English words, such as *stow* and *stead*. However, the English meaning now has a broader (!) meaning than its Romance cognates *place* (French), *piazza* (Italian) and *plaza* (Spanish), all of which refer to wide, open spaces and town squares. Another word from the *pele- (2) root is Greek πέλαγος (*pelagos*) "open sea". This is the root of *archipelago*, as well as being the ancestor of French *plage* and Spanish *playa*, both meaning "beach". Other flat open spaces from this PIE root include Old English *folde* "earth, land", Modern English *field*, German *Feld* and Afrikaans *veldt*, and on the Slavic side other words for "field", like Russian поле (*póle*) and Polish *pole*. In fact, *Poland* means "land of the field dwellers" after the West Slavic tribe the *Polans* (the Polish ethnonym is *Polanie* "those of the fields") who lived there from the 8th century.

Ethnonyms are words applied to given ethnic groups. Sometimes, the term used by the people themselves – the *endonym* – is the same as that used by outsiders to refer to the ethnic group – the *exonym*, but sometimes it is markedly different. As countries are most commonly named after their people, this can mean that their names are very familiar or that they differ widely from country to country. A famous European example is Germany, whose endonym is *Deutschland*, but is also known by the Norwegians as *Tyskland* (which is actually from the same Proto-Germanic root), by the French as *Allemagne*, by the Czechs as *Německo*, by the Romanians as *Germania,* by the Estonians as *Saksamaa* and by the Lithuanians as *Vokietija*. This diversity is thought to be a result of the wide variety of distinct tribes that have moved in and out of the region in recorded history.

Other interesting ethnonyms include Barbados, "the bearded ones", from Portuguese *barbados*, which either comes from the bearded Carib natives of the islands or the dense, hanging roots of the indigenous bearded fig tree; Belgium is the land of the Belgae tribe, whose name comes from the Proto-Celtic root *belg- "swollen, bulging with anger/battle fury etc." from PIE *bhelgh- "swell", ultimate source of *belly*, *budget*, *bulge* and *buckle* – so Belgium could belie its uninteresting reputation with its "land of those swollen with anger" ethnonym; Burkina Faso, formerly Upper Volta, is "the land of honest men", taking its name from the Mossi word *burkina* "honest, upright" and the Dyula word *faso* "homeland". Mossi (also known as Mooré) and Dyula are two of the most widely-spoken languages in that country.

Pakistan is a twentieth century coinage, which combines the Persian and Pashto word *pak* "pure" with the suffix –*stan* "land of, place of". Hence, it is "the land of the pure", but it was coined as an acronym of the five northern regions of the British Raj: Punjab, Afghania, Kashmir, Sindh, and Baluchis*tan*. Most of these lands would be incorporated into the new country of Pakistan following Indian independence and partition in 1947. The letter *i* was added to *Pakistan* to ease pronunciation.

Russia – "land of the Rus'" is also interesting, as the leading theory has it that the Rus' were Vikings from Sweden who were seafarers or rowers. Rus' is believed to be derived from Old Norse *rods*- "men who row", and describes the Swedish oarsmen who navigated the river systems of Eastern Europe and became rulers of the city of Veliky Novgorod from the ninth century and subsequently the state of Kievan Rus'. This theory is consistent with the contemporary Finnish name for

Sweden, *Ruotsi*, indicating that the founders of the Russian state were of North Germanic rather than Slavic origin.

Surprisingly, the derivation of *plant* is also from PIE **plat-*, which gave Latin the verb *planto* and noun *planta*. It seems that the idea behind this is that cuttings and newly planted shrubs, herbs etc. were driven into the ground with the soles of the feet and flattened into the soil. Indeed, one of the obsolete meanings of *plant* in English is "sole of the foot", as demonstrated by Ben Jonson in his 1611 masque *Oberon, the Faery Prince* in which he refers to "knotty legs and plants of clay". This is linked to the fact that humans, like bears and rabbits, but unlike most mammals, walk with *plantigrade* locomotion, that is, with the toes and metatarsals flat on the ground. We are *plodders*, walking on the soles of what the Cockneys refer to as our *plates of meat* – phonosemantic pl- making this particularly apposite. Ironically, the *platypus* from Greek πλατύπους (*platúpous*) "flat-footed" actually engages in knuckle-walking like chimpanzees and gorillas and so is not a plantigrade mammal species.

Another group of pl- words derive from the idea of smoothing things over, calming the waters. Latin *placare* "appease, soothe" gives us *placate*, *placid* and *implacable*, while the related verb *placere* "please, satisfy" gives us *pleasure*, *complacent*, *plea* and *please* amongst others. The word *placebo* also comes from the latter source, meaning "I will please" in Latin. It was used in the Catholic Church's Office of the Dead ritual "*placebo Domino in regione vivorum*" – "I will please the Lord in the land of the living". In France, the custom was that the mourning family would hand out food and drink to the congregation immediately after the Office of the Dead rite. Groups of so-called *placebo singers* would come to funerals and feign homeopathic grief and anguish in the hope of capitalising on this largesse. In this way, *placebo* came to mean "worthless sycophant, simulator".

The Greek verb πλάσσειν (*plássein*) "fashion, form, mould" but originally "spread thinly" is another descendant of *pele-* (2) and introduces the idea of flattening or folding substances into shape. It is the source of πλάσμα (*plásma*) "something formed" and the suffix –*plasm* as in *ectoplasm*, *cytoplasm* and *neoplasm*. Other English words which can be traced back to the same Greek source include *plastic* literally "from moulding" and *plaster*.

A final PIE root which captures the idea of folding is *plek-* "plait, braid, fold". This is the ancestor to *plait*, *pleat* and *flax*, as well as the Frankish form *flaska* "braid covered bottle", which gives us *flask* and *flagon* and German *Flasche* "bottle". Slavic pleats and plaits also carry the pl- cluster. The noun *pleat* is плисе (*plise*) in Bulgarian and *plisé* in Slovak and Czech. Similarly, *plait* is плитка (*plítka*) in Bulgarian, *pletenec* in Czech and Slovak and *pletenica* in Croatian.

The *plek-* root is the source of Latin *plecto* "weave, twist" and thus the *plexus* "area of the body where nerves and blood vessels intertwine". A cognate of *plecto* is *plico* "fold, flex" which has given English *ply*, *pliant* and *pliers* and a host of Latin based derivatives such as *apply*, *reply*, *replicate*, *comply*, *duplicate*, *complicate*, *employ*, *deploy* etc. which have the shared idea of folding and layering or bending to a higher power *implicit* in their root concept. *Plywood* is made up of thin layers of wood, or *plies*, stuck together with glue. Yet, if things are too *complex*, they are entwined, tangled up, so they need to be *simplified* to become *simplex*, i.e. *simple* "folded once", not *multiple* times. A *diploma* was a state paper or document folded *double*, so a *diplomat* would carry an official diploma of authority. Although the PIE roots are thought to be the same, the Germanic equivalent of *ply* is the Grimm's Law affected *fold*. Hence, *double* and *twofold* are basically the same word, as are *multiple* and *manifold*.

The combination of the *plosive p* and the lateral *l* in the pl-cluster has a *pleasantly* full and rich *plop* to it. This fullness aspect of pl- is covered by the descendants of PIE **pele-* (1) "fill" and its Indo-European descendants. These include Ancient Greek πολύς (*polús*) "much, many", Latin *plere* "fill" and *plenos* "full", German *viel* and English *full*. These have given a further *plethora* of words to the vocabulary of English. By borrowing here, there and everywhere, English has been *supplied* (Latin *supplere* "fill up") with a *plenitude* of synonyms to *replenish* our word stock and exasperate language learners, who must learn words which are seemingly *surplus* to requirements.

From Greek, English has taken the prefix *poly-* "many", while from Latin it has borrowed *plus* "more" and from *pluralis* – via Old French *plurel* – *plural*, literally "belonging to more than one". Other pl- words describing fullness which we have taken from Latin via French include *plenty, complete, deplete, replete, supplement, implement, complement* and *plenipotentiary* "one with full power". As well as anglicising linguistic borrowings, we are happy to take loanwords as they are if we see fit. Examples of this are the term *hoi polloi*, directly from the Greek οἱ πολλοί – "the many", and its Latin equivalent *plebs* "the multitude, the lower classes".

20.   sm- smears and smacks

Once-ler! You're making such smogulous smoke!
My poor Swomee-Swans... why they can't sing a note!
No one can sing who has smog in his throat.

Dr Seuss, *The Lorax*

Sm- is the cluster of *smile*, *smoke* and *smell*. This cluster often applies to things that start in one place and emanate outwards. Sometimes, this is contact that spreads across a surface, in which case, the initial pressure starts locally but then opens out into an unsightly *smudge* or *smear*. Similarly, the localised pain of a *smack* on the kisser will soon start to *smart* and will spread across the whole of the unfortunate recipient's face – it's far better to indulge in a *smooch*, though perhaps not with the kissersmacker. *Smiles* radiate outwards as conflict is *smoothed* over; fragments of a glass which is *smashed* to *smithereens* can travel seemingly impossible distances; *smells* emanate from one place but pervade the immediate area; and *smoke* can spread to envelop and *smother* the unwary.

PIE **sme-* "smear" and its derivative **smeru-* "grease" are responsible for many of the more unctuous sm- words in Indo-European languages. This includes Proto-Slavic *smetana* "cream", which is still current in Russian, Bulgarian and Czech among other Slavic languages, and its parallels in German *Schmant* "sour milk", and Austrian German *Schmetter* "cream". The German word *Schmetterling* "butterfly" comes from the belief that witches would transform themselves into butterflies to drink milk and cream from the pail. English *butterfly* may also reflect the idea that butterflies ate milk and butter, which is a cut above the decidedly earthier Dutch equivalent *boterschijte* "butter shitter" relating to the colour of the butterfly's excrement.

Equally pleasantly, PIE **sme-* is the antecedent of Greek σμῆγμα (*smêgma*) "soap, unguent", from which English borrowed *smegma* and the vulgarisms *smeg* and *smeghead*, popularised by the UK sci-fi comedy series *Red Dwarf*. The same Greek root gives us *smectites*, a group of absorbent clay minerals and *smectic* liquid crystals, which form in layers that can slide over each other like soap – they can be *smeared*. The Swedish for "butter" is *smör*, a cognate of *smear*, and the first element of the famous *smörgåsbord*, a compound of three words: *smör* "butter", *gås* "goose" and *bord* "table", so it literally means "butter-goose-table". The "goose" element comes from the small pieces of butter that floated to the top of cream when it was being churned, which reminded Swedish peasants of fat geese. These bits of butter were ideal for spreading on bread, and over time *smörgås* became the word for buttered bread, so *smörgåsbord* at its most basic was just "buttered bread table". Dishes kept being added to the table as time went on, until it became the feast of dishes that it is today. Nowadays, of course, *smorgasbord* in English has also acquired the extended meaning of "miscellaneous group", as in "chapter 20 has a veritable smorgasbord of eclectic etymologies".

Other more common English words from the PIE **sme-* root include *smirch*, *smudge*, *smooch* and *smarm* (and its variant *smalm*), meaning "bedaub". Surprisingly, *smite* also seems to come from this origin. Its Old English form *smitan* is attested to only as "smear on; soil, sully". The semantic link has been suggested as being "slapping on mud in wattle and daub construction" (Watkins, 2000). This seems plausible with a look at the many close Germanic cognates: Danish *smide* "smear, fling," Old Frisian *smita*, "cast, hurl," Dutch *smijten* "fling," German *schmeißen* "cast, fling," and

Gothic *bismeitan* "spread, smear". *Smite* was once used far more profusely than it is today. It occurs 133 times in the King James Bible, as the Lord strikes down those who incur his wrath. Sinners are routinely *smitten* for such heinous crimes as being from the wrong tribe or city, having the temerity to look in the Ark of the Covenant, mocking the prophet Elisha's bald head and most wantonly making a tinkling sound with their feet. This violent sense of *smite* has probably influenced the imitative *smack* and *smash*, both of which also have the familiar onomatopoeic endings *–ack* and *–ash*, associated with "striking" and "collision", as in *crack*, *whack* and *hack* and *bash*, *thrash* and *dash*.

Working in heavy industry – whether in the *smithy*, in mines, factories or on the railways – means *smelting* metals, working over *smouldering* furnaces, and encountering *smuts* and *smoke*, as the *smog monsters* (inhabitants of Middlesbrough) will no doubt confirm. In such conditions, *smudging* surfaces with dirty fingers is commonplace. Up until the mid-18th century, when the practice was outlawed, miners would scavenge for scrap lumps of ore, which were exempt from taxes. These lumps were known as *smitham*, or in the Northumbrian dialect *smiddum*, from which *smidgen* "very small amount" is derived. Dirt and grime are also found with the sm- cluster in other Germanic languages, for example with the familiar German *Schmutz*, Swedish *smuts*, Yiddish שמוץ (*shmuts*) and Danish *smuds* "dirt, grime" to which English *smut* and *smutty* are cognate.

Smock has survived the centuries almost unchanged from the Old English period when it was spelt *smoc*. Although now used to denote a protective garment worn over the clothes, a smock was originally a woman's undergarment. In fact, *smock* was tied up with the concept of womanhood – a man with a *smock-face* looked effeminate, while a *smocker* was a man who spent all his time with women. We think that *smock* comes from words for "press close", like many of the sm- words featured here, as it carries the idea of a piece of clothing to slip or creep into, (as did the words *slip* and *sleeve* originally). In Bulgarian, смок (*smok*) means "grass snake", though this is thought to be a descendant of Proto-Germanic *snako-*, the source of *snake*. Certainly, there seems to be some crossover between the sm- and the sn- clusters here, as with the close parallels between *smuggle* and *snuggle* (see also chapter 6).

Old English *smugan, smeogan* meant "creep" or "sneak", whilst in Norwegian it is *smjuga* and Swedish *smuga*. The word *smuggler* – a person who would spend a lot of time sneaking in and out of tunnels and caves with contraband goods – is also thought to be related to this source. The German verb *schmiegen* meaning "press close, nestle" is from this root too. It is predominantly in Germanic languages where the sm- cluster keeps the idea of "pressing close", as in the Dutch word for "smother", *smeren*, and its German equivalent, *schmoren*.

JRR Tolkien studied philology, worked for the Oxford English Dictionary, was a professor of Anglo-Saxon at Oxford University for twenty years from 1925-1945 and was then professor of English language and literature until his retirement in 1959. With such a wealth of experience, he was most definitely a man who knew his etymology and indeed invented his own languages from his youth onwards. His constructed languages feature heavily in his classic Middle-Earth works *The Hobbit, The Lord of the Rings,* and *The Silmarillion.* Tolkien said that his languages, particularly Quenya, the language of his elves, were designed according to their "phonaesthetic" considerations. Hence, the meaning behind the names of many of his places and characters is significant and reflects his knowledge of philology and awareness of phonosemantics.

The sm- cluster has two excellent examples of this. The character *Sméagol* in *The Lord of the Rings* is the creature who will later be known as Gollum after he is enslaved by the power of the One Ring. Tolkien says that the derivation of *Sméagol* is from the Old English *smygel* meaning "burrow; place to creep into". (Gollum is a so-called *stoor hobbit*, from the Middle English word *stoor* "large, strong" (see the sturdy st- words in chapter 1). A related Tolkien sm- is the dragon *Smaug* in *The Hobbit* – the very similar *smeág* is the preterite (past simple form) of the OE verb *smúgan* "creep, crawl into a hole" and is also reminiscent of the PIE root **smeug-* "to smoke", so altogether a perfect name for a cave-dwelling dragon!

The word *smart* comes from Old English *smeortan* "be painful" and can be traced back to PIE **(s)merd-* "to bite, sting". The meaning of *smart* as "clever" came with the idea of "smarting injuries" producing "cutting pain"; it is not a large leap from here for the word to acquire the idea of "having a biting wit". The Scandinavian languages all now have the adjective *smart* to mean "clever" but *smarting pain* still exists in most Germanic languages too, e.g. German *Schmerz*, Danish *smerte* and Swedish *smärta*. The word *sharp* had earlier followed the same evolution in English from "having a cutting edge" to "possessing keen intelligence".

The reconstructed PIE root **(s)mei-* "smile, be glad" is believed to be the source of a great number of smiling Indo-European cognates, including Sanskrit स्मयते (*smayate*) "laugh, smile" and Ancient Greek μειδάω (*meidáō*) "smile". Its descendant, Proto-Italic **smeiros*, gave Latin *miros* "wonderful", itself the source of *admire*, *miracle*, *marvel* and *mirror*. Other language families also have a smiling sm- cluster, e.g. Slavic with Bulgarian смея се (*sméja se*) and Baltic with Latvian *smieties*, both of which mean "laugh".

The Old English word for *smile* was *smearcian*, from which we get *smirk*. *Smile* began to be used more commonly in the Middle English period, having entered the language from a North Germanic source (the leading candidate for obvious reasons is Danish *smile*). After *smile* became widespread, *smirking* gradually lost its positive senses and was left with the meaning of "grinning in a jeering or *smug* way" – the sense which remains today. This is the less attractive side of smiling, a superior, self-satisfied look which is more in tune with many of the more negative words associated with the sm- cluster.

People may also seem self-satisfied or superficial when wearing ostentatious jewellery or through *smearing* (or *smalming*) pomade in their hair. Again, Germanic languages have parallel sm- cognates as in German *schmücken*, Danish *smykke* and Swedish *smycka*, all meaning "adorn, embellish". Such preening can make people seem *smarmy* or slippery: calling someone a *smooth-talker* is a backhanded compliment. It is only a short step away from being labelled a *smart-aleck*, *smart-ass* or *smarty-pants*, too clever for your own good, and in danger of a smiting!

21. str- stretchy straws

And he that striues to touch the starres,
Oft stombles at a strawe.

Edmund Spenser, *The Shepheardes Calender*

If **str-** was an animal, it would be a cat at full *stretch*, a combination of flexibility and tautness. *straining* yet supple. Str- is the cousin of the upstanding st- cluster outlined in chapter 1, and is equally *strong*. However, words in the str- group may denote objects that are malleable, or at least, not *stiff*: the unyielding rigidity of st- is compromised by the addition of the liquid *r* of str-. In contrast to the *staunch sturdiness* of st- words, the *strands*, *straws*, *streamers* and *straps* of str- are narrow, flat and *straight* but have little depth or solidity. *Strings* may be *strummed*, *stroked* and *struck*, but when plucked they are unresisting and vibrate. Nevertheless, there are a number of str- words which *straddle* the gap between static st- and stretchy str-. When objects are stretched to their full extent, they tighten up and become *stressed*: their flexibility is *constrained* at the point when they become taut. Other str- words *streak* ahead of the pack, *striding* away into the distance.

PIE **ster-* "to broaden, spread out" is the main source of the stretched out str- words. It is the root of *strand* in the sense of "shore, beach", a word which has close cognates throughout the Germanic languages e.g. Icelandic *strönd*, German *Strand* and Old Frisian *strond*, all meaning "beach". *Strand* was also formerly used to mean "river bank", which explains the name of the famous London *Strand*. This street, first recorded as *strondway* in 1002, ran alongside the north bank of the Thames until the construction of the Victoria Embankment, (1865-70). Several areas of open grassland in the north of England are known as *strays*, a word which also comes from this PIE root.

One Ancient Greek descendant of **ster-* is στορέννυμι (*storénnumi*) "scatter", whose Old English cognates included *strewian*, the ancestor of *strew*, and *streaw*, which became *straw*, literally "that which is strewn". *Strain* in the sense of "breed, line of descent" is probably from the same origin. Many unsuspecting males have received a Christmas present of *Blue Stratos* aftershave, a sure sign that the gift giver's creative or financial resources had reached breaking point. This concoction is liberally applied to the face by enthusiastic newcomers to the world of men's fragrances, or passed on next Christmas by wily old hands. *Στρατός* (*stratós*) is the Greek word for "encamped army, people, body of men" – literally "that which is spread out", and is another descendant of **ster-*. The leader of this army was the στρατηγός or *strategos*, a military general for whom a στρατηγία (*stratēgíā*) or *strategy* was essential. Similar tactical acumen may be required to dispose of the *Blue Stratos*.

Two important Latin verbs from the **ster-* root have also supplied English with large numbers of words. The first is *sternere* "spread out, stretch out, lay down, pave". This is the source of *stratum* and *strata*, which as well as describing horizontal layers, also meant "pavement" and "street". The Roman *via strata* "paved road" became *stret* in Old English, and *street* as "paved road" is one of the few words in English that has been in continuous use since the Roman invasion. The street was a cut above *roads* and *ways*, which were inferior unpaved routes on which one *rode* or *went on foot* respectively. Derived forms of *sternere* have also been passed on to English, giving us *consternation*, from the notion of being "thrown down in dismay" and *prostrate* "laid out, knocked flat". The second verb is the prolific *struere* "build, put together, arrange", again the original sense seems to be with the idea of extending and laying things down. *Struere* has given English *structure*, *construct*, *obstruct*, *destroy*, *industry*, *instruct*, and many, many others.

Descendants of **ster-* in other branches of Indo-European are remarkably widespread. Sanskrit has आस्तृ (*astr*} "spread", while Celtic languages are represented by Irish and Scottish Gaelic *srath* "wide river valley" (borrowed by English as *strath*, exemplified by the adaptation of Gaelic *Srath Chluaidh* as *Strathclyde*), and the similar Welsh *srat* "plain". Bulgarian has *строя* (*stroja*) "build", Russian has *строй* (*stroj*) "order, arrangement", the root of *перестройка*, or in Latin script, *perestroika,* the (economic) "restructuring", made famous by Mikhail Gorbachev.

Other English str- words come from ancestors that were related to "twisting and turning", as well as stretching. These words are likely to be descendants of PIE **streb(h)-* "turn, twist". This gave Greek στρέφω (*stréfo*) "twist", στρόφος (*stróphos*) "rope" and στροφή (*strophe*) "stanza, strophe", but originally "turning, moving". This came from the Greek chorus who would chant a section of an ode while turning and moving from right to left across the stage. The accent of elision or turning away was the *apostrophe*, while an overturning of the natural order was a *catastrophe*. Latin borrowed *stroppus* "strap, band, rope" from the Greek, which in turn was borrowed by Old English as *stropp* "thong, band, strap", which later morphed into *strop* and *strap*.

A word with an interesting origin is *stripling*, meaning "youth, youngster". The idea is that youths are slim and not filled out in their adult forms – they are "as slender as a reed", or a *strip* – a long, narrow piece. The cruder northern phrase "a lanky *streak* of piss" denoting a tall, thin, person who has yet to fill out has a similar idea behind it. The -*ling* ending is a diminutive from Old Norse where it is found in words like *gæslingr* "gosling".

In contrast with most other Indo-European languages, English uses diminutives rather rarely and in only limited circumstances, although some dialects, such as Scots use them more frequently. Native English forms are mainly confined to names as with *–s*: *Wills, Becks* or *–sy*: *Patsy, Betsy* etc. Similarly, the Geordie *–z* has recently gained a wider currency: *Gaz* for *Gary*, *Shaz* for *Sharon* etc. The frequentative *–le* often has a diminutive aspect too, as with *crackle* and *spittle*. A couple of other survivors are the *–ock* of *hillock, bullock, buttock* and *bollock,* and the *-en* of *kitten, chicken* and *maiden*.

The Norse *-ling* ending is still present in a small number of words, for example, *duckling, hatchling, fledgling, sapling, darling* (from *dear* plus *-ling*) and *underling* but it isn't very common. Another borrowed Germanic diminutive is the Dutch *-kin* of *catkin* (it looks like a cat's fluffy tail apparently), *lambkin, manikin* and *napkin* (which has the Dutch suffix on the borrowing of *nappe* "tablecloth" taken from French). The same suffix is present in the rather twee term of endearment added to names as in *Poppykins, Eddiekins*, and so on. There is also the very common Scottish-Dutch diminutive *-ie*, or *-y*: *Georgie* for *George*, *Sally* for *Sarah*, as well as *doggy, sissy, mummy, daddy, cookie* etc.

Diminutives taken from French and other Latin languages are by far the most widespread and productive in Modern English. One of the most common is *-let/-lette*, as in *booklet, tablet, piglet, leaflet, hamlet* ("little village" – the *ham* is of Germanic origin), gauntlet (from French *gant* "glove"), *roulette* (from French *roue* "wheel") etc. Similarly, we have borrowed the *-et/-ette* endings from French: *kitchenette, courgette* (from *courge* "marrow"), *cigarette, clarinet* (either from *clarine* "little bell" or *clarin* "trumpet") and *puppet* (from *poupée* "doll"). Another Romance diminutive is the *-ina/-ino/-ine/-ini* diminutive of *farina* (from Latin *far* "spelt, a kind of grain"), *domino* (from Latin *dominus* "lord, master"), *figurine* (Italian *figura* "figure"), and *zucchini* (Italian *zucca* "pumpkin, gourd"). Several others entered the language at an earlier point and are thus less easy to recognise as diminutives – the pejorative *-rel* of *wastrel* and *mongrel* (from obsolete *mong* "mixture") and the *-ole* of *casserole* (from Provençal *cassa* "pan") being two examples.

The str- cluster also includes a number of words which relate to the idea of being stretched, tightened up or made *stronger*. These come from the Proto-Indo-European root *streig-* "press, rub" – antecedent of *stripe, strip, streak, stroke* and *strike* – and its nasalised form, *strenk-*, meaning "tight, narrow". Latin *stringo* "press, tighten" is derived from the *strenk-* root, as are its Old English cognates *strong* and *streccan*, the ancestor of *stretch*. From *stringo*, English borrowed a large number of words either directly from Latin or from Latin via French. Chief amongst them were *stringent, strict* and *strain*, and their numerous derived forms including *constrain, constrict, restrain, restrict, district, distress* and, via a more convoluted path, *prestige*.

Old English for *string* was *streng*, but *strings* in the Old English period also referred to tendons and ligaments. This sense survives in *heartstrings* and *hamstrings*. The str- of *string* is present in many North Germanic and Slavic languages, represented by *strengur* in Icelandic, *streng* in Danish and *struna/струна* in Slavic. Of course, *string* can be *stretched* and drawn out, until it is *straight*. In fact, *straight* is an old past participle of *stretch*, while the word *straightaway* originally meant "by a straight path". The phrase *keep to the straight and narrow*, "follow the righteous path", is based on a misreading of Matthew 7:14: "*strait* is the gate, and narrow is the way, which leadeth unto life". The *strait* in question here was borrowed from Old French *estreit*, (now *étroit*) meaning "narrow, restricted", a form which is still seen in the forms *straitjacket* and *strait-laced* – the latter first being used of bodices bound with stays. Other words from *strenk-* include *strangle, straggle*, and *distraught*, which is a merger of *distract* and *straught*, another past participle of OE *streccan*.

22.   bl- blooming and blazing

Everything is blooming most recklessly; if it were voices instead of colours, there would be an unbelievable shrieking into the heart of the night.

Rainer Maria Rilke

When it comes to consonant clusters carrying implicit meaning, **bl-** is a beauty. This cluster is another where Lawler (1990) has spotted three plausible phonesthemes. Sometimes bl- conveys the idea of contained liquid or gas under pressure, *blooming* and *bloating*. A second, related meaning involves colour, especially in connection with the eye – itself a coloured organ that is filled with compressed fluid and also sees in colour. Eyes may *blur*, *blink*, go *blind* and get *bleary*, while colours *blaze* in *blonds*, *blues* and *blacks*. A third phonestheme entails a sense of excess: a *blotto* person's *blustering blather* requires a *bleeper*!

Many words with this cluster carry combinations of two or all three semantic meanings: a raw, swollen *blister* could be shocking pink, full of serum and unbearably painful for its poor victim. Drinking to excess will give you *blurred* vision and a *blotchy* complexion; it will also make you more liable to become a *blabbermouth* and *blurt out* nonsense, as you lose your inhibitions and sense of restraint. *Blood* is not only brightly-hued, but also a compressed fluid and often associated with excessive violence.

Although the Proto-Indo-European origins of *blood* are not entirely clear, we think it goes back to the Proto-Indo-European root **bhel-* "swell, blow, bloom" and a Proto-Germanic form reconstructed as **bloþa*. This has close cognates in ancient languages – Gothic *bloþ*, Old Frisian *blod*, Old Norse *bloð* – and in contemporary Germanic languages – Dutch *bloed*, German *Blut*, and Swedish, Danish and Norwegian *blod*. Excessive vehemence is often accompanied by swearing, and *bloody* was used as a swearword from the seventeenth century. *Bless* originally meant "consecrate with blood", a descendant of Old English *bledsian*, from the ritual sprinkling of blood from sacrificial animals on pagan altars.

The word *bloody* has lost much of its shock value, but at one time was considered to be a very profane and taboo swearword, in part due to its association with menstruation. This led to a number of so-called *minced oaths* being coined; that is, using similar substitute terms to lessen the crudeness of a taboo term. In the case of *bloody*, minced oaths include *blinking, bleeding, ruddy, blooming, blessed* and *bally*. George Bernard Shaw shocked polite society in his 1914 play *Pygmalion*, when he had the protagonist Eliza Doolittle say "Walk? Not bloody likely!", and for a time the word was known euphemistically as "the Pygmalion word" or "the Shavian adjective".

The three most common ways of creating more acceptable minced oaths are through using alliterative substitutes, shortening the offensive or blasphemous words, or by using a rhyming equivalent. Alliteration is used in *darn* for *damn*, *frick* for *fuck*, *cripes* for *Christ*, *jeepers* for *Jesus*, *heck* for *hell*, and *shoot, shucks* or *sugar* for *shit*. English is by no means alone in this: the Spanish exclamation of surprise or pain *ay caramba!* is actually a minced oath for *carajo* "cock, shit, fuck". French does this too with its use of *bleu* "blue" for *Dieu* "God" in phrases such as *parbleu* "by God", equivalent to our own minced oath, "by Jove". More not really blue French words include *morbleu* for *mort de Dieu* "God's death", and *sacré bleu* "Holy God", similar to our "Holy Cow" for "Holy Christ". English also shortened phrases that were considered blasphemous as in *zounds* "by God's wounds", *drat* "god rot" (someone), *gadzooks* "by God's hooks" – referring to the nails on Christ's cross – *crikey* "Christ kill me", *cor blimey* "God blind me" and *struth* (now *strewth*) "by God's truth". Over time, such reduced phrases may lose their shock value altogether as with the phrase *I couldn't give a monkey's* for "I don't care". In the full phrase, the word after *monkey's* was usually one of *toss*, *shit* or *fuck*. Modern shortening may be as radical as abbreviating the offending word to one letter, *f* or *c*, for example (although this can inevitably be built on again to produce *effing cee*).

Rhyming substitutes can also tone down the offensive nature of an expletive. The word *berk* is now used as a mild term of abuse for "dolt, insensitive fool", but it is an abbreviation of *Berkeley Hunt* – rhyming slang for *cunt*. In 2016, British junior doctors overtly popularised rhyming slang for the decidedly unpopular Secretary State for Health, Jeremy Hunt, a move which was welcomed by singer James Blunt, who tweeted that he was officially handing his rhyming slang title over to the embattled politician. Rhyming slang also disguises *prick* with *Hampton Wick*, later abbreviated to *Hampton*, *balls* to *cobblers' awls*, later just *cobblers*, and even more obscurely *arse*, which became *bottle and glass*, and then *Aristotle* to rhyme with *bottle*, before settling on *Aris* to refer to the buttocks, which was almost back to where it had started!

Many words with the bl- cluster (or with the *b* and *l* and an interposed vowel) relating to compressed fluid and swelling have also been tentatively traced back to one of the senses of the PIE root **bhel-* and its parallel form **bhle-*. Examples include *belly*, *bellows*, *bole*, *blain*, *bleb*, *bleed*, *ball*, *balloon*, *blow*, *blast*, *blister*, *blubber* and *bladder*. In Latin and Greek, these *bulging* bl- words show the progression of consonant sounds consistent with Grimm's Law, with bl- becoming fl-. Hence, Latin has *follis* "bellows, leather bag, paunch, puffed cheeks". In Vulgar Latin the sense of *follis* expanded to mean "fool, empty-headed person", probably through the idea that a foolish person is a "windbag", though the puffed-out cheeks of a buffoon or jester is another possible source of the sense evolution. English borrowed *fool* and *folly* from Old French *fol* "madman, idiot, jester" and *folie*, both descendants of Latin *follis*. Greek has φαλλός (*phallós*), from the swollen **bhel-* root, borrowed as *phallus* by English via late Latin. This bl-/fl- separation is evident in the different words English has for *flower*: Germanic *bloom* and *blossom* and Romance *flower* from French *fleur* and Latin *flos*. More of these *flourishing* fl- words are outlined in chapter 3.

Old English *blæd*, which became Modern English *blade*, was most commonly used for "flattened part of a tool or bone", as in *shoulder blade*. However, the meaning "leaf" gradually became more usual, influenced by Old Norse *blað* "leaf, blade of a rudder, oar or knife". Germanic languages keep their leafy bl-: German has *Blatt*, Icelandic has *blaða*, and *blad* is "leaf" in Swedish, Danish, Norwegian and Dutch. The same PIE root gave Latin *folium* "leaf", French *feuille* and Italian *foglia*. An Italian carrying case for loose leaves (or sheets) of paper is a *portafoglio*, giving us *portfolio*. Over time, however, English *blades* have narrowed and sharpened: we still have blades of grass and cereals, but not broad-leaved blades.

One instance of a recent bl- coinage which seems to have maintained the blown up phonestheme of bl- is *blimp* "non-rigid airship", used since World War I. The cartoon character *Colonel Blimp* – a puffed-up, pompous caricature of the stereotypical British reactionary – was named after the airship, and perfectly fits the bl- for *bluster* phonestheme. Colonel Blimp appeared in Lord Beaverbrook's right-wing *London Evening Standard* in the 1930s and 1940s and often poked fun at the owner's less than progressive views, and those of the British political establishment. Another modern bl- example is the thankfully short-lived British TV character *Mr Blobby*, a bulbous goggly-eyed pink and yellow figure who achieved the impossible feat of being even more irritating than TV host Noel Edmonds. This bl- for *bloating* is still common in Germanic languages. *Bloated* in German is *aufgebläht*, in Icelandic it is *uppblásinn* and in Danish it is *opblæst*. A *bloom* is *blom* in Swedish, *Blüte* in German and *bloem* in Dutch. *Bladder* is *blåsa* in Swedish, *blaas* in Dutch and *blære* in Norwegian.

As we saw in chapter 3, the most influential sense of the PIE root **bhel-* "shine, burn, be bright" is in words to do with brightness, such as *blaze*, *blush*, *blitz* and *blizzard*. Scandinavian cognates are also very common: Swedish *blick* "lightning", *bläs* "blaze" and *blossa* "flare", for instance. English took *blitz* "lightning" from German, initially through *Blitzkrieg* "lightning war", which was used by journalists during World War II to describe the fast, powerful waves of German attacks aimed at securing a swift military victory. *Donner und Blitzen!* "thunder and lightning!" was also known to generations of readers of boys' comics as a fearsome German oath. In the Slavic world, *Blesk* "lightning" is the top-selling Czech tabloid, while other related blazing bl- words include Slovenian *blisk* "flash, lightning", Polish *błyskawica* "lightning" and Ukrainian блискавка (*blyskavka*) "lightning, bolt". *Bhel-* and its extended form *bhleg-* "burn" are also the ancestral roots to much of the *flamboyant flaming* fl- vocabulary that English borrowed from Romance languages.

In addition, PIE *bhel-* is responsible for the bl- words in English that denote colour. Although it may be hard to comprehend that these words come from the same source, *bhel-* is a wide-ranging root and perception of colour and naming of colours differs markedly across cultures, and in fact, some colour names are surprisingly recent. English only adopted *orange* from Old French in the late Middle Ages, when the fruit of that name had been introduced. *Orange* was unknown as the name of a colour before this time, as can be seen from *robin redbreast*, a bird with a bright orange front. The best Old English had come up with for this colour was *geoluread*, literally "yellow-red". *Pink*, attested from the end of the 16th century, was even later on the scene. This name comes from *pink* being a common name for the carnation and similar flowers of the Dianthus genus, which have pink petals. Prior to this time, the colour was described as "like a pale rose", or *incarnation*, that is, "flesh colour".

It does seem to be the case that many of our colour words share a common origin. If we take the word *blue*, it is first seen around 1300 from the Old French *blo*, which meant "pale, light-coloured", but also "blue". Modern cognates of *blue* include *blau* (German), *bleu* (French), *blau* (Catalan), and *blå* (Danish). *Blo* entered French from the Germanic language of the Franks and can be traced back to a PIE root of **bhle-was*, also "light-coloured, blue, blond, yellow," again from the PIE form **bhel-*, "shine, burn, flash". The breadth of meaning encompassed by this root can also be seen in Welsh *blawr* "grey", Latin *flavus* "yellow", Middle High German *bla* "yellow", Old Spanish *blavo* "yellow-grey", Spanish *blanco* "white" and words for "white" in all contemporary Slavic languages, for example, Czech *bílý* and Bulgarian *бял* (*bjal*). It also gave Old Norse *blá* "livid, blue, lead-coloured", from where English has the phrase "black and blue" for someone who is very bruised. The source of the second element of this expression is the Viking "livid" *blá* rather than the Old English *blaw* "blue".

Fire is thought to be the connecting element behind the palette of colours **bhel-* has produced. When *ablaze*, fire is *blindingly* bright, but what is scorched or burned is *black* – and indeed *black* is another of the **bhel-* root's bafflingly multi-coloured offspring. From this root, Proto-Germanic took **blakaz*, meaning "burnt" and Old English *blæc*, from which we have *black*. However, Old English also had *blac*, meaning "bright", "glittering" or "pale". Unsurprisingly, *blac* did not survive into Modern English with its closeness to *blæc* and the high potential for confusion. Even so, close cognates can be found in words for "pale" in other Germanic languages, e.g. Swedish and Norwegian *blek*, Danish *bleg*, German *blass* and Dutch *bleek*. Many English "pale" words do endure from *blac* and later borrowings from Old Norse and French. These include *bleak*, *bleach*, *blank*, *blanch*, *blemish*, *blight*, and even *blanket*, which comes from French *blanquette*, a diminutive of *blanc* "white". The word *blancmange* comes from Old French *blanc mangier* "white food". It was originally a savoury dish of white meat in a sauce made of cream, eggs and rice and often sugar and almond milk. Over time, the meat content was omitted, gelatine was added and blancmange became a blobby dessert.

It is believed that Old English *blind* also comes from an extended form of the PIE *bhel-* root. As well as meaning "sightless", it referred to "mental blindness" meaning "confused" and "obscure" and this is where *blind alley* and *blind drunk* may have originated. The words *blunt* and *blunder* also come from *blind*, the latter first having the narrower meaning of "stumble around blindly". *Blend* is also from the same PIE source, originally meaning "make cloudy", rather than the more general "mix". *Blaand*, a traditional fermented drink in the Shetland Islands, also fits this mould. It is a cloudy blend of the whey of churned milk and water, and was apparently so popular that it was the last request of all Shetlanders on their deathbed. Or perhaps it just finished them off!

A number of bl- words may have "leaked" into the br- cluster, as there is certainly a crossover in some bl-/br- themes. Regarding colour, br- has *bright*, *brass*, *bronze* and *brown*. The latter comes from the PIE root *bher-*, which is very close and probably related to *bhel-*, and also means "shine". *Brass*, *bronze* and *burnished* metals still shine, although *brown* is not usually considered to be radiant any more! Then there is *bruise*, which seems to encompass all three of the main themes of the bl- cluster: colour, excess and compressed fluid. Some movement between the lateral alveolar /l/ and the rhotic post-alveolar /r/ (see appendix) is to be expected as there seems to have been a good deal of fluidity between these two liquid consonants throughout history. Anyone who has stumbled over the tongue-twister "red lorry, yellow lorry" will attest that there can still be a bit of a *blurring* of the sounds.

Finally, we come to the words with the bl- cluster that relate to the phonosemantic theme of excess. Many of these relate to prolonged, uncontrolled chatter. In fact, there are such a great number of these that many must have come about through mimetic analogy with similar existing words: *blather, blether, bleating, blab, blabber, blurb, blarney, blatter, bluster, blah, blah, blah*. An honorary mention should also come here for the *bling* culture despised by the conservative press. In the 1990s, hip-hop popularised the term *bling* or *bling-bling* referring to showy, ostentatious jewellery, especially diamonds and precious metals. The word then entered mainstream culture as new celebrities, footballers and other flashy individuals wishing to show off symbols of their wealth brought *bling* to the public attention. There is even the striking Bling-Bling building in Liverpool, built for Herbert Howe, the so-called "King of Bling" and "hairstylist to the rich and famous".

23.   dr- drenching and dragging

And then he only had eyes for the pie. Watch any man, he could be ninety years old and drooling spit, but at the sight of homemade pie every last one of his wits will spring to attention.

Elizabeth Hay, *A Student of Weather*

The dr- cluster fronts hundreds of words in English, but one of its main uses is with words to do with falling or flowing liquid. Babies and toothless old crones *dribble* and *drool* when taking food and *drink*. If you get caught in the rain, you are liable to get *drenched*, though of course, you have more chance of staying reasonably *dry* if it's only *drizzling* rather than raining cats and dogs. You may go to a pub for a "*drop* of the hard stuff" or a refreshing *draught* ale, possibly for fun, or possibly to *drown* your sorrows. *Draining* too many glasses will end up with the imbiber being as *drunk as a lord* or *as drunk as a skunk*: a *dribbling* mess hanging on to the bar, spouting *drivel* at anyone within earshot. Let's leave this squalid image behind and move on!

Some of the dr- words have fascinating origins. The Greek *drachma* was both a silver coin and a unit of weight in Ancient Greece. Literally, *drachma* means "handful" and the drachma coin was equivalent to a handful of six lower denomination obols. *Drachma* is also the source for *dirham*, which was a unit of weight used in the Ottoman Empire, and is currently the unit of currency of the United Arab Emirates and Morocco. Closer to home, *dram* is another word that ultimately comes from *drachma* and a *dram* was also a unit of weight, at one eighth of an apothecary's ounce. A fluid dram was therefore a small drink of liquor, often purchased in *dram shops*, establishments which sold booze by the shot. *Angel's dram* is the alcohol which evaporates through the porous wood of whisky barrels in the aging process.

Proto-Germanic *drengkan* is the source of *drink* and its Germanic equivalents such as Dutch *drinken*, Icelandic *drekka* and Danish *drikke*. *Drown* and *drench* are from the same source, the latter originally being the causative form "make drink" (see boxed text below), before it gained its current sense of "soak thoroughly". Although the etymological evidence isn't clear, it is believed that *drengkan* is a descendant form of Proto-Indo-European *dhrag-* "carry along, draw, drag". If so, the underlying idea behind *drinking* is "drawing in water" or "sucking a liquid up". Arabic, a Semitic, non-Indo-European language, has this lexical link: the verb شرب (šaraba) means "drink", but is also used for "smoke", so Arabs "drink cigarettes", much as the English might *drag*, *draw* or *pull* on their ciggies.

Draught is interesting as it links the idea of "drinking" with that of "drawing". *Draught beer* is drawn from the barrel, and the other senses of *draught* also come from a sense of "pulling": draughty air currents are drawn through gaps, and in the game of draughts, pieces are drawn across the board. The variant *draft* has the basic meaning of "something drawn", hence the extended senses of "preliminary sketches", "outlined plans", "cheque drawn from a bank" and "military conscription" whereby new recruits are "pulled" into the army, sometimes kicking and screaming.

Descendants of PIE *dhrag-* are ubiquitous across the Indo-European world. It is the source of Russian дроги (drogi) "cart, wagon, hearse", and its more familiar diminutive *droshky* "low carriage", Sanskrit ध्रजस् (dhrájas) "gliding course or motion" and Albanian *dredh* "revolve, spin". Its Proto-Germanic offshoot was *dragana* "draw, drag, pull", clearly the source of *draught*, *drag* and *draw*. English retains the "pull" element of *draw* in *withdraw*, *drawing room* (where people withdrew after dining), *drawers* (pulled on or off if underwear; pulled out if inside furniture). *Draw* also means "pull" in its sense of "attract", while the idea of drawing on paper developed from the idea of "pulling" a pencil or brush across a surface. Other Germanic descendants of **dragana* are closer in meaning to the source root, although there has been some sense evolution here too. Hence, Gothic *dragan* means "draw, accumulate"; German *tragen* and Dutch *dragen* both mean "carry", and also "wear clothes"; but Swedish and Norwegian *dra*, along with Faroese and Icelandic *draga* still mean "pull".

Other words from the Proto-Germanic *dragana* root passed down from Old English or borrowed from other Germanic sources include *dragnet*, *dredge*, *drawl*, *drail* "weighted fish hook", *bedraggled* (originally "dragged through the mire"), *dray* "sled or low cart without sides" and *drayman*. The latter term is still used for a brewery deliveryman, despite the fact that horse-drawn deliveries of beer have practically died out. In the past, barrels were rolled onto the low flat-bed wagon or *dray*, which would then be driven by the drayman, who would guide teams of horses or mules to the thirsty pub.

When too much water is *drenching* the streets, it needs to be *drained* away and *drawn* into the sewers. *Drain* derives from the Old English form *dreahnian* "drain, strain" and its primary focus is on drawing water out, i.e. making something *dry*. Thus, it should come as no surprise that *drain*, *dry* and *drought* share a common Proto-Germanic ancestor, **draug* "dry", which in turn descends from the PIE root **dherg-* "become hard, strengthen", something that happens to parched soil. This has given rise to hard or dry cognates, such as Dutch *droog* "dry", West Frisian *drege* "long-lasting", Swedish *dryg* "lasting, hard" and Latin *firmus* "strong, stable", from which English has borrowed *firm*. Fundamentally, *drought* means "dryness", and used to carry the -th suffix in its Old

English form *drugaþ*, in the same way as other abstract nouns formed from adjectives, such as *length*, *breadth* and *sloth* (see chapter 17). Later, the –th ending was reduced to –ht, in the same manner as *height*, producing *drought*.

Causative forms like *drench* (from *drink*) and *lay* (from *lie*) have a specific type of vowel change in common with abstract nouns from adjectives like *depth* (from *deep*), *width* (from *wide*) and *strength* (from *strong*). This particular change is known as i-umlaut or i-mutation. This occurs either when a back vowel is fronted (pronounced further forward in the vocal tract) or a front vowel is raised, before a syllable starting with /ɪ/, /iː/ or /j/. This was a particular feature of early Germanic languages like Old English and Old Norse, and its effects can still be seen today in some of our most basic words, even though the suffixes themselves may have changed dramatically or disappeared altogether. The irregular plurals *feet*, *men* and *mice* show the influence of i-umlaut. In West Germanic, these were bisyllabic **fōtiz*, **manniz* and **mūsiz-*. When the inflection –z was lost, the final vowel raised the first vowel and later the final –i was also lost as these plurals became monosyllabic, the mutated vowel serving as the only plural marker. The singular forms were unaffected and retained (at that time) their original vowels. Hence, we have the following sequence: **fōtiz* → **fōti* → **føti* → *føt* → *fēt* (the attested Old English form). The Great Vowel Shift then altered *fēt* to today's [fiːt] – *feet*. This history of change contrasts markedly with the West Germanic monosyllabic singular form *fōt*, which remained remarkably constant until the Great Vowel Shift and its movement to [fʊt]– *foot*.

Verbs that were formed from noun or adjective roots by adding *–jan* were similarly affected by i-umlaut. We can see the process in the ancestors of Modern English *deem* and *doom*: Proto-Germanic **domjan* "judge, think, compute" is reflected in Old English *dōm* "judgement". However, the *–jan* suffix brings about i-umlaut, so the Old English verb form is *dēman* – *deem* is the result. *Blood-bleed, full-fill, food-feed, hale-heal* and *tale-tell*, are indicative of the same evolution. *Elder* and *better* have their /e/ sound from i-umlaut, being comparative forms descended from PG *aldaz and, somewhat confusingly, PIE *bhad "good". Of course, these paragraphs on i-umlaut are in the language of the Angles – Ænglisc, the -isc suffix bringing about i-umlaut by raising the initial vowel, and so producing English, rather than Anglish.

The *dripping* dr- words originate from the PIE root *dhreu- "break off, fall, drop, crumble". Etymologically speaking, the words in this group derive from the idea of *dropping*, but their phonosemantic connection to the other liquid dr- words mentioned above seems very close. Words that can be traced back to *dhreu- include *drop, drip, droop, drowsy, dribble, dribs and drabs*, and *drizzle*. More surprisingly, *dreary* fits into this group too. Its Old English form *dreorig* meant "gory, dripping with blood". The word then went through a number shifts in sense from "horrible" to "sad, gloomy" to "dull, drab". *Drab* itself is a more recent borrowing from Middle French *drap* "cloth" (the source of *drape, draper* and *trappings*) and was used to refer to the rather nondescript colour of natural, undyed cloth. A few words with this theme have a voiceless tr- rather than a voiced dr- (see appendix). These include *trickle, trough, trench*, and many words in Modern German, such as *trinken* "drink", *triefen* "drip, ooze" and *tröpfeln* "dribble".

The less hygienic end of the dripping spectrum takes us to a smaller subset of dr- words descended from the PIE root *dher- "darken, make muddy". In this group we have *drool, dregs, dross* and *drivel*, as well as *dark*. Strands of this PIE root have been found in many Indo-European languages from the Albanian words *ndrag* "make dirty" and *dra* ""sediment of dairy products or liquids" to Latin *fraces* "olive oil dregs" and Old Norse *dregg* "sediment" – which brings us back to rivers that need *dredging* of their bottom sediments.

24.   tr- travelling and treading

"Eeyore", said Owl, "Christopher Robin is giving a party."
"Very interesting," said Eeyore. "I suppose they will be sending me down the odd bits which got trodden on. Kind and Thoughtful. Not at all, don't mention it."

A.A Milne, *Winnie the Pooh*

Tripping, traipsing and *tramping* where angels fear to *tread*, here comes **tr-**, our valiant phonosemantic *traveller*! Whether *trotting* gamely along *trails*, or *trudging* across *tracks*, if you are on your travels, you are likely to encounter the consonant cluster **tr-**. From various sources, English has accumulated dozens of words beginning with tr- that pertain to *travelling* and *treading*. Should *traipsing* the countryside on foot not appeal, you could opt for one of the numerous forms of *transport* that will speed up your *trip*. Stop a *truck*, catch a *train*, hop on a *tram* or hail a *trolley-bus*: if your destination is a bit of a *trek*, these vehicles will take you wherever you want to go. This even applies if you are "to boldly go where no man has gone before" and go *"star-trekking* across the universe" aboard the Starship *Enterprise*, splitting infinitives with gay abandon.

Travel also goes hand-in-hand with *trade*. From the itinerant pedlar *tramping* up hill and down dale with a sackful of goods on his back, to the global logistics firms trading items across the globe, words with the tr- cluster are to be found in the business of commercial *traffic* and the *transportation* of tradeable items. The tr- cluster carries the idea of "stepping out" – crossing the threshold and setting out on life's journey.

One of the most basic elements of the tr- cluster is the large number of near synonyms related to putting one foot in front of the other. The reconstructed PIE root of these words is *der- meaning "step" or "walk", which in turn became *tremp- in Proto-Germanic. This is very close to *tramp*, and its frequentative form *trample*, not to mention close cognates in other Germanic languages like Swedish *trampa* "tread, pedal", German *trampeln* "trample" and Danish *trampe* "stamp, trample".

In fact, a number of tr- words have been connected with the lives of soldiers, wanderers and vagabonds in several European languages. The German verb *traben* means "tramp" or "plod", but can also be used for *trot*, a verb that seems to have spread around the Germanic and Romance languages from Frankish *trotton* "go, flee" to Latin *trottare* and beyond. Old French *troller* "wander, stroll" gave English the verb *troll* "saunter, roll from side to side", though this is unrelated to the trolls of Scandinavian folk-tales or internet misanthropes. *Truant* appears to be of Celtic origin, the Welsh adjective *truan* means "poor or wretched", and its first attested meaning in English is "beggar". From there the sense developed to "lazy rogue", which is a short step away from the pupil skiving off school to hang aimlessly around shopping centres. *Traipsing* and *trudging* are also part of everyday life for the footsore gentlemen of the road.

It is a similar story with *tread*, a word almost unchanged from the Old English strong verb *tredan*, which had its counterpart in Old Saxon *trada*. The noun *trade* was a Low German descendant of *trada* and at this time meant "track, course". *Trade* joined *tread* in English when it was introduced by Hanseatic merchants in the 14th century. They used *trade* to denote "the track or course of a ship". The verb led on from this, as people with a trade *trod* a particular well-worn path in life and, like the Hanseatic merchants, often ended up trading their goods for other commodities or for money.

The flip side of *trade* is English *trap*, also from the stepping **der-* root, basically meaning "that into which you step", in this case, unwittingly.

Historically, long journeys had to be undertaken on horseback, or by horse-drawn transport, such as a pony and *trap*. *Trek* has its origins in the Dutch verb *trekken*, which means "journey, march", but was originally "pull, draw". (*Trekken* is also the source of English *trigger*, and has cognates in Germanic languages, where German *trecken* and Danish *trække* both mean "pull, draw"). Obviously, your trotting steed will inevitably leave *tracks*, borrowed from Old French *trac* "track left by horses, set of footprints" itself a borrowing – either from Dutch *trekken* or from its cognate, Middle Low German *treck*.

However, *trail* and *trace* are not Germanic, and are among hundreds of tr- words to do with travel that have entered English via the Latin verb *trahere*, and its Latin and French derivatives. *Trahere* also means "pull, draw", and by now, this linguistic trail should rightly have aroused your suspicions. Didn't we deal with this in the last chapter? Indeed we did, and with the shifting of Germanic dental sounds (see appendix), it should come as no surprise that the tr- and dr- clusters share many features, or that both *trahere* and *trekken*, along with Ancient Greek τρέχω (*trékhō*) "run" are thought to be descendants of last chapter's PIE **dhrag-* "carry along, drag, draw", and its variant form **tragh-*. When we consider the tired vagrant *dragging* his feet from town to town, the link becomes even clearer.

From the *trahere* stem comes Latin *tractus*, literally "a drawing out", which came to mean "track, space, duration". This is the source of *tract*, *tractor* and *traction*, as well as *trait* from its sense of "a line drawn out, a feature". A large number of prefixes were attached to the *trahere* stem to create new verbs. English happily adopted these derivatives as verbs ending in –*tract*. In this group, we can see *ad-* "to" giving *attrahere* "draw to" and English *attract*; *con-* "with, together", *contrahere* "bring together" and *contract*; *de-* "of, from", *detrahere* "draw off, deprive" and *detract*; *dis-* "apart", *distrahere* "pull apart" and *distract*; *ex-* "out", *extrahere* "draw out of, remove" and *extract*; *sub-* "under", *subtrahere* "draw from beneath" and *subtract*, and also *re-* "again", *retrahere* "undertake again; decline", which gave English both *retract* and *retreat*. There are other less literal more *abstract* borrowings from this origin, but we will curtail them here to prevent this paragraph from becoming even more *protracted*!

The frequentative form of *trahere* is *tractare* "drag about, tug, pull towards". This gained the extended sense "manage, handle, deal with". If you think of guiding and controlling a horse, you can see how this evolution came about. From this (via French *traiter*), we have *treat*, *treatment* and *treaty*. The notion of *treating* someone to food or drink has a related origin. Important envoys would be given a *littera tractora*, or "treatment letter" entitling the bearer to material support – essentially food, accommodation and means of transport – during travel. French *traiteurs* and Italian *trattorias* spring up from this idea: they are places where travellers would be treated to good food and service.

The word *train* has several points in common with *treat*, which is unsurprising as it is another descendant of *trahere*, again coming to English via Old French. *Train* was first used as a noun to describe the trail of a gown or robe. Next came the idea of "linear progression", so this led to "a train of thought", and then "a train of carriages pulled by an engine along rails". *Train* as a verb comes from the idea that something is drawn out and manipulated in order to reach the desired form. From here we come to the person who achieves this, i.e. the *trainer*, the one who will pull working animals, people, and ultimately *trainees* into shape.

Aside from the words above, a wave of English tr- travel words entered the language from Latin due to the preposition and prefix *trans-* meaning "across, over". Objects that are going across or going over an area are basically "travelling", so many of the *trans-* words in English relate to moving from one point to another. The *trans-* element has been traced back to the PIE root **terh-* "cross over, pass through", which also gave Old English *þurh*, which with a little metathesis became *through* (see chapter 4). Examples include *transit* from Latin *transire* "go across, go over"; *traverse* and the surname *Travis* "toll collector at a bridge or crossing point" both from Latin *transversare* "cross, throw across" by way of French *traverser*; and *trespass* via French *trespasser* "pass over, transgress" from Latin *trans* and *passus* "step".

Still more tr- travel words have arrived in English from a hotchpotch of different origins. *Trawl* was borrowed from Middle Dutch *traghel*, itself taken from the Latin *tragula*, meaning "dragnet". *Traffic* entered English over 500 years ago from French *trafique*, which was taken from Italian *trafficare* "carry on trade". *Truck* is also related to trade, borrowed from Old French *troquer* "barter, trade by exchange". This sense is preserved in the phrase "have no truck with" i.e. "have no dealings with". *Truck* as a vehicle is not attested until the 17th century, when it appears with the meaning "small wheel" particularly with regard to the wheels on which ships' guns were mounted. It came from Latin *trochus* "iron hoop", which came from Ancient Greek τροχός (*trokhos*) "wheel". Related to this is *truckle bed* or *trundle bed*, namely "a low bed on small wheels that can be slid under a higher bed". From this notion of being "beneath something", we have railway trucks and trucks as in "lorries" supporting loads and carrying cargo, as well as the verb *truckle*, meaning "act in a servile or submissive way".

Lastly, there is the word *travel* itself. Ironically, unlike other *treading*, *trailing*, *tramping* tr- words, *travel* cannot be tracked back to a travel-related root. Instead, it goes back to the medieval Latin *trepalium*, an instrument of torture made of three sharpened stakes (*pali*). This passed into Old French as *travailler* "put oneself to pain or trouble", which would certainly be the case if you were skewered by a trepalium. The sense then moved on to "take pains" and thence "work hard", with its noun *travail* "toil". In turn, *travail* was borrowed by English, meaning "painful effort". A new sense "journey" rapidly evolved – travel in the Middle Ages really was a painful effort, a laborious and troublesome task, whether you were on foot or riding along the rudimentary roads. As French influence came to bear on English, *travel* replaced the Old English verb *faren* (the twin of German *fahren* "travel" and still present in *ferry*, *fare* and *farewell*), showing how fed up travellers were getting with the arduous journeys on English roads! Modern travellers may well empathise!

Although unrelated to travel, another fascinating root, is PIE **deru-* "firm, solid". This has provided Indo-European languages with a number of common tr- and dr- words connected with *trees*. English *tree*, *tar*, *tray* and *trough* come from this root as does Sanskrit द्रु (dru) "tree" and Greek δρυς (*drus*) "oak" and δένδρον (*dendron*) "tree" – the former being the source of those wood nymphs the *dryads*, and the latter the source of *rhododendrons* and *dendrochronology*. Other descendants include Old Church Slavonic дрѣво (*drěvo*) "tree, wood"; Gothic *triu* "tree, wood"; Old Irish *daur* "oak" and Welsh *derwen* "oak". The latter is found in the names of a number of British rivers – Derwent, Darwen, Darent and Dart – evidently, there were many rivers among oaks in Brythonic Celtic times.

From the same root we have *druid* "knower of the oak". Both Old Celtic (**derwos*) and Old English (*treow*) had identical words for *tree* and *truth*, indicating their common PIE **deru-* ancestor: the truth being solid and firm, and in this sense tree-like. On the "true" side of **deru-*, English has *trust* and *truce* both of which carry the idea of "good faith", or "that which can be relied on", *trim* "well-prepared", and *tryst* and *betrothal*, with their connotations of trusting each other to be in a certain place at an appointed time!

Latin descendants of **deru-* include *durus* "hard" and *durare* "harden, last". Further derivatives in Latin and French have given English *durable, during, duration, obdurate, duress, endure* and *dour* among many others. Again, the connotations of this root have been picked up on by marketing departments: *Duralumin* is an age hardenable aluminium alloy; *Duracell* batteries have "durable cells" and so last a long time; *Dura Lube* is an engine lubricant used to prolong the life of truck engines; and *Durex* is an acronym for "**Du**rability, **R**eliability, and **Ex**cellence", guaranteeing the trustworthiness of their condoms, though perhaps not performance duration or tree-like solidity!

25.   pr- proper prodders

Papa, potatoes, poultry, prunes and prism, are all very good words for the lips: especially prunes and prism.

Charles Dickens, *Little Dorrit*

Pr- is a satisfyingly expressive cluster that will come up to you in full view and *prod* you in the ribs. Pr- focuses on things that stick out: *protruding* one-dimensional objects that *probe, prick* and *prod*. Of course, one-dimensional is an exaggeration – nothing is really 1D – but the objects used for prodding and probing are long and narrow – you can *prod* someone with a finger, or *prise* something open with a lever, but the flat of your hand wouldn't do. How far *protuberant* pr- goes is debatable – many things can be made to stick out if you arrange them carefully enough or search for a phonosemantic connection! For example, *profiles, pretzels* and *prawns* are pretty flat with sticky-out bits, while triangular *prisms* have flat surfaces and end in a point. Even so, other words like *prong, prickle, privet, prop* and *pricket* "spike on which to stick a candle" closely fit the phonosemantic model.

A number of simple *prickly* pr- words seem to be limited to Germanic. Middle Dutch *proppe* "vine prop, support" seems to be the source for *prop* in the senses of *clothes props, prop forwards* holding up the rugby scrum and *prop up. Stage props*, on the other hand, may well support actors, but *props* here is an abbreviation of *properties* and thus from a Romance source. *Prong*, along with its derivatives of the natural world, the *pronghorn* and the *prong-billed barbet* – a bird with a noticeably pointy beak, come from Middle Low German *prange* "stick".

You can find Germanic *pricks* everywhere, without needing to look too hard! Dutch has the nouns *priem* "pricker, piercer" and *prikkel* "prickle" and the verb *prikkan* "prick" amongst others. The verb *prick* is a descendant of the Old English *prician* – "prick, pierce, sting", which comes from West Germanic *prikojan*. Modern Germanic cognates include Low German *pricken*, Swedish *pricka* and Danish *prikke*. Of course, the noun *prick*, as well as "pricking instrument, point" has meant "penis" for the best part of five hundred years. However, in the early sixteenth century, *prick* was used as a term of endearment for "boyfriend", so girls at the time would be happy to tell their parents that they were going to take a walk with their pricks. As the century came to a close, and *prick* acquired its penial sense, it was considered more decorous to use the term "sweetheart". Shakespeare, who could get fairly earthy, notwithstanding his genius, was well aware of the different meanings of *prick*, as he demonstrates in *Romeo and Juliet*:

Romeo: Is love a tender thing? It is too rough, Too rude, too
            boisterous, and it pricks like thorn.
Mercutio: If love be rough with you, be rough with love. Prick
            love for pricking, and you beat love down.

Although *probes* also stick out, the origin of *probe* is from Latin *probare* "to test", which has several Indo-European cognates, such as French *prouver* "prove" and *éprouver* "test", Bulgarian пробвам (*probvam*) "try out, test" and German *prüfen* "check, examine". From the same root, English has *proof*, *probability* and *probation*, all words involving concepts that are testable.

The *prow* of a ship juts out into the water. This word came to English via Middle French *proue*, from Genoese *prua* – Genoa being a great seafaring republic – from earlier ancestors Latin *prora* and Ancient Greek πρῴρα (*proira*) "prow". The word *prone* from Latin *pronus* "turned forward, inclined" is a close cousin. Ultimately, both *prow* and *prone* can be traced back to the PIE root **per-* "go over, go forth, go before". PIE **per-* was passed down across the Indo-European world in related word-forming elements which tended to be used as prefixes and prepositions. They include प्र (*pra-*) in Sanskrit "forward, near, before", *pro-* and *prae-* in Latin (see below), πρό (*pro*) "before, in front of" in Greek, and *fore-* in Old English. These are all forward-facing prefixes; at the forefront, they stand out from the crowd.

Words like *prominent, promontory, propeller* and *projectile* carry the Latin prefix *pro-*, which means "before, forward, forth" or "in advance", so the idea of "jutting forward" is entrenched in the *prefix* of these words and many others like them. Hence, *prominent* is made up of *pro-* and *minere* "project", from *minae* "threats, projections"; *promontory* is made up of *pro-* and *mons* "mountain"; *propeller* consists of *pro-* and *pellere* "push, drive"; while *projectile* comes from a combination of *pro-* and the verb *iacere* "throw", so literally means "object thrown forwards". Greek also had the πρo- (*pro-*) prefix to mean "in front of", as in προβοσκίς (*proboskis*), literally "elephant's trunk" from *πρo-* and βόσκω (*bóskō*) "feed", which was passed on to Latin as *proboscis* and then on to English.

A more nebulous phonestheme shows a link between pr- and what Lawler (1990) calls "human (social roles)", but I would reclassify as "propriety in society", be it at the *prom* or on the *prowl*. In *private*, people *pray* and *preen*, with other people they *promise* and *praise* – we all have our *price*. For millennia, the *precepts* of what constitutes civilised behaviour have been determined by social norms on what is considered right and *appropriate*. This notion of *propriety* is inherent to pr-. Sticklers for the rules are *prim and proper*; *proud* of *practising* what they *preach*. Yet, if this goes too far, these guardians of public morals tend to become *priggish*. They could become *prissy, prudish* and *precious* – more concerned with social niceties and old-fashioned notions of chivalry and etiquette than the *practicalities* of modern life. *Prigs* have never been looked upon favourably. Former senses of the word include "tinker", "pickpocket" and "fop". George Eliot gives one of the most cutting indictments of such characters in *Middlemarch* (1871), when she states "a prig is a fellow who is always making you a present of his opinions". Ouch!

Latin is also the source of many pr- words relating to social *primacy* and *prestigious* roles in society. This is largely because the Romans had a bewilderingly wide array of official positions, and many of these were prefixed with *pro-*, or else *prae-*, (later *pre-*) which means "in front of in time or place". From the Roman legal system there are the familiar *praetor* "elected magistrate", famous for the *Praetorian Guard*, the bodyguard troops of the Emperor; *proconsul*, a magistrate who served first as a consul and then as governor of a province; and *procurator* "overseer, agent", with its contracted form *proctor*. Other top posts borrowed from Latin are *prince* and *princess* from *princeps* "chief leader, sovereign"; *president* from *praesidentum* "president, governor"; *provost*, from *propositus* "chief, superintendent", *principal* from *principalis* "first in rank"; *prefect* from *praefectus* "public overseer" and *professor*, literally "one who professes knowledge".

Many words to do with ecclesiastical roles and rites also entered English from Latin, which was, of course, the language of the early Church. A *primate* was an archbishop long before it denoted apes and monkeys, but in both cases the notion is that of the "highest rank". Other *praiseworthy prelates* include *preachers* and *priors*, always ready to guide the faithful in *prayer*. Given the hostility between Protestants and Catholics over the centuries, it is ironic that *Protestant* also derives from Latin, the language of the Roman Catholic Church. *Prophets*, *priests* and *Presbyterians* were also borrowed from Latin, but are of Greek origin, the latter two descendants of πρεσβύτερος (*presbúteros*) "elder, older".

PIE *per-* is also the source of a number of words pertaining to proper roles in the social order through its offshoot *prow-* "right judge, master". A Proto-Germanic descendant of this was *frawjo*, which gave Old English *frea* "lord, king" and Old Norse the fertility god *Freyr*; Latin descendants include *provincia* "province, dominion, duty" and hence the Roman *province* of *Provence* with its language *Provençal*; while the Proto-Slavic descendant *pravъ* gave cognates such as Polish *prawo* "law", Bulgarian прав (*prav*) "right, straight", Russian право (*pravo*) "right, claim, justice" and of course, правда (*pravda*) "truth".

Late Old English *prud*, the forerunner of *proud*, meant "splendid and brave" rather than "arrogant and haughty", although the latter sense soon developed. It is possible that the Anglo-Saxons attributed this negative sense to the Norman knights who called themselves *prud*, i.e. "valiant", as they *pranced* around on their steeds, sitting *pretty* on their horses. Such knights would take *pride* in their *prowess* on horseback, or more accurately, their *prouesse* "skill, bravery". *Prized* positions in society depended on the *proper* breeding, exemplified by *prudent*, *proportionate* behaviour and correct gentlemanly etiquette – eminently *preferable* to the boorish manners of the common horde, the lumpen *proletariat*.

The *proletariat* were the lowest class of Roman citizens, those without *property*, contributing nothing to the society other than by bearing children – future Roman citizens who could colonise the lands conquered by Rome. Again, Latin *pro-* "forth" is the key here: this class *produced proles* "offspring", in fact they were *prolific* at begetting *progeny*. Karl Marx studied Roman law at the University of Berlin, and used the term *proletariat* for those in contemporary society whose only means of subsistence was to sell their labour power in return for wages. George Orwell later popularised the term *proles* in his novel *1984* for members of the uneducated labouring classes in the superstate of Oceania.

As we have seen with the example of *proud* (above), adjectives are often problematic for searchers of phonosemantic meaning in that the sense development can evolve very rapidly. *Pretty*, for example, is from Old English *prættig* "tricky, sly" (from the same root as *prat* "trick", which later became "buttock" and then "fool"). The sense next moved to "gallant", then "fine" and then "attractive", as well as developing an ironical sense as in *come to a pretty pass*.

Silly has moved even more dramatically from its Old English form *gesælig* "happy, prosperous" (still found in German *selig* "happy, blessed"). It passed through a number of senses, from "blessed" to "pious" and "holy" then on to "innocent" and "naïve" before reaching "feeble-minded" and then arriving at "foolish, lacking in judgement" and "stupefied" with *knocked silly*, *drink yourself silly* etc. This type of semantic shift, where a word acquires negative connotations, is called *pejoration*, and is quite a common phenomenon. This can be seen by the quote variously attributed to King Charles II, King James II and Queen Anne on the new St Paul's Cathedral as, "amusing, awful and artificial" at that time meaning, "pleasing, awe-inspiring and skilfully-crafted"! German *schlecht* "bad" has shifted in a similar vein from its Old High German form *sleht*, meaning "smooth, even", which is a cognate with English *slight* (see chapter 17).

Nice has undergone *amelioration*, and has gained positive connotations, and so moved in the opposite direction to *silly*. *Nice* originates from the Latin *nescius* "ignorant, not knowing" from the negative *ne* and the verb *scire* "know". It was borrowed by English in the early medieval period from Old French *nice* "ignorant, simple". Next, the sense developed to "timid" and then quickly through "fussy" to "delicate" and then "precise" – still found in "a nice distinction", and then via "respectable" to "agreeable", "delightful", "pleasant" and "kind".

26.   gr- groaning, grinding and growth

God have mercy on the sinner
Who must write with no dinner,
No gravy and no grub,
No pewter and no pub,
No belly and no bowels,
Only consonants and vowels.

John Crowe Ransom, *Survey of Literature*

Grrr, you might think, leaves you in little doubt of its rank hostility. Yet despite its *gruff grouchiness*, the consonant cluster **gr-** is actually very common in English and so its sound symbolism is not confined to *grizzles*, *grunts* and *gripes*. Gr- words embrace the good – *great*, *grand*, *graceful*; as well as the bad – *groan*, *grudge*, *gruesome*; and the ugly – *gross*, *grotesque*, *grotty*. There are a number of other concepts which can also be associated with the gr- cluster. One group deals with *growth* and *greenness*; another focuses on *grains* and coarse *granules*; and a third is similar to one of the main semantic associations of the consonant cluster cl- (see chapter 8), dealing with "holding on tightly", *grabbing*, *gripping* and *grappling*.

As might be expected from such a large body of words, there is a certain degree of crossover between some of these disparate elements. *Grapes*, *grapefruit* and *pomegranates* that *grow* to ripeness have to be *grasped* by fruit pickers. However, while *grapes* and *grapefruit* share an etymology with *grapple*, *pomegranate* means "apple filled with grains". *Grains* are, of course, seeds, and seeds will germinate so seedlings will *grow*.

Undoubtedly the most evocative gr- group contains words with negative connotations: the *grotty*, the *grumpy* and the *grisly*. For instance, the *Grim Reaper* has been the personification of Death for hundreds of years. *Grim* "mask" was also one of the names given to the Norse god Odin, as was *Grimnir* "the masked one", when he was travelling in disguise among mortals. The town of *Grimsby* is named after Odin rather than the baleful demeanour of the town's inhabitants, the *Grimbarians*, popularly known as "codheads". Although Odin is a complicated, multi-faceted god, he certainly has a number of decidedly dark characteristics. He is referred to by over two hundred different names in Norse mythology, but for every *Faðr galdr* "Father of Magical Songs" or *Sigtýr* "God of Victory" there is a *Hangadrottinn* "Lord of the Hanged" or *Gapþrosnir* "the one in gaping frenzy". In fact, the Old Norse adjective *óðr* "furious, mad" comes from the same root as *Odin*. The sound symbolism of gr- is not lost on writers of fiction, as gr- has been associated with the downright nasty throughout the ages, from the monster *Grendel* in the Anglo-Saxon epic *Beowulf* to Dr Seuss's *Grinch* stealing Christmas and Steven Spielberg's *mogwais* turning into psychotic *gremlins*.

Proto-Indo-European **ghrem-* "thunder, angry" is the likely source of *grim* and its cognates. These include German *Grimm* "wrath", Swedish *grym* "cruel, vicious", and the Russian word for "thunder", греметь (*gremet'*). *Grime* comes from the sense of *grim* as a mask, and soot covering the face. Other English words from the same root include *grimace*, *grumble* and probably *growl*, which may be an onomatopoeic approximation of the rumbles of thunder or indeed, the belly!

Gripe comes from the Proto-Indo-European root **ghreib-* "to grip" and as a noun referred to a sharp pain in the bowels – something that it is natural to *gripe*, *groan* and be *grumpy* about. Similarly, flu sufferers would *grouch* about *grippe*, an archaic word for "influenza", which comes from the French verb *gripper* "to seize, grip", as flu grabs hold of its victims. An epidemic of flu in the Seven Years War (1756-1763) spread not only the virus, but also the word *grippe* throughout the European nations involved, so there is *грипп* (*gripp*) in Russian, *Grippe* in German, *gripe* in Portuguese and *grippe* in French.

West Germanic **gripjan* also descends from **ghreib-* and is the source of Old English *grippan* and its contemporary cognates *grip*, *gripe* and *grope*. Similarly, gr- also *grasps*, *grabs* and *grapples*. This time the origin is Proto-Germanic **krappo* – "hook", which is also the source of many cr- words, such as *crampon*, *cramp* and *crook* and a descendant of PIE **ger-* (see chapter 12). As outlined above, the word *grape* comes from the same root; it originally referred to a bunch of grapes, and the underlying notion is of the bunches "hooking on" to the vine.

Animals use their talons, claws and fingers to *grab* on to surfaces. The French for "claw, talon" is *griffe*, familiar through the hook-nosed, sharply taloned *griffin* of legend. Talons, claws and fingers also scratch, and many languages have scratchy gr- forms, including English *grate*, French *gratter* and Italian *grattare*. Germanic cognates scratch with a kr- cluster rather than a gr- cluster due to the First Germanic Consonant Shift (see chapter 3), so German *kratzen*, Danish *kradse*, Dutch *krassen* all mean "scratch", while one of the most famous grabbers and scratchers is the *crab*. Still with the *grating* gr- forms, the PIE root **gerbh-* "scratch" is not only the source of *carve*, but is also, through its Ancient Greek descendant γραφειν (*graphein*) "scratch, etch", the source of a large number of English gr- borrowings. Γραφειν was originally used for "scratching" on clay tablets with a stylus, and so came to mean "write". Among the numerous borrowings are *graph* and its derivatives such as *autograph* and *photograph*, *graphic*, *graphite, grammar, graft, graffiti* and *gram* with its derivatives *diagram, program* etc.

Scratching deeper brings us to the PIE root **ghrebh-* "dig". This produced *groove, grave* and possibly *grub*, as well as Albanian *gropë* "pit", and other cognates for "grave", such as Bulgarian гроб (*grob*), Dutch *graf*, German *Grab*, Danish, Norwegian, Swedish *grav* etc. This naturally brings us to *grief* and *gravity*, weighty matters derived from the PIE root **gwere-* "heavy, serious" that may cause us to feel *aggravated* or *aggrieved*. Descendants of **gwere-* can be found across the Indo-European world, from Baluchi گران (*giran*) "heavy" to Persian گران (*gerân*) "expensive", Latin *gravas* "heavy, serious" and Gothic *kaurus* "heavy". Another English descendant is *quern* "millstone", and from here we *gravitate* along the gr- trail to another group of gr- words to do with "grinding".

PIE **ghreu-* "rub, grind" has given English a set of *grinding* words with the gr- cluster that depict two-dimensional friction. These include *grind*, along with *grindstone* and *grounds, grit, gritty, gravel* and possibly *gristle* and *grist*. In heraldry, a wheat sheaf is a *garb*, and the original sense of *garbage* may have come from this source, meaning "wheat chaff for horses". Latin *frendere* "to gnash the teeth", Lithuanian *grendu* "to scrape, scratch" and Greek *khondros* "corn, grain," are further European descendants of **ghreu-*. This leads us from the mill back out to the *grain* fields, where the wheat sheaves are waiting for the scythe.

Gr- for "grain" goes back to the PIE root **grhno-*, which is also the ancestor of *corn* and *kernel*. Cereal is *ground* to get *groats* and *grits*, while *grout* is probably from the same origin, due to its resemblance to *grainy* porridge. Later imports entered English in the Middle Ages via Latin *granum* "seed, grain" and its Romance descendants. The verb *garner* "accumulate, gather" originally had the narrower sense of "reap, harvest grain". This would then be stored in a *granary* or a *grange*. *Granite, granita* and *granule* also come from *grain*, as a result of their grainy appearance. Oddly enough, *grog* can also be traced back to *grain* through its association with *grogram*, a rough textile fabric the name of which derives from French *gros grain* "coarse grain or texture". A cloak made of this material was habitually worn by British Admiral Edward Vernon (1684-1757), and so he was given the nickname *Old Grog*. In 1740, he ordered that his sailors' rum be watered down, so the name *grog* was given to the rum-water ration issued daily to the *groggy* sailors of the Royal Navy. I still remember how pleasantly surprised I was, living through a freezing Czech winter, when I came across a catering van in a small Prague square selling glasses (well styrofoam cups) of steaming *grog*. It warmed the cockles of my heart.

The first use of *grain* in English was with the sense "red dye made from insects", as in the verb *engrain*. *Grain* was also used as "seed" or "pip", as in *pomegranate* "apple with many seeds" and thus *grenadine* "syrup of pomegranates". The Spanish city of *Granada* (whose heraldic emblem is a pomegranate) was apparently named after the fruits that Arab settlers found growing in the vicinity. *Grenade* gets its name from its supposed resemblance to a pomegranate, and *grenadiers* were originally the soldiers most dexterous at throwing grenades. The gemstone *garnet* also takes its name from the dark red colour of pomegranate pulp.

The origin of *gravy* is less clear. Some believe it comes from *greaves*, the sediment of melted tallow, while others assert that it comes from French *grané* – "grained, seasoned". In slang, *gravy* came to mean "good money gained through little effort" and *riding the gravy train* was "earning a lot of money in exchange for minimal work and little risk". On the flip side of *gravy*, there is *gruel*, a thin meal porridge that has never seemed fancy or luxurious. In the 18th century, if you *got your gruel*, you received your punishment, and *gruelling* work is physically taxing or punishing.

The gr- cluster for *growth* and *greenness* derives from the PIE root **ghre-* "grow". Animals *graze* on *green* shoots in *groves* of trees, and on plants and spring *grasses*. There is a clear semantic connection between *green*, *grass* and *grow*, and these words have not moved very far apart in English's Germanic sister languages. *Grænn* is Icelandic for *green* and it is *grønn* in Norwegian, *grøn* in Danish and *grien* in Frisian. *Grass* is *gräs* in Swedish, *Gras* in German and *gras* in Dutch. *Grow* is less clear cut: while there is *groeien* in Dutch and *oangroeie* in Frisian, German and the Scandinavian languages have words similar to the English verb *wax*, which is now only commonly used to describe the waxing and waning of the moon, and in a small number of expressions like "wax lyrical". *Gro* does exist in Norwegian and Swedish, for example, but it is with the narrow meaning of "sprouting" and "germinating", while their all-purpose "grow" verbs are *vokse* and *växa* respectively.

The greenness of spring and the new growth that it brings are also tied up with the fertility of the season. *Grass widow* is first recorded in the early sixteenth century and referred to an unmarried woman who has had sexual intercourse out of wedlock, and thus outside of the marital bed. *Green* and *grass* had sexual connotations in the Middle Ages and expressions like "give a girl a grass gown" and "give a girl a green gown" were in common parlance for what is euphemistically termed "a tumble in the grass". The traditional English ballad *Greensleeves* is believed to refer to the grass stains on the dress of a woman after al fresco sex, but sadly it is not now thought to have been written by Henry VIII for his lover, Anne Boleyn, despite apocryphal rumour. Remaining in the meadow, the German for *grass widow* is *Strohwitwe* – "straw widow", while contemporary English has the slang idiom "a roll in the hay" for a casual quickie.

A word with a similar origin is *bastard*, which has recognisable cognates in most European languages. One widespread theory is that this word combines the French *fils de bast* – "son of the packsaddle" with the pejorative ending -*ard* as in *coward*, *drunkard* and *dotard*. Packsaddles were often used as makeshift beds by travellers, and so casual encounters on the packsaddle could lead to illegitimate children. *Batman*, as in the officer's servant who was in charge of the packsaddle, (as opposed to the "Caped Crusader" superhero), also comes from *fils de bast*. A second, not dissimilar, theory pinpoints Proto-Germanic **bandstiz* "cow stall, barn" as the likely origin of *bastard* – perhaps a drier location for a roll in the hay.

27.   shr- shrinking and shreds

I'm searching for a shred of humanity in that shriveled tangle of
arteries you call a heart.

Rachel Vincent, *Blood Bound*

Shr- words are often small, the *shrivelled* remnants of what has
gone before. Other shr- words are high-pitched and *shrieking*,
piercing to the eardrums. There is some crossover between these
two themes: *shrews* are tiny mammals, which *shrink* away from
danger, but they also squeak *shrilly*, *shredding* the nerves of those
in the vicinity. The shr- consonant cluster is unusual in that it is the
only native English cluster with the /ʃ/ sound combined with
another consonant. The exception to this is words taken from
Yiddish such as *schmuck* "fool", *schnook* "sucker" and *schlep* "loser,
drag", although English has equivalent sm-, sn- and sl- clusters.
However, a sr- cluster, which is existent in some Indian languages –
as the names *Srinagar*, and *Sri Lanka* attest – does not exist in
English, leaving a niche for a cluster with sibilant + /r/ (see
appendix). This is neatly filled by shr-, which seems to be easier than
sr- for English speakers to pronounce.

The shr- cluster shares several features with other clusters,
notably scr- and squ-. As we saw in chapter 15, there has been
extensive movement between sk-/sc- /sk/ and sh- /ʃ/, as English
pronunciation has evolved. It may be the case that shr- has
developed by analogy with other clusters, or more simply has come
into being through leakage from them. Shr- is certainly less
common than both scr- and squ- in English, and the assumed Proto-
Indo-European roots of many words from across these three
clusters bear a strong resemblance. The high-pitched noise in *shriek*

and *shrill* is covered by the squ- cluster in its *squeaking* and *squealing* and also by the scr- cluster in *screeching* and *screaming*. In addition, *shrinking*, *scrunching* and *squashing* are not hugely dissimilar and there isn't much between *scraps* and *shreds*, while *shrive* and *scribe* are pairs too, with German *schreiben* "write" almost identical (see chapter 16). Nevertheless, shr- has existed as a separate English cluster since at least the Middle English period, so we will focus on the shr- words here, while noting similarities with other clusters.

The word *shrink* meaning "contract, wither, shrivel up" has been in English for a very long period, from Old English *scrincan*, with its recognisable *scranc*, *scruncen* preterite and past participle equating to Modern English *shrink, shrank, shrunk(en)*. There also used to be a causative verb *shrench* meaning "make shrink" in a similar relationship with *shrink* as *drench* is to *drink* (see chapter 23). *Shrink* meaning "psychiatrist" or "psychotherapist" has been around since the mid-20th century. It is actually an abbreviated form of the equally uncomplimentary *head-shrinker*, presumably because clients and patients felt that their heads were being shrunk in their therapy sessions! Ultimately, *shrink* goes back to the Proto-Indo-European *(s)ker-*, meaning "turn inwards, bend, wrinkle". *Shrivel* and *shrimp* are also believed to come from the same root, as does *scrimp*, which now means "be thrifty, economise carefully", but as we have seen, was earlier an adjective meaning "scant, shrunken". Shr- for "shrivel" has cognates in several Germanic languages, e.g. German *schrumpfen*, which has the /ʃr/ sound as in English, or Norwegian *skrumpe* which has the hard unpalatalised North Germanic /skr/, (see chapter 15). Old Norse *skrælna* "shrivelled" also gives us *scrawny*, again showing the close link between scr- and shr-. *Shrug* also fits the phonosemantic model, being cognate with Danish *skrugge* "stoop, crouch".

Modern English prefers *periphrasis* – the use of separate words to express a grammatical relationship – to *inflections* – changes to the forms of words which convey their role in a sentence. The word order typically determines the meaning, rather than inflected forms. In a Modern English sentence such as "the horse bit the queen", we are in no doubt about who did the biting and who was bitten. Old English, as a highly inflected language, was very different. The sentence *se hors bāt ðā cwēne* means "the horse bit the queen", as a modern reader might expect, but *þone hors bāt sēo cwēn* means that "the queen bit the horse"! It is the inflections, not the word order, which tell us the subject and object of the sentence. Some modern languages have a lexical causative. For example, Arabic سَخُنَ (*sakuna*) means "be hot", whereas سَخَّنَ (*sakkana*) means "make hot, heat" – the doubling of the middle consonant makes the verb causative. However, in Modern English, we use periphrasis to show causation. We usually use two verbs and two clauses: *it made them weep; she compelled him to leave* etc. While Old English had similar structures, it also had many examples of a lexical causative – the causative factor was in-built in the verb.

Verbs tended to come in pairs, one of which was causal and transitive and the other non-causal and intransitive. Some pairs, like *sceawian* and *seon*, the ancestors of *show* (basically "make see") and *see* and *fedan* and *etan*, the ancestors of *feed* ("make eat") and *eat*, seem entirely unrelated, but most were etymologically linked with very similar spellings and pronunciations. For example, Old English had *settan* as the causative of *sittan*, now *set* and *sit*, along with *fellan* and *feallan*, the predecessors of *fell* (as in *fell a tree*) and *fall*. Similarly, OE *lecgan* and *licgan* produced *lay* and *lie*, while Middle English *raisen*, borrowed from Old Norse *reisa*, combined with OE *risan* to give us the modern pairing of *raise* and *rise*. Typically, the vowel in each pair will differ, with the vowel of the causative verb being raised and fronted due to i-umlaut (see chapter 23).

Many of these lexical pairs have followed a similar route to *drench* and *drink* e.g *clench* and *cling* from OE *beclencan* and *clingan*. However, many of the causal forms are becoming increasingly rare or obsolete: *shrench* "make shrink" (see above), *sench* "make sink", *stench* "make stink" and *wend* "make wind, turn, proceed on a course", for instance.

This is because Modern English prefers to use periphrasis to express causative forms: *make him drink* rather than *drench him*! In addition, over time, verbs tend to become ambitransitive: as well as *the ship is sinking* (intransitive), we have *the captain is sinking the ship* (transitive), so in this case, *the captain is senching the ship* is redundant.

As we saw in chapters 15 and 16, the principal meaning of PIE *(s)ker-* was "cut, shear", and as such it is the ancestor of both *shear* and *sharp*. *Shrub*, another *(s)ker-* descendant, not only means "brushwood, dwarf tree", but was also used in the past as a verb meaning "lop off, prune". This is similar in meaning to the Old English *screadian*, "peel, prune", which became Modern English *shred*. *Shred* as a noun carries the idea of "piece cut off" and as such is a close cousin of *scrap*. A related PIE root *skreu-* "cut, cutting tool" was followed by Proto-Germanic *skruda*, the source for Old English *scrud* "garment", i.e. "the thing that was cut to size", which is the forerunner of the word *shroud*. Modern Swedish still has the word *skrud*, meaning "attire". *Shrew* is also believed to come from the *skreu-* root, possibly because its pointed snout resembles a cutting tool and because it was thought to have a vicious bite.

Other shr- words fit the shredded phonestheme, but are more recent additions to English. The obscure neologism *shralp*, found in skateboarder, surfer and snowboarder slang is used for "rip, shred, tear up", which apparently means "do something really well" in their impenetrable jargon. *Shrapnel* "fragments of exploded artillery shells" may seem to be related, but is actually named after Lieutenant General Henry Shrapnel (1761-1842), a British Army officer who invented the shrapnel shell. Despite the huge technological developments in explosive weapons, the noun *shrapnel* lives on, possibly because of its phonosemantic aptness. Its extended meaning "low value loose change" is another ideal fit for the near worthless cast-offs of the shr- cluster.

High-pitched shr- words are less common than their shrinking shr- counterparts, but there are still a number of *shriekers*. *Shrikes* are birds thought to be named after their *shrill* call. The word *scric* existed in Old English, meaning "shrike" or "thrush". This strongly resembles the Swedish *skrika*, which means both "jay" and "scream". These two bird species are very different, but both have shrieking calls. Shrikes may also make their victims and onlookers shriek. It is with good reason that shrikes are known as "butcher birds" – they are from the family *Laniidae* (Latin *lanius* – "butcher, executioner") – because of the way they catch insects and small vertebrates and then impale their bodies on thorns, spiky bushes and barbed wire fences. The skewered animals then serve as a cache so the shrike can return to uneaten food later – the avian version of meat hanging. The animated movie character *Shrek*, also fits the shrieking shr- phonestheme perfectly. As a physically intimidating green ogre, he induces fear and loathing in the people that live around him, so they run off, shrieking in terror. The name *Shrek* comes from either German *Schreck* "fright, terror" or its Yiddish equivalent שרעק (*shrek*).

28.   kn- knobs and knockers

Mind you, I've always been musical... Mother used to sit me on her knee and I'd whisper, 'Mummy, Mummy, sing me a lullaby do,' and she'd say: 'Certainly my angel, my wee bundle of happiness, hold my beer while I fetch me banjo.

Les Dawson

Kn- is our knobbly cluster, home of objects that that stick up or out, such as *knees, knots, knuckles* and – as anyone who has watched a *Carry On* film can attest – *knobs* and *knockers*. In the Middle English period, kn- was pronounced /kn/ rather than with the silent *k* that it has today. This means that contemporary homophone pairs like *knight/night, knead/need* and *knave/nave* were easy to tell apart until relatively recently. Other Indo-European languages with the kn- cluster have maintained the /kn/ pronunciation, and it is still common in Germanic and Slavic. For example, German has *Knie* [kni:] "knee" and Dutch has *knap* [knap] "smart", "handsome", while the *k* is pronounced in Russian книга (*kniga*) "book" and Slovene *knéz* "prince".

Knees run the gamut of social positions in English-speaking cultures. The devout kneel to pray and the respectful genuflect in obeisance to the sovereign; they bend the knee. On the other hand, a Cockney *knees-up* is probably a little less decorous. (And a *knee trembler* is unmentionable in polite society.) *Knuckles* are also down the social scale: *knuckleheaded* gang members use *knuckledusters* when fighting their counterparts. *Knuckle-draggers* are even more uncouth, displaying manners and behaviour more suited to the Stone Age.

Knolls are also protuberant geographical forms. Once rather uncommon, and seemingly destined to be used only in crossword puzzles as an obscure synonym for "hillock", *knoll* came back into prominence upon the 1963 assassination of John F Kennedy when investigators tried to ascertain whether the fatal shots had come from the Texas School Book Depository or the adjacent grassy knoll. *Knoll* does have knobbly cousins in other Germanic languages: contemporary cognates include Swedish *knalle* "knoll", Danish *knold* "tuber, clod" and Dutch *knol* "turnip".

The kn- of *knowledge* is a descendant of the PIE root **gno-* "know", the ancestor of knowing words across the Indo-European spectrum from Russian знать (*znat'*) "know", to Latin *gnoscere* "know, recognise", French *connaître* "know, be familiar with", Sanskrit जानाति (*jānāti*) "know, acknowledge", Kurdish *zanîn* "know" and the Greek γνωρίζω (*gnorízo*) "know, be aware of" (see chapter 31). The Proto-Germanic descendant of **gno-* was **kunnana* "know" which produced German *kennen* "know, be familiar with", *Kunst* "art" but originally "skill, knowledge", Old Norse *kenna* "know" and Scots *ken*. It also gave English a number of words relating to knowledge and *know-how*, such as *kith* "kinsmen, family", from the notion of "the known, the familiar" and several descendants of Old English *cunnan* "know, be able to", now familiar as *can*. These include *canny* "astute, knowing", *cunnan*'s present participle *cunning* "skilful", later "crafty", its past form *couth* (of *uncouth* knuckle-dragging fame), and *couth*'s modern doublet *could*. English also borrowed heavily from the Romance descendants of **gno-* giving us *cognition, incognito, recognise, ignorance, note, notice, connotation* and many, many more.

The Old Norse form *kenna* is the root of the figure of speech known as a *kenning* which is common in Old Norse and Anglo-Saxon poetry and riddles. Kennings are expressions made up of compound words or phrases with metaphorical meanings. The Old English epic poem *Beowulf* features a large number of kennings, including *weorðmyndum* "mind's worth" for "honour" and *segl-rad* "sail-road", *swan-rad* "swan road" and *hwæl-weg* "whale's way" for "sea". The name *Beowulf* itself is a kenning, made up of *beo* "bee" and *wulf* "wolf, hunter", hence "hunter of bees" or "bear". Sometimes, poets would place a kenning within a kenning as in the 9th century skaldic poem *Glymdrapa*, where the poet Þorbjörn Hornklofi employs the grisly kenning *grennir gunn-mas* "feeder of war-gull". Here *gunn-mas* "war-gull" equals "raven", and the whole kenning means "warrior", alluding to carnivorous birds scavenging on the battlefield on the corpses of the fallen – dead warriors become raven food.

Kn- for knobbly things is common in Germanic languages. German has *Knauf* for "pommel" and *Knopf* for "button", for example, while Dutch has *knobbel* for "lump" or "knot" and *knop* means "button" or "knob". The Icelandic knobbly cluster is hn-, as in *hnappur* "button", *hné* "knee" and *hnútur* "knot". The other Scandinavian languages stick to kn-: *knuckle* is *kno* in Danish, *knoge* in Swedish and *knoke* in Norwegian. Old Norse *knútr* "knot" led to *knut* or *knop* in Swedish, *knude* or *knast* in Danish and *knute* in Norwegian. The name *Knut*, anglicised as *Canute* or *Cnut*, as in Cnut the Great, *ealles Engla landes cyning* – "king of all England" also means "knot". Cnut ruled from 1016 to his death in 1035, and also became king of Denmark, Norway and parts of Sweden, in a reign characterised by the winning blend of sagacity and extreme brutality. Russian borrowed *knútr* "knot" from Old Norse to make кнут (*knut*) "knout", the infamous scourge used in imperial Russia.

Knouts were used to flog criminals and political offenders. They came in different forms, but all comprised multiple whips attached to a long handle. Often wires, rings or hooks were attached to the rawhide thongs, the hide having been soaked in milk and left to dry in the sun to make it harder. Even twenty lashes of the knout could maim, and the victim's spine was often broken in the flogging. Sentences of a hundred or more lashes were usually equivalent to a death sentence. Alexei Petrovich Romanov, Tsarevich of Russia, was knouted to death on the orders of his father, Peter the Great in

1718. He had been found guilty of conspiring rebellion against Peter and he died after receiving forty lashes of the knout.

A number of knobs and lumps have *n-* rather than the kn- cluster. Some, for example, *nub* – from earlier dialectal *knub* "knob" – come from earlier kn- words in which the *k* has been dropped from spelling as well as pronunciation. Others, including *nose*, *nipple*, *nugget*, *navel*, *node* and *nuzzle*, have never begun with a /kn/ sound, as far as we know. This *kn-* or *n-* question can be rather confusing and not only because of homophones like *knot* and *not*. For instance, there is the informal term *nob* for a person of high social standing. This may have come from the earlier and equally informal term *nob* meaning "head", or else be an abbreviation for "noble". Be that as it may, care should be taken. As there is also the vulgar term *knob* meaning "penis", your observations could be misconstrued if you say "Cameron was hobnobbing with a bunch of nobs last night"! Or possibly not.

A smaller group of kn- words is connected with pinching, pressing or striking. *Knocking* is obviously done with the *knuckles*, which may also be used when punching dough in between squeezes in the *kneading* process. *Knell*, the slow tolling of a bell, fits into this category too. The word *knack* "special skill" is a descendant of Middle English *krak* "sharp blow", a cognate of the Modern German verb *knacken* "crack". The English word *knap* also comes from striking, in this case the action of breaking flakes off minerals such as flint to shape them. In some dialects *knap* means "bite off, eat" and from this we get the related term *knapsack*, "backpack for food, clothes and other supplies", as in the English version of the German song *Der fröhliche Wanderer* (*The Happy Wanderer*) featuring "my knapsack on my back". This use of *knap* is echoed by *snap*, which means not only "break off" but also "light meal, snack" in many British dialects (see chapter 6).

Other kn- words which at first glance seem to have unrelated meanings come from common pinching origins. Many objects that are pinched or pummelled into shape end up being kneaded into a ball or knocked into a knobbly form of some description. Hence, we can find German *Knödel*, Swedish *knödel* and Czech *knedlik* all meaning "dumpling". The ancient Proto-Indo-European root *gen-* "squeeze, ball up, pinch" is the source of *knock* and *knead*. Amazingly, *gen-* is also thought to be the source for *knight*, via Old English *cniht* "boy, youth"; *knave*, via Old English *cnafa* "boy, youth, servant" and *knife* via Old English *cnif* "knife". All these words diverged from their common ancestor *gen-* through metaphorical leaps resulting in dramatic sense evolution many centuries ago.

29.   kw- (qu-) quaking and quivering

Right as an aspen lefe she gan to quake.

Geoffrey Chaucer, *Troilus and Criseyde*

Kw- words are all *aquiver*; they have a shaky, trembling quality. These words are dynamic and pulsating, *quirky* and *quaking*. Other related words are more inclined to *quash* any undue agitation, *quenching* thirst, *quelling* uprisings or subduing any stirred-up sentiment from *quarrelsome* elements in society.

Although now written with a consonant and a vowel as **qu-**, this spelling usually has a /kw/ sound, and is thus made up of two consonants. The letter *q* is still the most seldom used of all English letters with the exception of *z*, but in the Old English period it was even more of a rarity, as the sound /kw/ was usually represented by the letters *cw-*, as in *cwen* "queen", *becweþan* "bequeath" and *cweorn* "quern". However, in the Middle English period, English began using *q* more frequently due to the massive influence of French, which used it much more. *Q* took on two sounds /kw/ and /k/, the latter sound often being spelt *qu-* in French, as in *plaque* [plæk], *clique* [kliːk] and *cheque* [tʃek], which English has borrowed from that language. In this chapter, we will concentrate on words where qu- represents a /kw/ cluster.

From the time of their emergence in 17th century England, the *Quakers* were often seen as quarrelsome or blasphemous and a threat to the social order. Dissenting Protestants, the Quakers are said to have got their name because they bade people to "tremble in the way of the Lord". *Quake* goes back to the Old English *cwacian* and prior to that to Proto-Germanic **kwakona* "shake, swing, tremble", which also influenced the onomatopoeic *quack* and cognates such as German *quaken* "croak, quack" and Danish *kvække* "croak, ribbit". *Quaver*, frequentative of the obsolete *quave* "tremble", *quetch/quitch* "stir, shake, flinch" and possibly *quail* can also be shakily traced back to "shaking" roots. (In the course of researching the etymology of *quail*, I was interested to discover that the *California quail* – a good-looking bird with an extravagant curving *quiff* – is *Colin de Californie* in French, and a most elegant fowl. This is a step up from the usual group of losers and deadbeats named *Colin* in the literary/TV stock character catalogue. It's also certainly a little more exotic than the run of the mill French *colin* "hake".)

Quiver is probably related to both *quaver* and *quick* in its "rapid trembling" sense, as are its trembly Modern German cognates *quabbeln* "wobble" and *quabbelnder* "wobbly pudding, blancmange". *Quagmire* is a pleonasm (see chapter 17) made up of two words meaning "bog": *quag* – a variant of Middle English *quabbe*, plus *mire* – from Old Norse *myrr*. *Quag/quabbe* goes back to Old English **cwabba* "shake, tremble like a flabby soft thing" or indeed, like a bog. *Kwab*, a contemporary Dutch word meaning "blubbery soft mass or tissue", is clearly related to this. Another link is the rare English word *quab* (also *squab*) denoting an "unfledged bird" especially a fat young dove or pigeon.

On the autocratic side of this cluster, *quash* can also be traced back to a "shaking" ancestor, as it comes from Old French *quasser* "smash, break" from Latin *quatio* "shake, agitate, harass" and all the way back to the Proto-Indo-European root **kwet-* "shake". On this side of qu-, the shaking is causative – these qu- words are shaking someone else. Further qu- suppression comes with *quench*, *quell* and *qualm*, all of which have attested Old English cw- equivalents: *cwencan* "extinguish", *cwellan* "kill" and *cwealm* "death, murder, plague". *Cwencan* is an example of a causative form which has endured (as *quench*), while the non-causative partner *cwincan* "go out, be extinguished" has not survived – we have *drink* with *drench*, but no *quink* with *quench*. The sense development of *qualm* "misgiving, feeling of unease or sickness" is not clear, although the connecting notion of "fit of sickness" from the "plague" sense of *cwealm* is a possibility, as is influence from Dutch *kwalm* or German *Qualm*, which now mean "steam, mist," but earlier meant "daze, bemusement".

We noted in chapter 2 that the PIE form **kwo-*, the stem of relative and interrogative pronouns throughout the Indo-European world is the origin of *who, which, what, why, where, when* and *how*. As such, it is the source of a vast number of Latin *question* forms, including Latin *quis/quid*, which, depending on context, can be "in what respect", "what", "who", "how", or "why,"; *qua* "where, in what direction, which way"; and *qui/quae/quod* "who, which" and thence numerous words with the qu-cluster which English has since borrowed. English has also invented words by combining Latin forms with existing English words, for instance, by putting the Latin *quando* "when" together with the Middle English *wandreth* "plight, difficulty, trouble" to produce the *quasi*-Latin form *quandary*.

Some examples of qu- words borrowed from Latin include *quibble*, a derivative of *quibus*, the ablative and dative plural form of *quis*; *quorum*, "minimum number of members present for a valid vote to be cast", is the genitive plural form of *qui*; and *quip*, "sarcastic rejoinder", comes from *quippe* "indeed", from *quid*. The English word *quid*, a colloquial term for "pound, guinea", derives from the Latin phrase *quid pro quo* "this for that", used in exchanging money for goods and services. *Qualis* "what kind" gives us *quality* and *qualify*, *quantus* "how much" gives us *quantum* and *quantity* and *quot* "which, how many" gives us *quota* and *quotidian* – from *quot* and *dies* "days" – How many days do you do something in a quotidian life? "Every day".

Quick is dynamic, nimble and vigorous. *Cwic* in the Old English period had the main meaning of "alive" and figuratively "swift", a double sense which is captured by *lively* today. However, *cwic* was more often paired with "dead" than with the ancestors of "slow" in the Old English period, as with the phrase "*cwicum* and *deadum*" which appears in Alfred the Great's ninth century translation of Pope Gregory's *Liber Regulae Pastoralis*, commonly known in English as *Pastoral Care*. This sense is maintained in phrases like *cut to the quick* and *stung to the quick*, where *quick* refers to the most vital, sensitive area of feeling. It is often used in relation to the flesh beneath the fingernail, the level of living tissue under the dead, insensitive nail. *Quick* also had the idea of shifting, flowing movement, hence *quicksand* – which will rapidly submerge anything that presses on top of it, *quicksilver* "living silver" (mercury) because of its constant liquid movement, *quicklime* "living lime" (calcium oxide) and the Old English *cwicfyr* "living fire" (sulphur).

The word *quick* comes from Proto-Germanic **kwikwaz* and ultimately PIE **gwey-* "to live", still recognisable in modern Lithuanian **gyvas* "alive". Descendants of **gwey-* in Indo-European language groups are still numerous, but the majority have stuck with the "living" sense of the root: Greek βίος (*víos*), Old Church Slavonic животъ (*životu*), Latin *vita* and Sanskrit जीवित (*jivita*) all mean "life", for example. On the other hand, most Germanic descendants of **gwey-* now mean "quick". Among the many modern Germanic cognates, Dutch *kwiek*, Swedish *kvick* and Icelandic and Faroese *kvikur*, all mean "quick" in the "fast" sense.

A final qu- word of phonosemantic interest is the coinage *quisling*, to mean "traitor". Vidkun Quisling was the leader of the Nasjonal Samling, a Norwegian fascist party modelled on the German Nazi Party prior to World War II. He attempted to garner support for the occupying Germans after their invasion of Norway in 1940 and served as the country's Minister-President from 1942-45 in the collaborationist pro-Nazi puppet government. The London

Star of 10 July 1940 stated that "the Norwegian traitor was cursed with a name which by its very sound conveyed all the odious, greasy wickedness of the man", while an editorial in *The Times* from 19 April 1940 entitled *"Quislings everywhere"* had gone much further:

> Major Quisling has added a new word to the English language. To writers, the word Quisling is a gift from the gods. If they had been ordered to invent a new word for "traitor", and given carte blanche with the alphabet, they could hardly have hit upon a more brilliant combination of letters. Aurally it contrives to suggest something at once slippery and tortuous. Visually it has the supreme merit of beginning with a Q, which (with one august exception) has long seemed to the British mind to be a crooked, uncertain and slightly disreputable letter, suggestive of the questionable, the querulous, the quavering of quaking quagmires and quivering quicksands, of quibbles and quarrels, of queasiness, quackery, qualms and Quilp.

Here both newspapers overtly refer to the idea of phonosemantic meaning, although *The Times* covers its back with its "one august exception" – the Queen. Charles Dickens is again on hand with the last entry in *The Times* article with *Quilp* – Daniel Quilp, a vicious, cantankerous dwarf, is the phonosemantically appropriate villain of his novel *The Old Curiosity Shop*.

30.   fr- friction, fractures and freezing

Free societies ... are societies in motion, and with motion comes tension, dissent, friction. Free people strike sparks, and those sparks are the best evidence of freedom's existence.

Salman Rushdie

Although **fr-** is quite common, it is one of the least phonosemantically coherent clusters: fr- can *fray, free, fracture,* and *freeze* and on the surface, seems as if it has a number of unconnected phonesthemes. Having said this, some surprising links can be traced by looking at etymological relationships and the tendency of fr- words to evolve and go off in different directions. Some fr- words also show evidence of the sound changes outlined by Jacob Grimm (see chapter 3), where Germanic br- has its equivalent in Latin fr-. This is the case with *fraternal, fraternity* and *friar*, which are derived from Latin *fräter* "brother", (and French *frère*). *Frater* comes from the PIE root **bhrater-* "brother", whose descendants include Sanskrit भ्रातृ (*bhratr*), Russian брат (*brat*) German *Bruder*, Persian برادر (barâdar), and Welsh *brawd*, none of which have gone so far from the PIE root.

A similar sound progression explains the correlation between Germanic *breaking* br- words (see chapter 5) and the Italic *fracturing* fr- words which comprise the largest phonestheme with the fr-cluster. Both groups stem from the PIE root **bhreu-* "break", which came to Gothic as *brikan*, but to Latin as *frangere* "break into pieces, shatter". From *frangere* and its descendants, English has borrowed *fracture, fractious, fragment, fraction, fracas, infringe,* and *fragile*, along with *fragile*'s doublet from French, *frail*. It is also very current as the source of *fracking*, or *hydraulic fracturing*. In the natural world, this root has given us the plant *saxifrage* "stone-breaker", so-called either because it grows in rock crevices, or because it has been used in medicine to dissolve gallstones; and the *ossifrage* "bone-breaker", a bird which gets its name because its diet is almost exclusively made up of the bone marrow of carrion. It is now more commonly known as the lammergeier or bearded vulture, but the name *ossifrage* lives on in *osprey*, which though an entirely different bird, is a conflation of *ossifrage* and the Anglo-Norman *ospriet*, from Medieval Latin *avis prede* "bird of prey".

PIE *bhreyh* "cut", is probably a related root and has given English a number of crumbly, *friable* words via Latin *friare* "rub, break into small pieces". These include *frayed*, *frazzle*, *fret*, *frivolous*, *friction* and possibly *fry* "young fish". But that's *small fry*. A French derivative of *friare* is *frotter* "rub", from which we have borrowed, to our prudish Anglo-Saxon horror, the highly questionable *frottage*. Here, the *frisky* "French" reputation for sexual adventure and *fricasseeing* goes before them – but I'm not *frigging* going there! Cognates of *friare* include Russian бpumь (*brit'*) "shave" and Persian بريدن (*boridan*) "cut".

The fr- cluster also has a large number of words which deal with the *frilly*. Aside from *frivolous* and *frayed*, we have *freckle*, *frizzy*, *fringe*, *frock*, *fritter*, *frond*, *froth*, *fraise* "ruff" and delicate *fretwork*. Although these words appear to have no common etymology, it is curious that frayed fibres, fronds, fringes and frills all conjure up similar imagery of wispy threads and the insubstantial. There may be some leakage at play here from the *flyaway* aspects of the fl-cluster (see chapter 3), although the influence of French *friser* "curl, graze, braid", and its Frankish forebear *fris* "curl" is another candidate.

Of course, the *French* got their name from the Germanic *Franks* who conquered Gaul in the 5th and 6th century CE, and the connection between *Franks*, *friends* and *freedom* goes to the heart of the fr- cluster. *Friend* and *free* have both been traced to PIE **preya-* "dear, beloved". Descendants include Polish *przyjaciel* "friend", Bulgarian *приятел* (*prijátel*) "friend" and Sanskrit प्रीणाति (*prinati*) "to please; to love". In Germanic descendants of **preya-* there is a connecting concept between words meaning "friend" and "free". This seems to stem from the notion that beloved members of the same clan were both friends and free, not in bondage, unlike captives, serfs or slaves attached to the tribe. A comparable idea exists with Latin *liberi* "free people and "children of a family", and with the idea of the Frankish tribes as freemen of the same clan (see box below).

The Franks were a confederation of Germanic tribes who controlled most of Western Europe at their height. From 800 CE with the coronation of Charlemagne as Holy Roman Emperor, their legitimacy was established as heirs to the emperors of the Western Roman Empire. They consolidated their possessions and are seen as the founding fathers of many of the states of Western Europe, but are particularly associated with the state to which they gave their name, *France*, or in German, *Frankreich* "realm of the Franks". They are named after their weapon of choice the Proto-Germanic **frankô* "javelin, spear", (OE *franca*), though the related **frankaz* "wild, fierce", (OE *fræc*) may also be relevant.

Other fr- words can be traced back to the Franks. Under Frankish rule in Gaul, only the Franks were free of taxation. Our word *frank* "free, liberal" comes from the Franks privileged status as freemen of the conquering class. From this root the monetary *franc* was obtained, as was the medieval *franklin* "landowner of free, but not noble birth", of the class below the gentry in feudal society. Similarly, the Eastern French region of *Franche Comté* (the Free County of Burgundy) takes its name from its sovereign's *Free Count* (*Freigraf*), a reference to his tax-exempt status, while *franking* a letter will mean that there is free postage. In most countries, all adults (who are not *disenfranchised*) now have the *franchise*, or right to vote. This term has narrowed from "freedom from servitude" to "privileged status, exclusive right" and then to "freedom to vote" and "exclusive authority to buy and sell". Finally, we have borrowed *frankincense* from Old French too – *franc encense* "noble incense" designated incense of the highest quality.

Germanic pairs for "free" and "friend" include Dutch *vrij* and *vriend*, West Frisian *frij* and *freon* and German *frei* and *Freund*. North Germanic languages show the link with the clan more closely, as their words with similar forms to *friend* mean "kinsman, male relative", e.g. Icelandic *frændi*, Danish *frænde* and Swedish *frände*. Many Germanic words for "peace" also have the same roots as those for "free". For example, there is Norwegian *fred*, German *Friede* – the source of *Frederick* "peace-rule" and *Godfrey* "the peace of God" – and Icelandic *friður*. The English equivalent is *frith* "peace, security", which though now practically obsolete, is still used by neo-pagans in Heathenry and featured in Richard Adams's *Watership Down* in "Lord Frith", sun-god and creator of the universe in the rabbits' creation myth. Related is Old Norse *Frigg* "beloved, loving; wife", the wife of Odin, queen of heaven and goddess of married love. *Frigg* gives us *Friday* – Old English *frigedæg* and thus an approximate Germanic translation of the Latin *dies Veneris* "day of Venus", as in Italian *venerdì*, Spanish *viernes* and French *vendredi*.

Surprisingly, *afraid* (Middle English *affrayed*) comes from the same PIE root as all these loving, friendly words. It is derived from Old French *esfreer*, which is made up of the prefix *es-* "separation from" and *freer* "secure the peace" – hence, "to separate from peace" becomes "to scare, make fearful". *Esfreer* was borrowed as the verb *affray*, which now only exists as a noun meaning "disturbance". The past participle of the obsolete verb eventually evolved from *affrayed* to *afraid*, perhaps due to conflation with *afeared*. Although *fear*, *fright*, *frenzy*, *fret* and *fraught* all seem to fit the mould of a fearful fr- phonestheme, none of them have been proven to have common etymological origins.

Two more minor phonosemantic themes can be perceived from the smorgasbord of the fr- cluster. The first is to do with the cold when the temperature is a little too chilly for *alfresco dining*, or even going outside. Imagine you have been sent out to play in the *frigid*, skin-searing winds from Norway in a small Northern English town on the North Sea coast, having been forced by your parents to "get some *fresh* air" – I'm not bitter, but the wind was. At this point, you may experience a little *frisson* (French "shiver") from the *freezing* cold although it could well just be dread. It may well feel as if you have just walked into a *freezer*, or, if you find a sheltered spot (there aren't any), as if you are merely sitting inside a *fridge*, as eloquently expressed by legendary Geordie songwriter Ronnie Lambert in *Coming Home Newcastle,* his *magnum opus*:

> It's cold up there it summer
> It's like sitting inside a fridge
> But I wish I was on the Quayside
> Looking at the old Tyne Bridge.

If you are lucky, you might be summoned back inside before the onset of *frostbite*. *Frost* and *freeze* can be traced back to PIE *preus-* "to freeze", and Germanic cognates look very familiar: Danish *frost* and *fryse*, German *Frost* and *frieren*, and Dutch *vorst* and *vriezen*. Yet, extremes meet in *preus-* as it also means "burn", as in Latin *pruna* "live coal", Albanian *prush* "ember", and in *prurient* "burning" curiosity. In fact, burning and freezing are not as far apart as they may appear. We often talk about the "burning sensation" of snow, and the effects of frostbite and burns on the body are very similar, and even described with the same terminology; first degree, second degree burns/frostbite etc. Other words that add to the freezing fr- group are derived from the Latin word for "cold", *frigidus.* These include *refrigeration, frisson, frigid* and French *froid* "cold", which gives us the chill in relations that is *froideur.*

Finally, we have a *fruity* little fr- phonestheme which comes from PIE **bhrug-* "enjoy" and has evolved in different directions. The Latin descendant of this root is *fruor* "enjoy" with its derived noun *fructus* "enjoyment, produce, fruit". The latter is the ancestor of *fruit, fructose, fructify, usufruct, frugal* and *tutti-frutti,* as well as French *froment* "wheat". The meaning of *fruit* has narrowed over time from "products and profits of the soil" to its modern meaning where it partners *vegetables. Frugal,* too, has developed dramatically, initially being akin to *fruitful.* The sense development seems to have been from "successful" to "profitable" to "useful" to "economical" and thus "sparing, thrifty". The Old English descendant of **bhrug-* was *brucan* "enjoy, eat, use", which has become *brook* "endure" through another chain of sense development from "use to eat" to "be able to digest" and then to "tolerate". German *brauchen* "need" and Dutch *bruiken* "use" are cognates.

31.   wr- wriggling and wrangling

That was a way of putting it – not very satisfactory:
A periphrastic study in a worn-out poetical fashion,
Leaving one still with the intolerable wrestle
With words and meanings.

T.S Eliot, *East Coker* from *The Four Quartets*

The **wr-** cluster twists and *writhes*, its words *wrap* themselves tight, *wringing* the life out of the poor *wretches* who incur their *wrath*. Although the *w* of the cluster used to be pronounced, wr- has been pronounced /r/ for the best part of four hundred years. Even so, it has a clear and distinct identity with its phonosemantic meaning implying distortion or twisting. The sound symbolism of words beginning with the wr- cluster can also be followed very neatly, because the vast majority of these words emanate from a single origin, the Proto-Indo-European root **wer³-* "turn, bend".

*Wer³- is a mega-root whose influence extends into thousands of words across Indo-European languages. Sanskrit has वृत् (*vartate*) "turn", Lithuanian has *virsti* "turn into, become", and Russian has вертеть (*vertet'*) "rotate, turn, twist". The Latin descendant is *vertere* "turn", source of numerous English borrowings, including *verse, version, vertebra, versus, versatile, universe, divert, convert, avert* etc. **Wer³-* is also the origin of the suffix *–ward*, from Old English *–weard* (spelt *–weardes* in the masculine or neuter genitive singular), which means "turned in the direction of", i.e. "toward(s)". This suffix makes its *wayward* presence felt in *forwards* and *backwards, windward* and *leeward*, and *awkward*, literally "in the

wrong direction" from *awk* "out of order, perverse" (see chapter 14 for more on this suffix). In the meantime, *onwards* and *upwards*!

That famous wriggler, the *worm,* from Old English *wyrm* "worm, snake, dragon" also comes from the **wer³-* root. It has its Latin cognate in *vermis* "worm", the base of *vermicelli*, literally "little worms". *Vermilion*, the scarlet colour similar to the dye made from the *Kermes vermilio* Mediterranean scale insect is also from this origin. Latin *vermis* is also the source of *vermin*, which was originally used to denote worms and snakes, before being used for any objectionable creatures, while its colloquial version, *varmint*, is a later addition to the language. The word *vermouth* comes from the French pronunciation of German *Wermut* "wormwood", which was traditionally used to fortify the wine base of vermouth, as well as in the manufacture of absinthe, beloved beverage of bohemians, poseurs and hopeless drunks.

The *wriggling* source PIE root **wer³-* "turn, bend" spawned a wealth of twisting daughter roots, all containing the wr- cluster or these two consonants with an intervening vowel. One such root is **wert-* "turn, wind". In Germanic languages, this has developed into words for "become", as in Old Norse *verða*, Dutch *worden* and the archaic English verb *worth*, still found in the expression *woe worth the day*. German *werden* is both "become" and the auxiliary verb for the future, combining what will befall us with the notion of "the twists and turns of fate". This is echoed in Old English *weorþan* "happen" and *wyrd* "that which happens, chance, destiny, fortune; the Fates". The three Fates or Norns are the goddesses of human destiny, and were known in Scots as the *weird sisters*. Shakespeare borrowed this term for the three witches in *Macbeth*, from which the "odd, uncanny, abnormal" idea of *weird* became prevalent. **Wert-* is also the likely ancestor of *Wurst*, "sausage" and famed staple in the diet of our German cousins. As well as being turned and twisted, *Würste* have a distinctly worm-like appearance.

The notion that *straight* and *right* = "good" and *crooked* and *left* = "bad" is widespread across Indo-European languages. Latin, for example has the contrast between *pravus* "crooked, wicked", source of *depraved*, and its antonym *rectus* "straight, right", from which English has *rectitude*, *correct*, *direct* and *rectify*. Similarly, Latin *tortus* "twisted, tormented" gave French *tort* "fault, error", and Catalan *tort* "crooked, askew", not to mention English legal *torts*, as well as *torture*, *torque* and *torch*, which was formerly a twisted roll of *tow* (flax or hemp prepared for spinning) that would be lit. Proto-Germanic **wrangaz* "twisted, warped, wretched" gives English *wrong*, Danish *vrang* "crooked, wrong" and Dutch *wrang* "bitter, tart", literally "something sour; that which distorts in the mouth".

Many languages still equate the left and the twisted with undesirable traits such as dishonesty, weakness, awkwardness, and all too graphically, cack-handedness. This has been reinforced by cultural prejudice against left-handedness, children being forced to use their right hands for writing, eating and other tasks they would naturally perform with the left. Hence, Old English distinguishes between the *riht* – the right and just – and the *lyft/left* – the weak and foolish.

The idea that the left signifies bad luck is also present in the use of Greek, Roman and Etruscan augury, whereby fortune-telling was conducted by observing the auspices, usually the flight of birds. Birds which appeared to the right foretold good fortune, *auspicious* events, whereas birds flying by on the left gave *sinister* omens, i.e. "evil" or "unlucky". Latin and French words for right and left have added further to our vocabulary. Latin *dexter* "skilful, right, proper" comes from the Latin word for right, and from this we now have the adjective *dexterous* (manually skilful) and the noun *dexterity* (skilfulness). If you can use both hands equally well, you are not bi-handed but are *ambidextrous* (doubly skilful) that is, you have two right hands!

Borrowings from French include the word for left, *gauche*, which in English means "awkward and clumsy". Related to this is the adjective *gawky*, meaning "ungainly and socially inept". This comes from *gawk*, Yorkshire dialect for "left hand", possibly from *gaulick* – the mistrusted "Gaulish", that is, French hand, and therefore both "gauche" and "sinister"! A synonym for *gauche* is *maladroit*, which means "badly-skilled", literally, "not right". *Adroit*, though, from *à droit* "according to the right" is another synonym for *dexterous*, or *skilful*.

Another daughter root of **wer³-* has been reconstructed as **wreit-* "turn, twist", which produced *writhe*, *wreath* and *wrath* (with its archaic *wroth* variant). *Wrath* comes to us via Old English *wraþ* "angry, irate", but is literally "tormented, twisted". Germanic cognates include Danish *vred* "angry", Icelandic *reiður* "angry" and Dutch *wreed* "cruel". A parallel root is thought to be **wreik-* "turn, wrap", which is the ancestor of *wrest*, its frequentative *wrestle*, and its non-standard form *wrassle*, as well as *wriggle* and that great turning joint, the *wrist*. Another descendant of **wreik-* is *wry*, whose sense has evolved somewhat to mean "dry, sardonic", but was formerly more commonly used for "twisted to one side, distorted" and was a verb meaning "contort, twist". This sense is preserved in the adverb *awry* "crooked, askew" and in the *wryneck,* a type of woodpecker that can twist its neck almost 180 degrees.

*Wergh- "turn, bind, squeeze", is yet another member of the *warped *wer³-* family of PIE roots, and gave Old English *wyrgan* "strangle, throttle". This gradually morphed in spelling and sense, passing through forms that meant "choke" and "harass" before arriving at the Modern English spelling and meaning, *worry*. This root's nasalised form, **wrengh-* is the predecessor of *wring*, *wrangle*, *wrinkle*, *wrench* and *wrong*, which originally meant "bent, crooked", and so "not right". Other European descendants of this PIE root include French *ride* "wrinkle" and its derivative *rideau* "curtain", from the notion of "plaited (or wrinkled) cloth", German *ringan* "wrestle, struggle", Old Norse *riða* "to wind", and Dutch *wringen* "wring, writhe, twist".

Most other English wr- words come from two possibly related PIE roots: **wreg-* "push, shove, drive" and **werg-* "do, make". The former is the source of *wrack*, *wreck* and *wreak*, as well as *wretch* –

literally "one who is driven out, exile". Interestingly, French *garçon* "servant, waiter, boy", can be traced to the same origin as *wretch*, which tells us a lot about historical attitudes towards the servant classes! *Garçon* is a French borrowing from Frankish or another Germanic source. Among the other descendants of **wreg-* are Gothic *wrikan* "persecute", German *rächen* "avenge" and the Slavic word враг (*vrag*), which in Bulgarian and Russian means "enemy" but in Serbo-Croat means "devil". The Latin descendant of **wreg-* is *urgere* "push forward, drive", from which we have derived *urge* and *urgent*.

Some sources also connect *urgere* to the PIE **werg-* root, which may ultimately be **wreg-* in a metathesised guise (see chapter 4), as people are driven to act, make or do things. The verb *work* with its archaic past participle *wrought* and personal noun *wright* are certainly traceable to the **werg-* root. Greek ἔργον (*ergon*) "work" is a cognate which has passed on the *ergo-* prefix to English, along with a host of derived forms, of which *energy*, *organ*, *orgy*, *allergy* and *argon* are just a few.

32.   waifs and strays

They have been at a great feast of languages, and stolen the scraps.

William Shakespeare, *Love's Labour's Lost (Act 5, Scene 1)*

There are a few rarer consonant clusters which crop up fleetingly in Modern English. These may be relics of clusters more frequent in the past or quirkily humorous clusters, which are often onomatopoeic, e.g. the **vr-** of *vroom*, or the whispered (and vowelless) *psst*, or else used only in interjections e.g. the /pʃ/ of *pshaw* or the frankly ridiculous /fw/ of sexual desire present in *phwoar*. **Gw-** makes the odd appearance in a few names of Brythonic origin – *Gwendoline*, *Gwyn* and *Gwynedd* – as well as borrowings such as *guano* and *guava* from American indigenous languages via Spanish. **Vl-** comes up occasionally too, through Slavic names such as *Vladimir* and *Vladka*, not to mention the recent appearance of the blend *vlog*, from *video + blog*.

As we have seen, the seventeenth century saw the reduction of **kn-** to /n/ and **wr-** to /r/. **Gn-** was reduced to /n/ at around the same time. All three of these clusters preserve their older spellings, but their pronunciation has been reduced to a single consonant sound, apart from in a few northern and insular Scottish dialects, such as the Shetland Islands where a distinction remains.

Other clusters have been borrowed from other languages, but in most cases, the pronunciation has been modified or reduced so that the loan word loses its unfamiliar cluster and is simplified to correspond to a commoner sound in English. Hence, the initial /p/ sounds of French *pneumatic* and Greek *psychopath* are lost to become [njuːmætɪk] and [saɪkəʊpæθ] respectively. Similarly, the

/ks/ of *xylophone* becomes /z/ and *pterodactyls* make people terrified rather than pterrified.

However, some unusual clusters in loan words have been retained, especially those from Latinised Greek sources. The **sph-** of *sphere*, *sphinx* and *sphincter* has maintained a /sf/ sound, and there is even a **sphr-** /sfr/ cluster in *sphragistics*, the study of seals and signet rings. Other rare clusters include **scl-** /skl/ in *sclerosis*, hardening of the arteries, **sth-** /sθ/ in *sthenic*, having an excessive level of vigour or strength, **thl-** /θl/ in *thlipsis*, the constriction of blood vessels from an external source, and the **tm-** of *tmesis*, the separation of parts of a word or phrase by other intervening words. (Tmesis may be an uncommon word, but you can find it everyfreakingwhere.) There are also several one-off clusters in other borrowings, such as the **bw-** in *bwana* "master" (from Swahili), **sv-** in *svelte* (from Italian via French), **schw-** in *schwa* (from Hebrew via German), **nw-** in *noire*, **pw-** in *puissance* and **vw-** in some pronunciations of *voyeur* (all from French), **zl-** in *zloty* (from Polish) and **kv-** in *kvetch* "endless whiner, moaner" (from Yiddish) etc.

In the Late Middle English and Early Modern English period, there was a trend for letters to be inserted into words to reflect their etymology. However, this was done in a rather haphazard manner and often letters were added in error. This process has given English some of its most unlikely letter combinations. One example of this is the *p* of *ptarmigan*, added by association with the Greek word πτερόν (*pterón*) "wing", despite being borrowed from Scottish Gaelic *tarmachan*. The most famous lexicographer of English, Samuel Johnson, was also guilty of this, changing the spelling of the Middle English verb *aken* to *ache*, believing it came from Greek ἄχος (*ákhos*) "pain" rather than its actual derivation from Proto-Germanic **akiz* "ache, pain, evil". In the same way, the erroneous late 16th century insertion of *s* in *island* is due to association with the similar, but unrelated term *isle*, ultimately from Latin *insula*.

Supposed Latin origins were usually responsible for this enthusiastic addition of superfluous letters. The c of *scissors* and *scythe* was added in the mistaken belief that both words were derived from Latin *scissor* "carver, cutter" and *scindere* "split, cut". *Scissors* (Middle English *sisoures*) actually comes from Latin *caesus*, the past participle of *caedere* "cut" via Old French *cisoires* "shears", while *scythe* (Middle English *sithe, sythe*) is a descendant of Old English sīðe "sickle" and not from Latin at all! *C* was also added to *scent* (previously *sent*), and *victuals* (previously *vitaylle*) as well as to Middle English *parfit* and *verdit* to produce *perfect* and *verdict*, with the *c* now pronounced in the latter two cases.

Other spurious changes included *ancor* to *anchor* (borrowed from Latin *ancora* in the Old English period) and *erbe* to *herb* (borrowed from Old French *erbe*, though originally from Latin *herba*). Adding to the confusion is the question of whether or not to pronounce the new letters – the Americans tend not to pronounce the *h* of *herb*, while it is generally pronounced in British English. The newly-acquired *d* of *adventure* and the *l* of *fault*, *vault* and *assault* are all now pronounced, but the *b* of *doubt* and *debt* stays resolutely silent.

The **gn-** cluster does seem to have some phonosemantic meaning in English, with several words relating to biting or nibbling, including the Germanic forms *gnaw*, *gnash* and *gnat*, etymologically "biting insect". The jaw is obviously important for a good gnaw, and English has borrowed the adjective *gnathic* and *gnathion*, the lowest point on the lower jaw, from the Greek for "jaw" γνάθος (*gnathos*). Away from biting, the Ancient Greek gn-form γνωστικός (*gnostikos*) "relating to knowledge" has given us *gnostic*, *diagnosis* and *gnomic*, while *gnarly* and *gnocchi* are related to the knobbly forms of the kn- cluster (see chapter 28). For example, *knurled* is the forerunner of *gnarled*, meaning "knotted, twisted", and was used by Shakespeare to refer to an oak in *Measure for Measure*:

Thou rather with thy sharp and sulphurous bolt
Split'st the unwedgeable and gnarled oak
Than the soft myrtle.

It is thought that this single use in Shakespeare brought this previously rare word into more common use in the 19th century, which shows the lasting influence of the Bard. Gn- is more widespread in other languages. Swedish, for example, has a number of different onomatopoeic gn- noises – *gnägga* "neigh", *gnälla* "whine, squeak", *gnissla* "creak, squeak" – as well as a phonestheme related to different ways of talking, e.g. *gnat* "nagging", *gnola* "hum" and *gnabb* "bickering" (Abelin, 1999).

Unlike gn-, the **dw-** cluster seems to have little in the way of a unifying theme, largely because words currently with an initial dw- come from very different sources and are the result of complex phonetic and semantic changes. For example, *dwell* is a descendant of Proto-Germanic *dwelan* "go astray", but shifted sense dramatically. Old English *dwellan* "deceive" became Middle English *dwellen* "stun, perplex", then "hinder, delay". This shifted again later in the Middle English period to "linger" as is still found when we *dwell on* something. The semantic jump from "linger" to "abide" and then "reside" is no longer so drastic. Smallness is perhaps a connection between the archaic and dialectal form *dwine* "wither, pine away, vanish" and its familiar frequentative form *dwindle*, and *dwarf*, but the two are not etymologically related, and it seems a bit of a stretch. Finally, *dweeb* "socially inept loser" is a US variant of *feeb*, a contraction of *feeble-minded*. As we noted in chapter 9, this has since been accorded the backronym **D**im-**W**itted **E**astern-**E**ducated **B**oor attacking the stereotypical Ivy League graduate.

As for **thw-** only two words are really current in modern usage: *thwack* and *thwart*. The former has been influenced by *whack*, but is a separate word with an etymology that has been traced back to Old English *þaccian* "pat, stroke, touch" and thus **tag-*, a PIE root which is the ancestor of Latin *tangere* "touch" and so *tango*, *tangent*, *tangible* and *tactile*. The latter is a distant relative of *twist* and *twirl* from PIE **terkw-* "twist, wind" (see chapter 14), and has its Old English form in *þweorh* "transverse, cross, contrary to" and cognates in English *queer*, Danish *tvær* "sulky, sullen" and Dutch *dwars* "diagonal, in a contrary direction to".

Conclusion

It is always delightful when a great and beautiful idea proves to be consonant with reality.

Albert Einstein

From what we have seen in the chapters of *Sl- is for Sleaze but Sn- is for Sneeze!* the evidence all points towards consonant clusters meaning something in and of themselves. Of course, onomatopoeia plays a significant part, with a few combinations, wh- and spl- in particular, which we could justly label as onomatopoeic clusters. Yet, this only goes so far: most of the clusters we have looked at are not obviously onomatopoeic, but the entrenched phonosemantic meaning is clear to see. The reason *why* sl- is a *sleazy slapper* and sn- is a *sneezing snoot* is more difficult to fathom. Why is a frog called a frog? Apparently, *frog* can be traced back to Proto-Germanic *fraubaz* and from there to Proto-Indo-European **prew-* "jump, hop", so a frog is, logically enough, "a hopper". But why does **prew-* mean "hop"? We are back to where we started.

Nonetheless, there does seem to be a link between the perceived softness or harshness of consonants and phonosemantic meaning, and this can be seen more clearly when the consonants are combined in clusters. The most common second elements of English consonant clusters are the liquid consonants *l* and *r*. As might be expected, there appears to be a fundamental difference between clusters with the mellifluous *l* and the rasping *r*. We have found that clusters with –*l* tend to be smooth, whereas –*r* clusters are associated with roughness. This goes way beyond onomatopoeia and is integral to the phonosemantics of the clusters themselves. We can see this by comparing phonesthemes: gl-

glides, while gr- grinds; fl- flows, while fr- frays; or simply by comparing word pairs where only the liquid consonant is different. If we make the contrast between *glaze* and *graze*, *bloom* and *broom*, and *cloak* and *croak*, the difference in smoothness and roughness is clear in each case.

We have also observed another interesting facet of the phonosemantics of consonant clusters in the way that three-part clusters narrow the focus and add specifics to their "mother" two-part clusters. St- is *upstanding*, *steadfast* and *stiff*; str- takes this stiffness and *stretches* it out, *straining* to make it into a *strap* or a *string*. Sp- *spits* outwards in an explosive jet, but spr- takes this burst of energy and *sprays* it in all directions, *spreading* the wealth. Sc- *scans* and has two-dimensional *scope*; scr- *scrapes*, *scrawls* and *scrambles* across this 2D expanse.

Other connections between cluster meanings stem from changes in pronunciation or due to extensive borrowing from other languages. The *scrawny* scr- with its *scrumpled scraps* differs only from the *shrivelled* shr- with its *shrunken shreds* by an unpalatalised Viking /sk/ as opposed to a palatalised Anglo-Saxon /ʃ/. Similarly, the *flames* and *flowers* of fl- are separated from the *blazes* and *blooms* of bl- owing to different pronunciations arising after Germanic and Italic languages diverged from a common ancestor. Still on fl-, its Old English *folds* and *flatness* find their parallel in the borrowed Romance *pleats* and *plains* that lie at the heart of the pl-cluster. Yet somehow, even with all these developments, the distinct meanings behind the clusters remain tangible.

The meaning within our consonant clusters goes back thousands of years to our Proto-Indo-European forebears and the roots of the ancient language or languages that they used. These roots have been altered and added to, but the consonant clusters that they produced have proved to be enduring and significant. These base meanings have been supplemented with the coining of new words, existing words converging around a theme by analogy, and by English's insatiable desire to borrow words from around the world. I believe that new and incoming words are accepted more readily when they match the underlying themes that are built-in to the existing words, morphemes, clusters and letters of the language. This reinforces the strength of the phonesthemes and gives all of us the sense that a certain combination of letters just "feels right". This is the essence of sound symbolism in relation to English consonant clusters. It feels right because it *is* right. It *means* something.

Appendices

Indo-European Languages

English is one of around 450 living Indo-European languages, all derived from a reconstructed Proto-Indo-European ancestor language thought to have been spoken about 5,500 years ago in the Pontic-Caspian steppe. There are over 3.4 billion speakers of Indo-European languages as of 2018, and eight surviving branches. Numbers given are for native speakers.

INDO-IRANIAN (c. 1.7 billion). The Indo-Aryan sub-group includes Hindustani (Hindi–Urdu), Bengali, Punjabi, Marathi, and Gujarati, while the Iranian sub-group includes Persian, Pashto and Kurdish. The ancient sacred languages of Sanskrit (Indo-Aryan) and Avestan (Iranian) are from this branch.
ITALIC (c. 850 million). Includes the Romance languages descended from Latin, such as Spanish, Portuguese, French, Italian, Romanian and Catalan, and a number of extinct languages from the Italian peninsula.
GERMANIC (c. 530 million). Includes English, German, Dutch, Danish, Swedish and Norwegian, as well as extinct languages like Gothic, Burgundian, Frankish and Old Norse.
BALTO-SLAVIC (c. 320 million). Includes Slavic languages such as Russian, Ukrainian, Polish, Czech, Serbo-Croat and Bulgarian, as well as the Baltic languages of Lithuanian and Latvian.
HELLENIC (c. 13 million). Modern Greek and its related varieties.
ARMENIAN (c. 11 million) Includes Eastern and Western varieties.
ALBANIAN (over 5 million) Spoken in Albania and large parts of Kosovo and Macedonia.
CELTIC (over 1 million). Once spoken over large swathes of Europe, but now confined to the North Atlantic fringe. Includes Welsh, Breton, Irish and Scottish Gaelic.

Extinct Indo-European branches include Anatolian and Tocharian.

English Consonants

Obstruents (speech sounds formed by obstructing airflow)

Manner of articulation	Voicing	Place of Articulation							
		bilabial	labiodental	dental	alveolar	post-alveolar	palatal	velar	glottal
stop (plosive)	voiceless	p			t			k	ʔ
	voiced	b			d			g	
fricative	voiceless		f	Θ	s	ʃ		(x)	h
	voiced		v	ð	z	ʒ			
affricate	voiceless					tʃ			
	voiced					dʒ			

Sonorants (sounds formed by free airflow through the vocal tract)

		Manner	Voicing	Place of Articulation							
				bilabial	labiodental	dental	alveolar	post-alveolar	palatal	velar	glottal
		nasal	voiced	m			n			ŋ	
approximant	liquid	lateral	voiced				l				
		rhotic	voiced					r			
		glide	voiced	(w)					j	(w)	

Voiced consonants are consonant sounds that are made by vibrating the vocal cords, whereas **voiceless or unvoiced consonants** do not require this vibration in the articulatory process. As can be seen from the diagram on the previous page, most English consonants come in pairs – the sounds are produced in the same place in the mouth, the crucial difference being whether the vocal cords vibrate or not.

Stop consonants or **plosives**, are consonants in which the vocal tract is blocked, so all airflow stops. The occlusion (block) occurs at the lips in bilabial stops (*p* and *b*); with the tongue blade at the alveolar ridge behind the teeth (*t* and *d*); with the back part of the tongue against the soft palate (velum), i.e. the back part of the roof of the mouth (*k* and *g*); or at the glottis (opening between the vocal cords) in a glottal stop (*ʔ*).

Fricative consonants are produced by forcing air through a narrow channel made by placing two points of contact in the mouth, or articulators, close together. These may be the lower lip against the upper teeth (*f* and *v*); the back of the tongue against the soft palate, with the tongue against the upper teeth (the *ϑ* of *think* and the *ð* of *that*); with the blade of the tongue against the alveolar ridge (*s* and *z*); with the blade of the tongue against the hard palate (the *ʃ* of *sure* and the *ʒ* of *pleasure*), with the back of the tongue against the soft palate (in the *x* of *loch*); or at the glottis (with *h*).

Affricates are consonants that start as a stop and release as a fricative, as indicated by their International Phonetic Alphabet (IPA) symbols. Hence the *tʃ* of *church* is a combination of *t* and *ʃ*, while the *dʒ* of *jam* combines *d* and *ʒ*. The alveolar and post-alveolar fricatives and affricates are also known as **sibilants**. This manner of articulation is made when the tongue pushes a stream of air towards the sharp edge of the teeth, producing an intense hissing sound. The hiss of sibilants often lends itself to onomatopoeic words, and is also prevalent in the phonosemantic themes of many English consonant clusters.

In contrast to the obstruents above, sonorant sounds allow a free flow of air to pass through the vocal tract to the place of articulation. The airflow of nasal consonants is somewhat different insofar as it is blocked through the mouth but air escapes freely through the nose. Like the other English sonorants, English **nasal consonants** are all voiced: *m* is bilabial, articulated with both lips, *n* is articulated with the tip of the tongue at the alveolar ridge, and the *ŋ* consonant of –*ing* forms is velar, articulated with the back of the tongue at the soft palate.

L, *r*, *w* and *y* (IPA /j/) are collectively known as **approximants**, speech sounds in which the articulators approach each other, but not enough to cause friction and turbulence to the airflow in the vocal tract. They are considered a halfway house between fricatives and vowels. *L* and *r* are the **liquid consonants**: *l* is an alveolar lateral, where the airstream is directed over the sides of the tongue, while English *r* is a post-alveolar rhotic liquid, more accurately transcribed as /ɹ/ in the IPA, where the air is directed down the centre of the tongue.

The **semivowels or glides** have sounds that are similar to vowels, but act as the syllable boundary rather than as the syllable nucleus. Hence, the palatal approximant /j/ of *yes* is close to the /i:/ of *feed*, and the labiovelar /w/ is close to the /u:/ of *food*. The term *glide* highlights the characteristic of semivowels to "glide" from the /i:/ or /u:/ vowel position to that of the following vowel which functions as the syllable nucleus. For example, in *yes* [jes] the movement is from /i:/ to /j/ to /e/.

English Phonotactics

The branch of phonology which relates to the permissible combinations of phonemes is known as *phonotactics*. Phonotactic limitations on the consonant clusters which are possible in the initial position in English are quite strict. We actually use a rather narrow range of consonant clusters when the number of sound combinations we *could* produce is considered. English avoids all three-part onset clusters unless they begin with /s/:

three-part consonant clusters

s + voiceless stop + approximant

	p	l
s	t	r
	k	w

All three-part clusters in English must conform to the pattern *s + voiceless stop + approximant*, giving us five three-part clusters with enough words from which we can perceive a discernible phonosemantic theme: **spr-** /spr/, **spl-** /spl/, **str-** /str/, **scr-** /skr/ and **squ-** /skw/. Elsewhere in Indo-European, other three-part s-clusters are commonplace. Slavic and Greek make extensive use of a /skl/ cluster as with Russian *склад* (*sklad*) "warehouse", Bulgarian *склон* (*sklon*) "slope" and Greek *σκληρός* (*sklērós*) "hard". Although there is a marked preference for s- in initial position in three-consonant onset clusters in many languages, there are plenty of other possibilities. Slovak, for example, has **zdr-** in *zdravie* "health", **vzr-** in *vzrast* "increase, growth" and brilliantly **zhl-** in *zhluk* "cluster", among many other combinations.

S also has the greatest range in English with onset clusters of two consonants, as can be seen below:

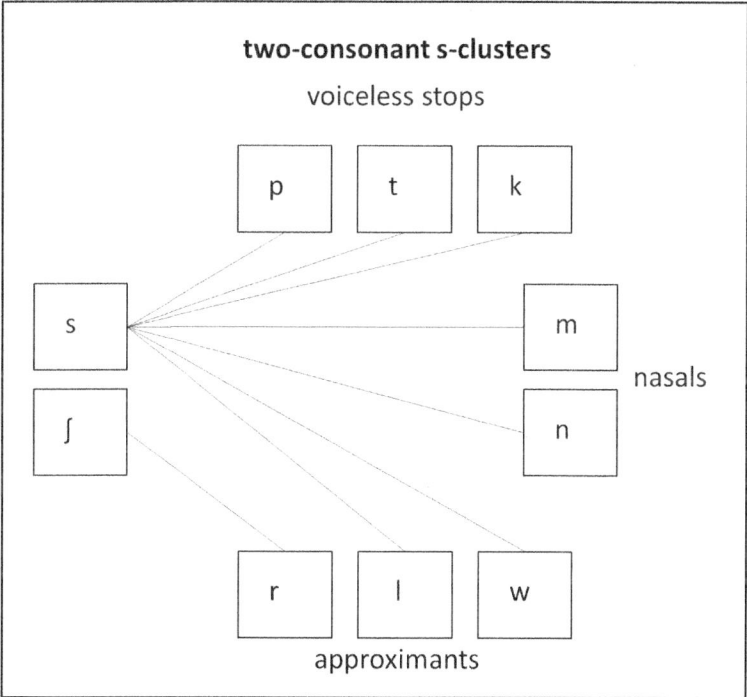

two-consonant s-clusters

voiceless stops

| p | t | k |

s

m

nasals

ʃ

n

r   l   w

approximants

S can be followed by the unvoiced stops /p/, /t/, /k/, and also the nasals /n/ and /m/, as with *spill*, *still*, *skill*, *snip* and *smitten*, as well as /l/ and /w/. ʃ (*sh*) takes the place of *s* in the *ʃr* cluster of *shrink* and *shrivel*. In other languages, even more combinations with *s-* are permissible e.g. Italian *sdire* "deny, retract", Czech *sbor* "board, committee, choir", and Bulgarian *свям* (*svyat*) "world".

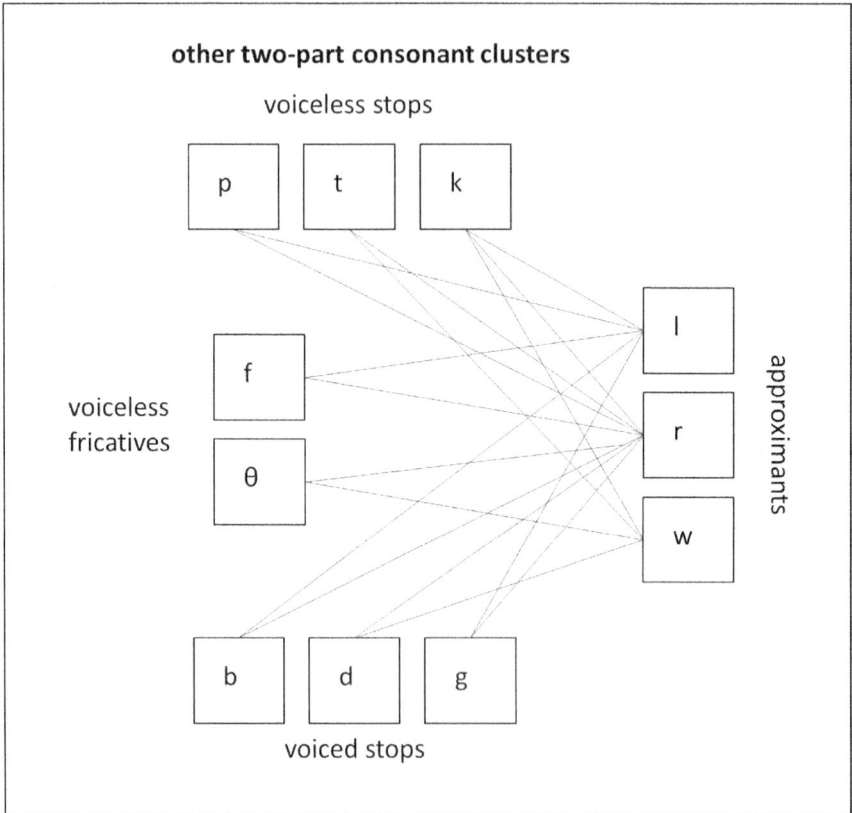

other two-part consonant clusters

voiceless stops

p t k

voiceless fricatives f θ l r w approximants

b d g

voiced stops

In Modern English onset clusters, consonants other than *s* must be followed by a liquid or a glide (semi-vowel), and even here some combinations are unlikely or impossible. As the above diagram also shows, the liquids *l* and *r* are by far the most common letters as the second element of English consonant clusters.

Again, English phonotactic rules are not universal – different languages have their own phonotactic rules, which often allow combinations that are not permissible in English: Macedonian *впечаток* (*vpečatok*) "impression" (voiced fricative + voiceless stop), German *pfropfen* "graft" (voiceless stop + voiceless fricative), Swedish *fnask* "hooker" (voiceless fricative + nasal), French *moitié* [mwatje] "half" (nasal + semi-vowel), and so on. Czech is particularly impressive with regard to consonant clusters, notwithstanding the fact that the syllabic liquid consonants *r* and *l* aid pronunciation, as beauties such as *cvrnkl* [tsvrŋkl̩] "flipped" and *čtvrtek* [tʃtvrtek] "Thursday" testify.

In other languages, nasals in particular are common as second elements in onset clusters. Examples include Serbo-Croatian *кмет* (*kmet*) "mayor", Russian *знак* (*znak*) "sign", and Greek's *τμῆμα* (*tmi:ma*) "segment" and the more recognisable *πνεύμονας* (*pnevmonas*) "lung", familiar to us from *pneumonia*. With German *gnädig* "gracious", Irish *gnéas* "sex", French *gnome*, Swedish *knop* "knot" and Slovenian *knjiga* "book", both the *g/k* and the *n* are pronounced. As we have seen, this was also the case in English until the seventeenth century, when kn- and gn- were reduced to /n/, although King Cnut, despite having attained minced oath status in some ruder quarters (see chapter 22), has not become a *nut* yet!

There are several other phonotactic constraints. English allows no affricate consonants in onset clusters, so /dʒ/ and /tʃ/ are absent in this position in combination with other consonants. This is unlike the case of Slavic languages where /tʃ/ is common as the first element of a cluster - Bulgarian *чрез* (*črez*) "through", Czech *čtrnáct* "fourteen" - and may even appear as the second element of a cluster - Russian *счётчик* (*sčetčik*) "account" and Serbo-Croatian *пчела* (*pčela*) "bee". In addition, English clusters must begin with an obstruent rather than a sonorant, so the nasals /m/, /n/ and /ŋ/, the two liquids /l/ and /r/, and the two semi-vowels /j/ and /w/ do not feature first in English clusters (although see chapter 31 on *wr-* for more on this). This constraint contrasts with Slavic languages where nasals often precede other nasals, liquids or semi-vowels e.g. Russian мнение (*mneniye*) "opinion", Croatian *mrziti* "hate", Polish *młody* "young". In other languages, nasals can have more of a free rein. The Indo-Aryan languages of Sinhala and Dhivehi, as well as languages in the Bantu group feature pre-nasalised consonants where a nasal is followed by an obstruent: Swahili *mti* "tree", *mkono* "hand, arm", *ndege* "bird" etc.

Although our available consonant clusters as prescribed by English phonotactics are very limited, we do routinely produce a wide variety of other clusters in rapid, everyday speech. This is especially noticeable with regard to the syncope of unstressed vowels when the second syllable carries the word stress. Hence, we have /tm/ in *tomato*, /pt/ in *potato*, /ft/ in *photography*, /dʒr/ in *giraffe*, /dl/ in *delicious* and many, many more. Similarly, rapid speech will also bring about unusual consonant clusters across word boundaries – the /km/ of *come here*, the /dʒg/ of *did you go*, the /zg/ of *'s good*, or the /zv/ of *'s very good*, for instance. Although this book concentrates on the pronunciation of citation forms of words and their phonosemantic themes, the actual number of consonant clusters a native English speaker will produce goes way beyond the scope of what I've been able to cover here.

Bibliography

The following books, websites and articles have been my pleasure to delve into during the course of my research for this book:

Abelin, Å. (1999) *Studies in sound symbolism.* Dissertation, Göteborg University.

Algeo, J. (1978) What consonant clusters are possible? *Word* 29 (3), pp. 206-224.

Arber, E. (ed) (1910) *Travels and works of Captain John Smith President of Virginia and Admiral of New England 1580-1631.* Edinburgh: John Grant, 1910.

Ayto, J. (1990) *Dictionary of word origins.* London: Bloomsbury.

Bergen, B. K. (2001) *Of sound, mind, and body: Neural explanations for non-categorical phonology.* Dissertation, University of California, Berkeley.

Bolinger, D. (1968) *Aspects of language.* New York: Harcourt, Brace, & World.

Boutkan, D. and Siebinga, S.M. (2005) *Old Frisian etymological dictionary.* Leiden: Brill.

Brown, J. (1964) *Flat Stanley.* New York: Harper & Row

Crystal, D. (1995) *The Cambridge encyclopedia of the English language.* Cambridge: Cambridge University Press.

Ferguson, R. (2016) *Scandinavians: In search of the soul of the north.* London: Head of Zeus.

Harbert, W. (2007) *The Germanic languages.* Cambridge: Cambridge University Press.

Harper, D. (2000-2018) *Online Etymological Dictionary.* (www.etymonline.com).

Holmquist, K. (2006) Shifting meanings, forgotten meanings: Metaphor as a force for language change. *DELTA* [online] 22, pp. 95-107.

Jespersen, O. (1922) *Language: Its nature, development and origin.* London: George Allen & Unwin.

Klein, E. (1971} *A comprehensive dictionary of the English language.* Amsterdam: Elsevier Scientific Publishing.

Lakoff, G. and Johnson, M. (2003) *Metaphors we live by.* Chicago, University of Chicago Press.

Lawler, J.M. (1990) Women, men, and bristly things: The phonosemantics of the BR- assonance in English. *Michigan Working Papers in Linguistics* 1, pp. 27-43.

Lawler, J.M. (2003) Style stands still, *Style* 37 (2), pp. 220-37.

Lewis, N. (1994) *The book of Babel.* London: Viking.

Merriam-Webster new book of word histories. (1991) Springfield, Massachusetts: Merriam-Webster.

O'Brien, D. (2012) *If houses, why not mouses?* New Generation Publishing.

Onions C.T, with Friedrichsen, G.W.S and Burchfield, R.W. (eds). (1966) *Oxford dictionary of English etymology*. Oxford: Oxford University Press.

Pollington, S. (1997) *First steps in Old English*. Hockwold-cum-Wilton: Anglo-Saxon Books.

Posner, R. (2006) *The Romance languages*. Cambridge: Cambridge University Press.

Rhodes, R.A. and Lawler, J.M. (1981) Athematic metaphors. In Hendrick, R.A. Carrie S. Masek, C.S. and Miller, M.F. (eds) *Papers from the 17th regional meeting, Chicago Linguistic Society*, pp 318-342.

Sapir, Y. and Zuckermann, G. (2008) Icelandic: Phonosemantic matching. In Rosenhouse, J. and Kowner, R. (eds). *Globally speaking: Motives for adopting English vocabulary in other languages*, Clevedon: Multilingual Matters, pp. 19-43.

Schlegel, F. (1808) *Über die Sprache und Weisheit der Indier*. Heidelberg: Mohr und Zimmer.

Schreier, D. (2005) *Consonant change in English worldwide: Synchrony meets diachrony*. Basingstoke: Palgrave Macmillan.

Shipley, J.T. (1984) *The origins of English words*. Baltimore: Johns Hopkins University Press.

Skeat, W.W. (2005) *An etymological dictionary of the English language.* Mineola, New York: Dover.

Sussex, R. and Cubberley, P. (2006) *The Slavic languages*. Cambridge: Cambridge University Press.

Watkins, C. (2000) *The American heritage dictionary of Indo-European roots* (2nd edition). Boston: Houghton Mifflin.

West, M.L. (2007) *Indo-European poetry and myth*. Oxford: Oxford University Press.

I can wholeheartedly recommend Douglas Harper's brilliant *Online Etymological Dictionary* (www.etymonline.com) as a great resource. It collates numerous print sources for its reconstructed etymological histories, and is extremely thoroughly researched. The very informative *Wiktionary* (www.wiktionary.org) has also proved invaluable for seeing how words have developed over time. In addition, the improving *Google Translate* (translate.google.co.uk) has been a useful starting point when trying to detect patterns of consonant clusters and phonesthemes in different languages.

Acknowledgements

First, I want to thank my students in Bulgaria who asked me (with great irritation!) why there were so many words in English beginning with gl- to do with light. They were the catalyst for my looking up consonant clusters in the first place, and set me on the road to writing this book. Four years later, I am still a consonant cluster aficionado, and there is so much more to discover!

I'd like to reiterate my thanks to John Lawler for the fascinating study 'Women, Men and Bristly Things: The Phonosemantics of the BR-Assonance in English', which introduced me to the theory of phonosemantics. Discovering his list of assonances was the eureka moment that made me look at consonants in a new way and spurred me on to research the material for *Sl- is for Sleaze but Sn- is for Sneeze!*

Most of all, thanks to my wife, who has given me some great ideas as well as having the thankless task of being my sounding board while not sounding bored. And to my kids, who have had to suffer me calling them *spangalangs* since the days they were born.

Printed in Great Britain
by Amazon